Series editors

David Knights, Department of Management, University of Keele

Chris Smith, School of Management, Royal Holloway, University of London

Paul Thompson, Department of Human Resource Management, University of Strathclyde

Hugh Willmott, Judge Institute of Management, University of Cambridge

This series offers a range of titles examining the broad areas of work and organisation within a national and global arena. Each book in the series is written by leading experts and covers a topic chosen to appeal to students and academics. Originating from the International Labour Process Conference, the series will be informative, topical and leading edge.

Published

Alan Felstead and Nick Jewson   *Global Trends in Flexible Labour*

Bill Harley, Jeff Hyman and Paul Thompson   *Participation and Democracy at Work*

Craig Prichard, Richard Hull, Mike Chumer and Hugh Willmott *Managing Knowledge*

Paul Thompson and Chris Warhurst   *Workplaces of the Future*

Andrew Sturdy, Irena Grugulis and Hugh Willmott   *Customer Service*

Chris Warhurst, Ewart Keep and Irena Grugulis   *The Skills that Matter*

Critical Perspectives on Work and Organisations Series

Series Standing Order

ISBN 0–333–73535–8

You can receive future titles in this series as they are published by placing a standing order. Please contact your bookseller or, in case of difficulty, write to us at the address below with your name and address, the title of the series and the ISBN quoted above.

Customer Services Department, Macmillan Distribution Ltd
Houndmills, Basingstoke, Hampshire RG21 6XS, England

Participation and Democracy at Work

Essays in Honour of Harvie Ramsay

Edited by
Bill Harley, Jeff Hyman and Paul Thompson

First published 2005 by
PALGRAVE MACMILLAN
Houndmills, Basingstoke, Hampshire RG21 6XS and
175 Fifth Avenue, New York, N.Y. 10010
Companies and representatives throughout the world

PALGRAVE MACMILLAN is the global academic imprint of the Palgrave
Macmillan division of St. Martin's Press, LLC and of Palgrave Macmillan Ltd.
Macmillan® is a registered trademark in the United States, United Kingdom
and other countries. Palgrave is a registered trademark in the European
Union and other countries.

ISBN-13: 978–1–4039–0004–3
ISBN-10: 1–4039–0004–3

This book is printed on paper suitable for recycling and made from fully
managed and sustained forest sources.

A catalogue record for this book is available from the British Library.

Library of Congress Cataloging-in-Publication Data
Participation and democracy at work : essays in honour of Harvie Ramsay / edited by
    Bill Harley, Jeff Hyman and Paul Thompson.
        p. cm.—(Critical perspectives on work and organisations)
    Includes bibliographical references and index.
    ISBN 1–4039–0004–3 (pbk.)
        1. Management—Employee participation. I. Ramsay, Harvie, 1949– II. Harley,
Bill. III. Hyman, J. D. (Jeffrey D.) IV. Thompson, Paul, 1951 Jan. I– V. Series.
HD5650.P3316 2005
331'.01'12—dc   222004062500

10   9   8   7   6   5   4   3   2   1
14   13   12   11   10   09   08   07   06   05

Printed in and bound in Great Britain by
Creative Print and Design (Wales), Ebbw Vale

In memory of **Harvie Ramsay** (1948–2000), Professor of International Human Resource Management, University of Strathclyde.

Until his untimely death, Harvie Ramsay was a leading scholar on issues of participation and democracy at work. This book honours Harvie's memory in the way most befitting his career – by bringing together critical and cutting-edge theory, practice and policy in his best-known field.

Contents

Notes on the Contributors

JOS BENDERS is Senior Researcher at the Nijmegen School of Management, Radboud University of Nijmegen, the Netherlands. His research interests include employment relationships; organisation concepts; medieval numismatics; and technology, work and organisation. He serves as Associate Editor Europe of *New Technology, Work and Employment,* is author of *Optional Options: Work Design and Manufacturing Automation,* co-author of *Useful but Unused; Group Work in Europe,* and co-editor of *The Symbiosis of Work and Technology* and *Mirroring Consensus; Decision-Consensus; Decision-Making in Japanese–Dutch Business.*

PAUL BOREHAM is Professor of Political Science and Director of the University of Queensland Social Research Centre. He has researched and published extensively on comparative political economy and the structure and organizational dynamics of economic and industrial relations institutions. He also has long-established interests in quantitative studies of labour market dynamics and unemployment.

ANDY DANFORD is Reader in Employment Relations at the University of the West of England, Bristol. He has published widely in the areas of trade union renewal and critical studies of lean production in the aerospace and automotive sectors. He is the author of *Japanese Management Techniques and British Workers* and co-author of *New Unions, New Workplaces.*

MARK HALL is Principal Research Fellow at the Industrial Relations Research Unit, University of Warwick, and co-editor of *European Works Councils Bulletin.* He has acted as a consultant to the European Commission and the Department of Trade and Industry concerning legislation on European Works Councils and related issues.

RICHARD HALL is Associate Professor of Organisational Studies and Human Resource Management at the University of Sydney. He was previously Deputy Director of ACIRRT at the University of Sydney. His recent research has focused on IT systems and organisational change, knowledge management, new skills in the services sector and critical approaches to international HRM. He has published in journals including *Work, Employment and Society, Industrial Relations* and *Economic and Industrial Democracy.*

BILL HARLEY is Associate Professor in Management at the University of Melbourne. His main areas of research are work organisation and the labour process, industrial relations, and changing occupational structures. His recent work has appeared in *Work, Employment and Society* and the *Journal of Management Studies*. He is currently conducting projects on work organisation in nursing and the impact of Enterprise Resource Planning (ERP) systems on the labour process among clerical and professional employees.

NIGEL HAWORTH is Professor of Human Resource Development at the University of Auckland. He has a long-established interest in the impacts of internationalisation on labour movements, in terms of both theoretical analysis and practical involvement with national and international labour organisations.

JEFF HYMAN is Professor of Human Resource Management in the Department of Management Studies at the University of Aberdeen Business School. His main research interests include the future of work, work–life balance, and industrial democracy.

EWART KEEP has been employed at the University of Warwick since 1985, first in the Industrial Relations Research Unit (IRRU) and, since 1998, as Deputy Director of the ESRC Centre on Skills, Knowledge and Organisational Performance (SKOPE). He has acted as an adviser to the National Skills Task Force, the Cabinet Office, the DTI, the DfES, and the Scottish Parliament, and has published extensively on UK vocational education and training policy; work-based learning for the young; the links between skills and competitive strategy; and the learning society and learning organisation.

MAREK KORCZYNSKI is a Reader in Employment Relations at Loughborough University Business School. Among his publications on service work is the Palgrave text, *Human Resource Management in Service Work*. He writes and researches in the areas of service work, social theory, and music in the workplace.

MICK MARCHINGTON is Professor of Human Resource Management in the new Manchester Business School at the University of Manchester. His research interests are in Human Resource Management and Industrial Relations, most specifically to do with employee involvement and worker voice as well as management approaches to employment. He has published some fifteen books and numerous papers in refereed journals. His most recent book is *Fragmenting Work: Blurring Organisational Boundaries and Disordering Hierarchies*, co-authored with Damian Grimshaw, Jill Rubery and Hugh Willmott.

PAUL MARGINSON is Professor of Industrial Relations and Director of the Industrial Relations Research Unit at the University of Warwick. He has researched and published extensively on European Works Councils. His recent co-authored book, *European Integration and Industrial Relations*, analyses the Europeanisation of industrial relations.

JONATHAN PAYNE is Senior Research Fellow with the ESRC's Centre for Skills, Knowledge and Organisational Performance (SKOPE), and is based at the University of Warwick. He has written widely on social partnership; the political economy of skill; workplace development; and vocational education and training (VET) policy in the UK and Scandinavia. He is currently conducting research into the Norwegian Competence Reform and Finland's National Workplace Development Programme.

ANDREW PENDLETON is Professor of Human Resource Management at Manchester Metropolitan University. He has degrees from the universities of Bath and Oxford, and has also held academic posts at the universities of Bath, Bradford and Kent. His main research interests are employee share-ownership plans, and the impact of finance and corporate governance on employment relationships. He has also written extensively on industrial relations in public transport industries.

HARVIE RAMSAY was Professor of International Human Resource Management at the University of Strathclyde before his death in 2000. He was the author of numerous works including *People's Capitalism? A Critical Analysis of Profit Sharing and Employee Share Ownership* (with Leslie Baddon, Laurie Hunter, Jeff Hyman and John Leopold), and *Information Technology and Workplace Democracy* (with Martin Beirne).

DORA SCHOLARIOS is a Reader in Organisational Behaviour at the Department of Human Resource Management in the University of Strathclyde, Glasgow, Scotland. Her research interests are in the areas of personnel selection and classification, social process perspectives of selection, and the effects of emerging forms of work on career patterns and employee well-being.

ANDREW STURDY is Professor in Organisational Studies at Warwick Business School, University of Warwick, and a Visiting Professor at the Tanaka Business School, Imperial College London. He has worked in a number of business/management schools in both the UK and abroad. His teaching and research are now focused on the global and local translation and diffusion of management ideas and practices, with particular interest in the role of management consultancy as well as training and education.

PAUL THOMPSON is Professor of Organisational Analysis at the University of Strathclyde. Among his publications are *The Nature of Work: An Introduction to Debates on the Labour Process*, *Work Organizations* (with David McHugh, 3rd edn), *Organizational Misbehaviour* (with Stephen Ackroyd), and the *Handbook of Work and Organization* (co-edited with Stephen Ackroyd, Pam Tolbert and Rose Batt). His research interests focus on skill, control and resistance, and work organisation.

List of Abbreviations

AEEU	Amalgamated Engineering and Electrical Union
AGM	Annual General Meeting
APEC	Asia-Pacific Economic Cooperation
CBI	Confederation of British Industry
CEO	Chief Executive Officer
CI	Continuous Improvement
CIPD	Chartered Institute of Personnel and Development
CWU	Communication Workers Union
CRM	Customer Relationship Management
DTI	Department of Trade and Industry
ECLA	Economic Commission for Latin America
EEA	European Economic Area
EI	Employee Involvement
EIP	Employee Involvement Program
EIRR	European Industrial Relations Review
EPOC	Employee (direct) Participation in Organisational Change
ERP	Enterprise Resource Planning
ESOP	Employee Share Ownership Program
ESRC	Economic and Social Research Council
EU	European Union
EWC	European Works Council
FDI	Foreign Direct Investment
FWDP	Finnish Workplace Development Programme
GATT	General Agreement on Tariffs and Trade
HCM	High-Commitment Management
HF-B	Norwegian Agreement on Development
HIM	High-Involvement Management
HPWO	High-Performance Work Organisation
HPWS	High-Performance Work Systems
HR	Human Resources
HRD	Human Resource Development
HRM	Human Resource Management
ICFTU	International Confederation of Free Trade Unions
IFI	International Financial Institutions
ILO	International Labour Organisation
IT	Information Technology
ITS	International Trade Secretariats
JCC	Joint Consultative Committee

JPC	Joint Productivity Committees
JSSC	Joint Shop Stewards Committee
kaizen	Japanese systems of continuous improvement of production
LO	Norwegian Trade Union Confederation
MNC	Multinational Corporation
NGO	Non-government Organisation
NHO	Norwegian Employees Association
OECD	Organisation for Economic Cooperation and Development
PIU	Performance and Innovation Unit
QC	Quality Circle
QWL	Quality of Working Life
R&D	Research and Development
RCN	Research Council of Norway
SBA	Norwegian National Work Life Centre
SCELI	Social Change and Economic Life Initiative
SKOPE	ESRC Centre on Skills, Knowledge and Organisational Performance
SNB	Special Negotiating Body
SOP	Standard Operating Procedure
STSD	Socio-technical Systems Design
TGWU	Transport and General Workers Union
TQM	Total Quality Management
TUC	Trades Union Congress
UK WON	UK Work Organisation Network
UMIST	University of Manchester Institute of Science and Technology
VET	Vocational Education and Training
WCC	World Cooperation Councils
WCL	World Council of Labour
WERS	Workplace Employee Relations Survey
WFTU	World Federation of Trade Unions
WIRS	Workplace Industrial Relations Survey
WTO	World Trade Organisation

1
The Paradoxes of Participation

Bill Harley, Jeff Hyman and Paul Thompson

> Looking back to the end of the 1960s . . . is rather like observing another world. A significant indication of the changes that have taken place over the last 15 years is that 'participation', the rallying call of a wide variety of social movements in most western countries in the late 1960s and early 1970s, is now rarely heard as a popular slogan. (Pateman 1983: 107)

Halfway through the first decade of the new century, a comparison with the 1980s reveals yet another world, or at least an apparent paradox. In comparison with the late 1960s and early 1970s, the general significance of participation and democracy in societal and workplace discourses is greatly reduced. As Heller (1998: 142) observes based on two twelve-country studies of industrial democracy: 'organizational influence sharing appears to have made only limited progress during the last 50 years'. Most significantly, its location as part of a broader notion of economic democracy or a citizenship framework has more or less disappeared. Expectations about the scope and purposes of participation have been scaled down and linked firmly to narrower, bottom-line and top-down outcomes.

Yet, apparently paradoxically, in the sphere of everyday work relations, participation practices have grown and proved much more durable than might have been expected. Mainstream business and management literature, at least, has convinced itself that:

> Employee involvement has now been accepted and understood by world class organizations . . . These same organizations, working predominantly in the fast-moving world of information and knowledge application, recognize the value of decisions made at the lowest qualified level and the payoff from smart workers who know their jobs. (Bennet and Bennet 2002: 11)

While this claim is situated within the discourse of 'the rise of the knowledge organization', it is not untypical (as we see in several chapters) of perspectives that link participation to new forms of competition and the associated requirements for flexibility, quality and innovation in the provision of goods and services. Of course, it is not difficult to make a sceptical

1

counter-argument, given the evidence on the scale and scope of contemporary employee participation.

We shall summarise and comment on that evidence later in the chapter. However, we want to start from an earlier, sceptical counter-case that has acted as a focal point for the whole book. Harvie Ramsay's 'cycles of control' thesis has formed a rallying point for nearly three decades for those who are sceptical about the emancipatory potential of employee involvement. In the next section of the chapter we outline Ramsay's argument and then, having reviewed the evidence on participation in the middle section, we consider how we might re-theorise participation in the light of contemporary developments.

Harvie Ramsay's 'Cycles of Control' Thesis

Since Harvie Ramsay published 'Cycles of Control: Worker Participation in Sociological and Historical Perspective' (hereafter 'Cycles') in *Sociology* in 1977, it has become one of the more influential works in the field of worker participation and involvement. In writing this piece, Ramsay sought to challenge the view that worker participation had arisen as part of a gradual and ongoing humanisation of capitalism. Instead, he argued that it was a cyclical phenomenon that emerged when management authority was under challenge and it was necessary to gain workers' compliance.

Ramsay's theoretical framework was Marxian and premised on a belief that relations between management and employees were fundamentally antagonistic. Accordingly, he challenged the unitarist assumption, found in much of the earlier literature on participation, that it was possible to generate 'win–win' situations in which both management and employees benefited from participation schemes, and argued that the conflict inherent in the employment relationship set limits on the viability of participation schemes.

In support of this thesis, he sought to demonstrate that participation initiatives in Britain had waxed and waned in a series of cycles since the early nineteenth century. In each case, he argued, employers introduced participation at times when labour sought to challenge managerial authority, and the initiatives declined because of the declining power of labour and/or economic pressures to cut costs and maximise profit. He argued that, at the time of writing 'Cycles', Britain was in the midst of another cycle of participation.

Ramsay argued that participation initiatives in the 1960s and 1970s were largely misunderstood because commentators failed either to put them into historical perspective or to understand the features common to each cycle. His claim was that the participation initiatives of the period reflected the combination of shop-floor militancy that had grown in a context of full employment and prosperity, and economic pressure on employers as growth slowed and profits fell. In these circumstances, it became increasingly difficult for employers both to maintain profitability and to meet the demands for wage increases. The solution, as it had been in similar situations in the past, he argued, was an attempt to incorporate labour by means of limited participation, which fell far short of the kind of largely union-based industrial democracy then advocated by the Labour Party and many unions (Ramsay 1977: 494–5).

Ramsay's argument was not that attempts to encourage participation were futile. He stated quite explicitly that he did not consider 'that the democratic control of industry by those who produce its goods is a worthless pursuit' (1977: 498). Indeed, he argued that the fact that management authority was challenged periodically provided evidence of the underlying strength of calls for increased worker control. Ultimately, he concluded that, because of the structural conflict inherent in capitalism, the wholesale transformation of economy and society would be required before genuine industrial democracy could prevail.

At the time that 'Cycles' appeared there was a good deal of optimism about the potential for participation, and Ramsay sought to correct what he saw as a misreading of the situation. Clearly, he saw such optimism as being based on a lack of understanding of both the cyclical nature of participation and the historical context. He observed that:

> we now find ourselves back in the midst of a strong current of interest in the concept of workers' participation in management. Once more one would think the idea was new; at the very least, we are told, this time 'the process of democratization' is reaching an inexorable peak and this time employers really mean it. (Ramsay 1977: 493)

'Cycles' must be understood as an attempt to correct the naïve optimism of those who cast their ahistorical gaze upon developments in the 1970s and saw them as part of a teleological process in which industry was becoming progressively more democratic.

If we accept Ramsay's argument that patterns of participation can only be understood in their historical and sociological context, then in assessing the value of 'Cycles' as a theoretical and empirical contribution to understanding employee participation, we must consider the context in which his thesis was developed. At the time when Ramsay was developing his thesis, the long post-war boom was coming to and end. A series of changes in the international political economy was rendering the Keynesian settlement increasingly unworkable and this was being manifested in slowing rates of growth, increases in inflation and a rise in unemployment levels across the OECD (for a useful summary of key changes, see Harvey 1989: 125–40). Most of the features of the 'long boom' were still observable, but the first signs of the changes that took place during the 1980s and 1990s were becoming evident.

At this time, support for participation was widespread. Pateman argues that: 'During the last few years of the 1960s the word "participation" became part of the popular political vocabulary' (1970: 1). During the 1960s, student and worker militancy had surged in many of the liberal democracies and the advocacy of participation at work and in society more generally had considerable legitimacy. In the realm of government policy-making and economic management, Keynesian, or at least quasi-Keynesian, thinking was dominant, although there were significant differences between OECD countries in terms of precisely how economic management was enacted (Harvey 1989: 135). There appears to have been a significant degree of consensus across the OECD that national governments should play a role in maintaining both stability and growth, and in regulating capital–labour relations. As part of this role there was considerable support in government circles in a range of countries for initiatives aimed at encouraging workplace participation.

Turning to the labour market, in the United Kingdom the official unemployment rate from the late 1940s until the mid-1970s was never higher than 3 per cent, although in the mid-1970s it began to climb towards a peak in the mid-1980s of around 11 per cent (Lindsay 2003: 136–7). A broadly similar pattern can be discerned in other parts of continental Europe (Mitchell 2003: 168–9). Union density in the United Kingdom was almost at its peak of just over 50 per cent in the late 1970s, before beginning a decline that has been maintained to the time of writing (Lindsay 2003: 140). This decline was also evident in other Anglophone countries and in parts of continental Europe (Adams 1995: 104). Manufacturing accounted for a very significant slice of employment at this time. Although its share of total employment had begun to drop by the early 1970s, in 1975 it still accounted for nearly a third of jobs (see ILO 1960, 1975, 1980). Reflecting this, discussion of participation at the time focused almost exclusively on manufacturing settings.

In important ways, the context in which Ramsay's thesis emerged had similarities with those surrounding earlier cycles. The growth of interest in participation had taken place in the context of economic prosperity and full employment. The economic environment, and particularly the state of the labour market, encouraged high levels of union membership. Organised labour was strong and employers were under a degree of pressure to seek co-operation. There remained a general consensus in political circles across the OECD about the appropriateness of Keynesian macroeconomic management and a variety of corporatist or quasi-corporatist mechanisms for economic planning and co-ordination. Thus, as in earlier upswings of the cycle, Ramsay discerned on the one hand a combination of forces conducive to participation and on the other a growth in participation.

The constellation of economic and political factors that had supported the growth of participation was just beginning to break down in the face of changes in the international political economy. Interest in participation began to wane at the same time as this breaking down of the factors that apparently facilitated it: this appeared to confirm that validity of the 'Cycles' thesis. According to the thesis, full employment, general prosperity and high levels of union density, which went hand-in-hand with union power and militancy, were key explanatory factors in the growing interest in participation. The declining interest in participation in the late 1970s and early 1980s, just as unemployment rose, growth slowed and union density began to decline was entirely consistent with the 'Cycles' view. Moreover, Ramsay was not claiming to have generated an iron law of participation with universal applicability. In later work, he sought to refine his thesis in line with developments in the 1980s and 1990s (for example, Ramsay 1983, 1992).

Assessing Contemporary Trends

The period since the publication of 'Cycles' has witnessed political, economic and sectoral upheavals, with the corresponding landscape of participative practice – and its surrounding discourse – now very different from that of 1977. The most visible manifestation of change has been the apparently inexorable rise in use of employer-initiated involvement programmes, articulated within a liberalised political economic framework. According to the 'Cycles' thesis, these voluntary actions would arise as a systematic management response to attempted or anticipated union incursions into management control.

Yet participative practices have apparently evolved in ways that the 'Cycles' theory has been unable to predict; techniques have been introduced or reinforced at times of no obvious threat to the hegemony of managers, and met with only subdued opposition or even active endorsement by employees and their union representatives (Roche and Geary 2002). How might these developments be explained? One possibility is that participation is neither a single practice entity nor derives from a singular ideology. Contributors to this volume generally endorse the Ramsay thesis that participation can be introduced by employers to prevent or weaken union mobilisation attempts during periods of tight labour markets (see Pendleton, Chapter 5 in this volume). Nevertheless, employers themselves readily oppose participative formulas which they interpret as inimical to their interests. In the UK, employers successfully resisted proposals for statutory worker directors; in Sweden, employers opposed wage-earner funds; and many international companies have still to implement European Works Councils. This suggests that participation is neither a single nor a continuous entity.

From her influential analytical perspective of democratic influence, Pateman (1970) identified three different variants of participation – namely, full, partial and pseudo, with only full participation offering equal rights to all organisational members. Pseudo-participation derives from management communication and persuasion initiatives and offers little influence to employees, while partial participation describes limited inputs offered on management terms to the weaker party in the relationship. Democratic citizenship, representing the 'full' participation described by Pateman, is untouched by employer-sponsored participative approaches. Apart from co-operative ventures, it has figured only peripherally in recent political debate, in which economic recession, market liberalisation and competitive values provide the combined driving forces behind labour market policy, practice and evaluation. The concentration of economic power and the associated issues of corporate governance, once central targets of advocates for workers' control, have long receded from activist or political pursuit agendas (Cole 1972).

At a more operational level, participation can also be classed along three dimensions, two of which can be directly associated with management interests, and the third aligned more closely with employee protection needs. The first is based on capital-sharing through employee share schemes. This was made popular during the Thatcher years in the UK as 'people's capitalism' (Baddon *et al.* 1989; Nichols and O'Connell Davidson 1992) and maintained during the New Labour years as a practical expression of partnership and mutual gains ideology. It was promoted as such by the government as a means to enhance labour performance (see Pendleton, Chapter 5 in this volume). Share schemes are commonly applied in North America and are found in most other developed economies (Vaughan-Whitehead 1995). An analysis of the US 2003 National Organizations Survey showed that one-third of North American private-sector companies offer shares to employees, rising to 75 per cent for publicly-listed companies (Blasi *et al.* 2003: table 2). Across Europe, profit-sharing, which relates employee remuneration to company performance but does not offer equity to employees, is more common than share ownership. The Employee (direct) Participation in Organisational Change (EPOC) study found that while more than a fifth of companies across the EU offered profit-sharing, only 7 per cent had employee share schemes (23 per cent in the UK). However, evidence of positive performance effects when share schemes are linked with other forms of participation suggest that with awakening EU and national government support, these proportions are likely to increase (Gill and Krieger 2000; Pendleton *et al.* 2001).

A second and closely related approach is also employer-initiated and driven, equating at best to Pateman's partial participation, embracing task-centred employee involvement in areas narrowly identified as being of 'direct interest' to employees (CBI 1991). Task-involvement is typified by direct exchanges between individual employees and managers and, as well as financial involvement can include information, communication, consultation and job-restructuring exercises, of which empowerment and team-working (see Benders, Chapter 4 in this volume) are well-known examples.

When applied in combination, these initiatives might be presented as high-performance (or high-involvement or high-commitment) work systems (HPWS) (see Harley, Chapter 3 in this volume). As employers purport to detach themselves from Taylorist models of work organisation towards the commitment agenda evangelised by writers such as Walton (1985) and Pfeffer (1998), various manifestations of task or direct involvement have expanded in usage in developed economies over recent years.

The third dimension of participation includes approaches that recognise and attempt to countervail the structural vulnerabilities of employees in contemporary, competitive and globalised economies by offering them regulation over employment rights that might otherwise be restricted or denied to them in a free market system. These approaches emerge directly from the efforts of employees, usually acting collectively, and/or through pluralistic political programmes initiated at state and super-state levels, such as the European Union. Initiatives include support for collective representation and negotiation; works councils, including supranational European Works Councils; and worker directors (Hyman and Mason 1995). As participation is implemented through representatives, it is sometimes referred to as indirect participation. Also, as it purports to influence or challenge aspects of corporate-level governance, it is also termed power-centred participation (see Hall and Marginson, Chapter 11 in this volume). In the prevailing liberalised economic climate, regulation through indirect participation has struggled against ascendant management, and individualistic and competitive values.

Evidence for each of these trends is readily available. The 1998 Workplace Employee Relations Survey (WERS) showed that practices such as team working, team briefing, attitude surveys and employee share schemes are now commonly applied in UK workplaces. From the same data, over half the establishments with over twenty-five employees claimed to operate five or more of these involvement practices (Cully *et al.* 1999). Across the pre-2004 European Union, the EPOC survey revealed that the vast majority of organisations had some form of employee involvement practice (Gill and Krieger 2000: 118). North American studies reveal similar trends (Cappeli *et al.* 1977; Smith 1997; Hodson 2001). As the WERS findings above demonstrate, there is increasing evidence of the use of bundles of practices in the UK (White *et al.* 2003), and this trend is well established in the USA (MacDuffie 1995; see also Harley, Chapter 3 in this volume) though it is perhaps less in evidence as yet in continental Europe (Gill and Krieger 2000). While task-centred involvement and financial involvement have demonstrated both growth and resilience, representative participation has been markedly less robust. In the UK, joint consultation and both the scope and coverage of collective bargaining have been in decline since the end of the 1980s (Millward *et al.* 2000). Employers remain suspicious of European representative arrangements, and progress over drafting statutes for

European Works Councils, the European Company (an EU statute regulating company law) and EU-backed information and consultation rights has been slow and tortuous. Once in place, the impact of recent representative participation has been questionable: in the UK, less than half the European companies covered by the European Works Councils directive have established councils and, according to one union officer, 'very few could be said to working effectively' (Richards 2004: 21). Management obstruction and manipulation are not uncommon (Royle 1999; Waddington 2003). Collective wage-earner funds, one of the mainstays of the Swedish Meidner plan and aimed at fundamental reform of labour–capital relations, soon withered in the aftermath of the election success of an economically liberal administration (Kjellberg 1998).

While usage of individual techniques might wax and wane (see Marchington, Chapter 2 in this volume), the aggregated incidence of employer-driven involvement appears to be both durable (Millward *et al.* 2000: 121) and continually expanding, though whether these initiatives arise from structured or strategic management orthodoxies is unclear. Some argue that employers' search for 'a "quick-fix", low-cost solution to problems of low productivity, poor quality, or whatever else ails the organization' (Heller *et al.* 1998: 13) is indicative of, and the prime explanation for, management's possibly faddish behaviour. Ramsay effectively demolished the idea of participation as a progressively applied humanitarian response to the inequities inherent in labour market relations, but pragmatic employer policies (if not practices) might reflect situations of acute labour market and skill shortages. Other explanations include the high turnover of senior management personnel, with successive incomers being keen to imprint their own individual management style, picked up increasingly from executive education programmes and textbooks; and growing manager awareness of the importance of employee commitment and a recognition that different techniques need to be adopted for changing circumstances (Ackers *et al.* 1992; see also Marchington, Chapter 2 in this volume). There might even be recognition that potentially superficial, manipulative or inexpertly handled devices are unlikely to influence employee behaviour towards closer alignment with employer interests. Nevertheless, while the range and coverage of Employee Involvement (EI) has undoubtedly expanded, the impact has been less certain, as demonstrated in this volume by Harley for HPWS, Payne and Keep (Chapter 8) for work restructuring and Pendleton with respect to share schemes. Further, where there have been employer gains, it is by no mean certain that task-centred EI or minority share-ownership have acted as the principal agents of change (see Ramsay *et al.* 2000; Legge 2001).

A central aim of this book is to examine these processes more closely and in particular to question the extent to which Ramsay's original and wide-ranging ideas are relevant in today's changed political landscape and increasingly internationalised economy. Appropriately, the substantive chapters open with Marchington's account of the 'Cycles' debate in the contemporary economy, and in particular a review and updating of the cycles versus waves debates of the early 1990s. Marchington offers a partial resolution through his dual-level analysis, suggesting that cycles can account for the macro-level decline of indirect participation, while organisational scrutiny indicates that individual organisational and managerial contextual factors can explain the character of micro-level waves of involvement. Nevertheless, recognising the still-unsatisfactory state of participative theorising, his chapter ends with a plea for greater terminological clarity located in longitudinal research. This chapter is followed by three chapters which take cycles as their specific empirical analytical focus. With financial and task-involvement, along with its high performance work systems, teamworking and partnership variants flying high in both policy and managerial discourse, the opening chapters focus on these practices, their inspiration and outcomes.

Thus using 'Cycles' as a prism to reflect current trends, Harley examines in depth one recent manifestation of management-inspired involvement – high performance work systems. He questions whether this is a temporary behavioural phenomenon, which in Marchington's terms is poised currently at the crest of a wave, or whether it represents a more structured Ramsayian shift in the topology of management practice or even strategy, explicable in terms of gaining employee compliance while reinforcing management control. The outcome is inconclusive: following Ramsay, it is entirely consistent that managers introduce initiatives intended to succour (or sucker?) employee attachment and goodwill, potentially at the expense of their collective loyalties. Equally, actual management activity can be pragmatic, uncoordinated and not apparently driven by rationality and consistency, a point well recognised by Ramsay (1996; Ramsay and Scholarios 1996). In Chapter 4, Benders unravels another contemporary and contested practice – team working – and argues once again that it constitutes at best a form of partial participation. As employers have moved towards objectives governed solely by 'bottom-line' performance, earlier views that involvement could in itself be a legitimate goal have largely disappeared.

Based on UK experience, Pendleton returns to one of the original source areas of cycles theory – namely financial participation – and subjects it to contemporary scrutiny. In particular, he asks whether the objectives of share schemes are directed against union organisation and activity. This would conform with the 'Cycles' thesis, but its application at a time of declining union potency would not. Identifying other motives (and other key actors), Pendleton argues that while evidence from share schemes since the 1970s is not supportive of cycles, it is not incompatible with it either. A key management objective at the time of writing is still to secure control of employees, though the approaches now might be wrapped in the rhetoric of empowerment, commitment and identification with company objectives at a time of reduced long-term company attachment to employees. Associated management shifts towards the concept of 'shareholder value' and an increased focus on 'market-based' forms of regulation and governance are mediated through the ideological application and material benefits associated with share schemes.

Nevertheless, other explanations for the ascendancy of financial and task involvement have been presented. One recent explanation is that the cult of the customer (du Gay 1996), allied with heightened competition based on quality standards in production, delivery and service, demands more enlightened management styles. These are designed to elicit company identification, commitment and the willingness to 'to go the extra mile' (Flecker and Hofbauer 1998) to serve the customer. The contribution of Sturdy and Koczynski to this book (Chapter 6) is especially valuable as they focus on the somewhat neglected area of participation in service work. They suggest that service work can be divided into three main categories: front-line sales; front-line service; and back-office sales/service. They further suggest that task-based involvement and discretion is informed by, and descends from, proximity to the consumer. In other words, the customer acts as an additional labour process actor, whose interaction with the material and ideational conditions of work helps to shape the nature and content of task involvement. The rise in task-based involvement could therefore be associated with the rise in customer-facing and service activities.

Emerging questions of worker heterogeneity and contextual framework are further explored in Chapter 7 by Ramsay and Scholarios. They point out that involvement and participation might serve to divide rather than unite disadvantaged employees as well as to offer differential benefits to the relatively advantaged. These issues are explored in the context of gender, an area in which untested assumptions of different orientations towards work by men and women can lead to questionable expectations about their participative interests, potential and activity. Based on an analysis of a Department of Trade and Industry (DTI) data set, the authors caution against both stereotyping and homogenising the experiences of men and women. Instead, they argue that the propensity to participate cannot simply be identified along gender lines: individual, domestic, sector and organisational factors all emerge as significant variables for both men and women.

Payne and Keep challenge directly the underlying assumption that working arrangements have been changed to offer greater responsibility and autonomy. They question the extent and depth of task involvement in the UK by relating it to the paucity of government and organisational policy designed to enhance the skills required of employees to engage with expanded responsibilities. Consistent with evidence presented by other contributors, they suggest that policy and practice follow a 'low road', based on minimum costs and supply-side market regulation. In other words, without appropriate training and insight, task involvement becomes little more than an empty shell. The authors specifically contrast the UK's extended and continuing lack of co-ordinated policy and practice with long-standing Scandinavian programmes for work reorganisation and job design. Though such experiences are themselves uneven, they can still inform a publicly-supported workplace development/quality of working life programme in the UK.

Following the initial analyses of forms of task-based employee involvement, the focus shifts in later chapters to an examination and critical appraisal of power-centred participation by Danford (Chapter 9), Haworth (Chapter 10) and Hall and Marginson (Chapter 11). Danford examines union attempts at gaining workplace influence in an inhospitable UK climate, while Hall and Marginson's analysis is located within a broader European framework. Haworth takes a broader, internationalised perspective. The three chapters question the extent to which labour can collectively regain influence in a period of market and management ascendancy, and all three chapters point cautiously to possible areas for advancement. Danford reflects on the decline in the power and influence of trade unions in developed countries, and specifically in the UK. Through three case studies in aerospace manufacturing, where organisational and labour process restructuring have been implemented by management, he explores the extent to which unions are still able to draw on resources of collective workplace organisation to influence workplace issues at the point of production. In particular, he asks whether the introduction of techniques such as partnership and HPWS close down or open up opportunities for worker influence. In a more pessimistic assessment of policy options, Danford concludes that it boils down to a choice between accommodation or resistance: from the case studies, he argues that not only resistance at the point of production but also broader oppositional collective strategies are feasible and potentially achievable.

Haworth, a close collaborator with Ramsay over a number of years, identifies his wider and highly percipient contribution in identifying and conceptualising worker struggles to gain influence in internationalised corporate settings, and in particular in areas of regional economic integration. While Ramsay was understandably cautious in his early appraisal of the capacity for labour to confront multinational power, Haworth argues that developments since the 1970s allow a (guardedly) more optimistic appraisal of labour's future. This optimism is based on a historical evaluation of the evolution of international capital, initially unrestrained in operating beyond the boundaries of nation states and their domestic regulatory procedures. Haworth argues that the recognition of capital's encroaching dominance led to a reaction in the form of multi-agency challenges for popular representation and multinational corporation (MNC) restraint amid growing concerns for forms of supranational regulation, an issue explored further in Hall and Marginson's assessment of European Works Councils.

In their chapter, these authors assess the impact of European Works Councils (EWCs), which they describe as 'the most significant institutional innovation in European-level company-based industrial relations' in confronting 'the internationalisation of capital's decision-making' (Ramsay 1997: 321). Two polar propositions are presented; EWCs function either as ineffective paper tigers or as Trojan horses paving the way for integrated European organisation and synchronised activity by trade unions. After ten years of EWC experience, the authors conclude, agnostically, that Ramsay's (1997) predictions of significant variation in practice and effects, influenced by a range of national, sector and organisational factors, remain pertinent. One positive precondition for greater worker influence is increasingly being met, however, through the international integration of company operations, whereas a second precondition, the capacity of unions to co-ordinate their organisation and activities across national boundaries, remains debatable.

Even within national boundaries, political ideology remains a key influence on material outcomes for workers. In an important essay, Boreham and Hall identify in Chapter 12 of this book different theoretical perspectives in their interpretation of the relationship between labour institution participation and macroeconomic state policies. Tracing the recent history of economic democracy, they first identify a dominant negotiated or regulated model, balancing competition and co-operation, emerging from left-of-centre political doctrines. They then raise the question of the value to labour of the economic outcomes of this form of political collaboration. Comparative studies in OECD countries, conducted from the 1980s, indicated that neo-corporatist models, typified by formal labour institutional intervention, had been instrumental in reducing unemployment and in raising the level of state welfare efforts. From the late 1980s, however, the fragility of the neo-corporatist agenda became increasingly exposed as business interests and international competitiveness undermined its principal regulatory supports and policy shifted in favour of neo-liberal economic nostrums. One practical consequence was the enforced decline of the institutions of organised labour, with corresponding deleterious effects for workers as systems of universal rights give way to fragmented expressions of market power. In turn, this shift has contributed to growing wealth and income insecurity, reduced welfare provision, growing employment insecurity, and reduced access to the public provision of training and skills (see also Payne and Keep, Chapter 8 in this volume).

Conclusion: Re-theorising Participation

We have argued that the available evidence indicates that something significant has happened to at least some forms of workplace participation, though the *outcomes* are not as significant as their managerial and academic proponents claim. Herein lies the apparent paradox that we observed at the start of the chapter: while participation of the kind espoused in the 1960s and 1970s has largely disappeared, managerially-driven involvement initiatives have become part of the industrial landscape.

How are we to make sense of contemporary developments? The emergence and spread of new practices, and their limitations, were clearly visible by the end of the 1980s. This led Ramsay (1991: 19) to argue that while competitive pressures had led to a modest emphasis on the need for employee co-opera-tion and some concessions on rights and humanisation at work, these initia-tives were short-lived and faddish in character. We agree to an extent with his assessment, but there is a danger of confusing the rise and fall of particular practices with a more enduring employer interest in involving employees following the crisis of Fordism and Taylorism in the early 1980s.

As we argued earlier, part of the solution to explaining the paradox of participation is to abandon any idea of tracking a single phenomenon against a single conception of participation. The relevant practices have always been too diverse, particularly when considered across national boundaries, to be captured through the lens of a particular explanation, cycles or otherwise. Whether considered as task- and power-centred, or direct and indirect, the need to unpack categories is paramount. We would argue, therefore, that we need to go beyond such categorising practices as 'pseudo-participation' or the like. Different types of participation should be evaluated against both their stated objectives and their underlying purposes as revealed through an analysis of intent and outcomes. Rather than assum-ing that particular types have fixed qualities or effects, we would seek, among other things, to identify the conditions under which management initiate different forms of participation; the dominant historical and compar-ative patterns; and the conditions under which particular practices have been successful or generated rejection and resistance.

With this in mind, the process of unpacking is predominantly about exploring the issues of actors, interests and contexts. With respect to actors and interests, at a very basic level, direct or task-centred practices have over-whelmingly been forms of participation initiated by employers, whereas power-centred or indirect measures invariably derive from employees, or at least from their organisations. In contrast, the prime actor in financial partic-ipation tends to be the state – through, for example, tax incentive legislation, which explains why its incidence is largely confined to particular countries (notably France and the UK). Employers tend to pursue participation because it can enhance organisational efficiency and productivity and/or because the practices and accompanying rhetoric have persuasive proper-ties. With respect to the latter, participation might be directed towards legit-imising painful organisational change, or might function to mask or give credibility to otherwise mundane or exploitative measures (empowerment is a case in point).

Labour also proceeds from predominantly pragmatic rationales. Voice mechanisms, whether direct or indirect, might be supported by labour where action alone is insufficient to exert influence in the regulation of the employment relationship. Employees might also gain degrees of autonomy and creativity that enhance the less tangible feelings of meaning, dignity and self-realisation at work (Hodson 2001).

By virtue of its role as an economic manager, the state also has an interest in the regulation of the employment relationship. As there are multiple states in capitalist societies rather than *the* capitalist state, preferences for promoting particular forms of participation by law or exhortation reflect specific ideologies and governance projects. It is worth keeping in mind, however, that states are often more sensitive to issues of legitimacy than employers, individually or collectively. Historically, governments of different ideological persuasions have responded to legitimation crises by initiating discussion and action on participation rights or work humanisation. With new forms of global and regional governance, outlined elsewhere by Haworth, the levels of state regulation are also becoming more complex.

That is not to say that capital and labour are homogenous or, along with the state, the only relevant actors:

> One of the important internal influences shaping participation is the range of values, beliefs and strategies held by the actors involved. These actors include the managers, individual employees, work groups and their representatives who are involved in the decision-making process of the organisation and the bodies concerned with participation (Poutsma *et al.* 2003: 51).

Such variations draw our attention back to *context*. Many of the contributors to this volume draw on varieties of institutional approaches that locate outcomes within, as Pendleton puts it, an interplay between actors in specific and contingent institutional contexts. Others draw on labour process or radical political economy frameworks within which asymmetries of power between capital and labour at the global and workplace level form the primary focus of analysis. There is room for both in understanding the patterns of consistency and constraint in workplace participation, particularly if, as Marchington observes, we are addressing the issues at different – macro and micro – levels of abstraction. Nor are these perspectives necessarily studying different things. Neither societal institutions nor capital–labour relations are fixed in form or content, and there is growing evidence of the remaking of traditional institutional boundaries within a globalising economy. Analyses of participation draw increasingly on a 'varieties of capitalism' framework, distinguishing, for example, between Anglo-Saxon, German, Latin and Japanese variants (Poutsma *et al.* 2003). Such models shape and constrain local contingencies. Furthermore, as Katz and

Derbyshire (2000) demonstrate, a common process of converging divergence in which the location of management of the employment relationship is pushed downwards, means that there is increasing variation of practices within and across the dominant employment systems of particular countries.

Within this variation, however, direct workplace participation appears to be central to the efficiency objectives of many employers, and such practices have, as has already been indicated, proved to be relatively durable. To what extent has this durability been based on the capacity of new practices to meet the interests of major economic actors? There is nothing in a labour process or other radical framework that a priori prevents recognition of mutual gains. A mutual gain is not predicated on shared objectives or interests, but rather on the understanding that the outcomes of practices generate sufficient benefits to each party, and that the accompanying rhetoric is sufficiently aligned with the practices as not to threaten significantly their legitimacy. The fact that what labour, capital and sometimes the state seek from participation might, and often does, differ is not in itself a barrier to their success.

This is not to say, however, that we are advocating a view of the world in which involvement invariably, or even usually, involves a 'win–win' situation. As Hodson notes, employee involvement is contested and negotiated continually, placing limits on the durability of practices and any associated mutual gains: 'Too often calls by management for increased participation are coupled with programs of work intensification and reduced job security under the guise of "increased flexibility" ' (Hodson 2001: 172). Any mutual gains are therefore not only circumscribed by divergent interests, but are also threatened by changes in the context of the political economy through which those interests are fashioned. One of the reasons why the scope and scale of HPWS are so limited is the unfavourable and unstable condition of corporate governance arrangements driven by shareholder value (Thompson 2003).

Admittedly, this is neither the only nor the most popular understanding of the broader workplace context. Pride of place here must go to the widespread theories of the rise of a knowledge economy. These are pertinent to our purposes, not simply for their optimistic view that what counts are skills, creativity and human capital, but also because of what the perspective implies for participation.

If proponents of the knowledge or new economy are correct then we should expect a much greater incidence of high autonomy work. As a result, there would be less need for either task- or power-centred participation. With respect to the former, such measures have largely been mechanisms for offsetting the effects of routine low-discretion work. In other words, we should see a rise in participative *jobs* and a decline in participation *schemes*. Highly qualified knowledge workers will not only be able to engage in their own version of direct participation, but will be able to rely more on self-representation, though these will be mediated by societal differences in collective forms of interest regulation (Pries and Abel 2004). At a rhetorical level, we can note that discourses of participation are already being partially displaced by those of learning and communities of practice.

However, there are a number of big 'buts' to this scenario. The first is that the numbers involved fall far short of the more optimistic claims that knowledge work is the engine of job growth and that soon more than 80 per cent of all jobs will be 'cerebral' in nature (Neef 1998). Summing up a range of evidence and their own rigorous (re)coding of occupational statistics, Brown and Hesketh (2004) arrive at a figure of around 20 per cent of jobs in the USA being in knowledge work. While the figure is a little higher in the UK, the fact remains that 47 per cent of UK employees are in routine jobs. Similarly, recent Australian work suggests that professional jobs are growing rapidly but they still account for less than a third of all jobs and there is concurrent, rapid growth in low-skill sales and service work (Fleming *et al.* 2004).

Second, it would be wrong to assume that those who are really doing knowledge-intensive work automatically experience high levels of autonomy. In the UK, the 2001 Skills Survey revealed a marked decline in task autonomy, with the sharpest fall being among technical and professional employees (Felstead *et al.* 2002). The language of knowledge management – capturing, converting, codifying – is indicative of the tension between the need to encourage creativity and innovation, and the growth of formal systems and metrics for monitoring and measuring such work.

What the above indicates is the enduring importance of both the concept of the frontier of control and the workplace as a contested terrain. In current circumstances, the emphasis of critical analysis is on the substantive rather than the temporal limits of workplace participation. While Harvie Ramsay's work is associated with the 'Cycles' argument, its underlying concern is with the constraints imposed by capitalist political economy and employment relations:

> As for management, the continuing battle to find an organizational answer to competitive and internal pressures seems likely to continue to emphasise the need for employee co-operation. The primary requirement though, will remain that of control, to achieve unit costs savings, quality improvement, flexibility and all the other imperatives. (Ramsay 1991: 20)

New competitive pressures, as well as social and material technologies, compel employers to experiment constantly with available 'best practices' and refashion the division of labour. Employee involvement and participation has always been an integral, if varied, part of that process. While the outcomes are what matter, their significance is continually inflated within managerialist discourses. Like Ramsay's work, this volume is part of the continuing requirement of sceptical scholarship, to bring discussion of involvement and participation 'down to earth'.

References

Ackers, P., Marchington, M., Wilkinson, A. and Goodman, J. (1992) 'The Use of Cycles? Explaining Employee Invovlment in the 1990s', *Industrial Relations Journal*, 23, 268–83.

Adams, R. (1995) *Industrial Relations Under Liberal Democracy* (Columbia: University of South Carolina Press).

Baddon, L., Hunter, L., Hyman, J., Leopold, J. and Ramsay, H. (1989) *People's Capitalism?* (London: Routledge).

Bennet, D. and Bennet, A. (2002) 'The Rise of the Knowledge Organization', in C. W. Holsapple (ed.), *Springer Verlag Handbook on Knowledge Management*, Vol. 1 (Berlin: Springer Verlag).

Blasi, J., Kruse, D. and Bernstein, A. (2003) *In the Company of Owners* (New York: Basic Books).

Brown, P. and Hesketh, A. (2004) *Playing to Win: Managing Employability in the Knowledge-Based Economy* (Oxford University Press).

Cappeli, P., Bassi, L., Katz, H., Knoke, D., Osterman, P. and Useem, M. (1997) *Change at Work* (New York: Oxford University Press).

CBI (1991) 'The UK's Employment Involvement Test', *Labour Research*, April, 12–14.

Cole, G. D. H. (1972) *Self-Government in Industry* (London: Hutchinson).

Cully, M., Woodland, S., O'Reilly, A. and Dix, G. (1999) *Britain at Work* (London: Routledge).

du Gay, P. (1996) *Consumption and Identity at Work* (London: Sage).

Felstead, A., Gallie, D. and Green, F. (2002) *Work Skills in Britain 1986–2001* (Nottingham: Department of Further Education and Skills).

Flecker, J. and Hofbauer, J. (1998) 'Capitalising on Subjectivity: The "New Model Worker" and the Importance of Being Useful', in P. Thompson and C. Warhurst (eds), *Workplaces of the Future* (Basingstoke: Macmillan).

Fleming, P., Harley, B. and Sewell, G. (2004) 'A Little Knowledge is a Dangerous Thing: Getting Below the Surface of the Growth of "Knowledge Work" ', *Work, Employment and Society*, 18, 725–47.

Gill, C. and Krieger, H. (2000) 'Recent Survey Evidence on Participation in Europe: Towards a European Model?', *European Journal of Industrial Relations*, 6, 109–32.

Harvey, D. (1989) *The Condition of Postmodernity* (Oxford: Basil Blackwell).

Heller, F. (1998) 'Playing the Devil's Advocate: Limits to Influence Sharing in Theory and Practice', in F. Heller, E. Pusic, G. Strauss and B. Wilpert (eds), *Organizational Participation: Myth and Reality* (Oxford University Press).

Heller, F., Pusic, E., Strauss, G. and Wilpert, B. (1998) *Organizational Participation: Myth and Reality* (Oxford University Press).

Hodson, R. (2001) *Dignity at Work* (Cambridge University Press).

Hyman, J. and Mason, B. (1995) *Managing Employee Involvement and Participation* (London: Sage).

ILO (International Labour Office) (1960) *Yearbook of Labour Statistics* (Geneva: ILO).

ILO (1975) *Yearbook of Labour Statistics* (Geneva: ILO).

ILO (1980) *Yearbook of Labour Statistics* (Geneva: ILO).

Katz, H. and Darbyshire, O. (2000) *Converging Divergences: Worldwide Changes in Employment Systems* (Ithaca, NY: ILR/Cornell University Press).

Kjellberg, A. (1998)'Sweden: Restoring the Model', in A. Ferner and R. Hyman (eds), *Changing Industrial Relations in Europe* (Oxford: Basil Blackwell).

Legge, K. (2001) 'Silver Bullet or Spent Round? Assessing the Meaning of the "High Commitment Management"/Performance Relationship', in J. Storey (ed.), *Human Resource Management: A Critical Text* (London: Thomson).

Lindsay, C. (2003) 'A Century of Labour Market Change', *Labour Market Trends*, 111, 133–44.

MacDuffie, J. (1995) 'Human Resource Bundles and Manufacturing Performance: Organisational Logic and Flexible Production Systems in the World Auto Industry', *Industrial and Labor Relations Review*, 48, 197–221.

Millward, N., Bryson, A. and Forth, J. (2000) *All Change at Work* (London, Routledge).

Mitchell, B. (2003) *International Historical Statistics: Europe 1750–2000* (Basingstoke: Palgrave Macmillan).

Neef, D. (1998) *The Knowledge Economy* (Boston, Mass.: Butterworth-Heinemann).

Nichols, T. and O'Connell Davidson, J. (1992) 'Employee Shareholders in Two Privatised Utilities', *Industrial Relations Journal*, 23, 107–19.

Pateman, C. (1970) *Participation and Democratic Theory* (Cambridge University Press).

Pateman, C. (1983) 'Some Reflections on Participation and Democratic Theory', in C. Crouch and F. Heller (eds), *International Yearbook of Organisational Democracy*, Vol. 1 (Chichester: John Wiley).

Pendleton, A., Poutsma, E. van Ommeren, J. and Brewster, C. (2001) *Profit Sharing and Employee Share Ownership in the European Union* (Dublin: European Foundation).

Pfeffer, J. (1998) *The Human Equation: Building Profits by Putting People First* (Boston, Mass.: Harvard Business School Press).

Poutsma, E., Hendrickx, J. and Huigen, F. (2003) 'Employee Participation in Europe: In Search of the Participative Workplace', *Economic and Industrial Democracy*, 24, 45–76.

Pries, L. and Abell, J. (2004) 'Shifting Patterns of Labour Regulation: Highly Qualified Knowledge Workers in German New Economy Companies', Paper prepared for the International Workshop, Studying New Forms of Work: Concepts and Practices in Cultural Industries and Beyond, Berlin, March.

Ramsay, H. (1977) 'Cycles of Control: Worker Participation in Sociological and Historical Perspective', *Sociology*, 11, 481–506.

Ramsay, H. (1983)'Evolution or Cycle? Worker Participation in the 1970s and 1980s', in C. Crouch and F. Heller (eds), *Organizational Democracy and Political Processes* (Chichester: John Wiley), 203–25.

Ramsay, H. (1991) 'Reinventing the Wheel: A Review of the Development and Performance of Employee Involvement', *Human Resource Management Journal*, 1, 1–22.

Ramsay, H. (1992) 'Recycled Waste? Debating the Analysis of Worker Participation: A Response to Ackers *et al.*', *Industrial Relations Journal*, 24, 76–80.

Ramsay, H. (1996)'Managing Sceptically: A Critique of Organizational Fashion', in S. Clegg and G. Palmer (eds), *The Politics of Management Knowledge* (London: Sage).

Ramsay, H. (1997) 'Fool's Gold? European Works Councils and Democracy at the Workplace', *Industrial Relations Journal*, 28, 314–22.

Ramsay, H. and Scholarios, D. (1996) 'Cognition in the Machine: On the Development of Dialogue in Management Research between Disciplines and Levels of Analysis', Paper presented at the 4th International Workshop on Managerial and Organisational Cognition, Stockholm, 29–30 August.

Ramsay, H., Scholarios, D. and Harley, B. (2000) 'Employees and High Performance Work Systems: Testing Inside the Black Box', *British Journal of Industrial Relations*, 38, 501–31.

Richards, B. (2004) *People Management*, 11, 21.

Roche, W. and Geary, J. (2002) 'Advocates, Critics and Union Involvement in Workplace Partnership: Irish Airports', *British Journal of Industrial Relations*, 40, 659–88.

Royle, T. (1999) 'Where's the Beef? McDonald's and Its European Works Council', *European Journal of Industrial Relations*, 5, 327–47.

Smith, V. (1997) 'New Forms of Work Organization', *Annual Review of Sociology*, 23, 315–39.

Thompson, P. (2003) 'Disconnected Capitalism: Or Why Employers Can't Keep Their Side of the Bargain', *Work, Employment and Society*, 17, 359–78.

Vaughan Whitehead, D. (1995) *Workers' Financial Participation: East–West Experiences* (Geneva: International Labour Office).

Waddington, J. (2003) 'What Do Representatives Think of the Practices of European Works Councils? Views from Six Countries', *European Journal of Industrial Relations*, 9, 303–26.

Walton, R. (1985) 'From Control to Commitment in the Workplace', *Harvard Business Review*, March–April, 77–84.

White, M., Hill, S., McGovern, P., Mills, C. and Smeaton, D. (2003) ' "High Performance" Management Practices, Working Hours and Work–Life Balance', *British Journal of Industrial Relations*, 41, 175–96.

2
Employee Involvement: Patterns and Explanations
Mick Marchington

Introduction

The amount of published material on participation and democracy at work continues to grow, albeit under many different titles and with varying attention both to theory and decent-quality empirical research. Unfortunately, little of this adds to existing knowledge and is likely to be forgotten in a few years. Such a state of affairs would have saddened, but perhaps not surprised, Harvie Ramsay. The impact of his 1977 paper on a generation of scholars – including me – was immense, and it helped to stimulate further research during the following two decades, as well as to an exceptionally amicable exchange of views in the *Industrial Relations Journal* in the early 1990s (Ackers *et al*. 1992; Ramsay 1992). Although the UMIST team (John Goodman, Adrian Wilkinson, Peter Ackers and myself) had sharply contrasting views on the subject from Harvie, my respect for his research (and I think his for mine!) was considerable. In recent years, he and I wrote less about participation and more in the broader area of employment relations through our respective Future of Work projects. Nevertheless, we both continued to show an interest in participation and democracy, and the purpose of this chapter is to review contemporary developments in the context of his work on cycles, as well as to propose some new lines of enquiry. I hope – for his sake, if nothing else – that this chapter will encourage other students to develop these ideas further and, whatever their perspective, to continue investigating participation at work with the enthusiasm as we both did.

With this in mind, the remainder of the chapter is structured as follows. In the next section we examine the dynamics of participation, specifically restating and reviewing the cycles versus waves debate. While both interpretations have strengths, albeit at different levels of analysis, it is argued here that 'Cycles' ignored explanations for patterns of participation at workplace level while 'waves' paid insufficient attention to the influence of broader societal forces that may promote isomorphic tendencies in a range of different organisations. Both explanations agreed that the evolutionary view was misguided, and that participation was unlikely to evolve over time into more radical forms, but that it would wax and wane in significance over time – as it had in the past. The rest of the chapter then examines three issues thrown up by this debate: the meanings of participation; the extensiveness and centrality of participation; and macro and micro explanations for participation. The third section reviews briefly the meaning of participation, focusing in particular on task-based or direct employee involvement at the workplace level. This aspect of participation is widely acknowledged to have become substantially more extensive since the late 1980s, not just in the UK but also in other industrialised countries, as employers have struggled to find ways of improving competitiveness, quality and customer service. Following this, the fourth section argues that the focus on extensiveness and numbers of schemes in operation, often brought about by statistical analysis of survey data, leads us to ignore the much more important issues of how central and meaningful participation is within particular organisations, and its impact on both employees and organisations. Here, recent work undertaken at UMIST by Annette Cox, Stefan Zagelmeyer and myself (Cox *et al.* 2003) is presented; this proposes that participation can vary in terms of both breadth and depth, and that there are statistically significant links between these and employee outcomes. In the fifth section, one of the most obvious differences between the cycles and waves concepts is addressed directly by examining participation in its macro and micro contexts, suggesting that combining these produces a much better understanding. It is also suggested that analysis of capital–labour relations may continue to offer at least part of the explanation for the dynamics of indirect, if not direct, participation.

Waving Goodbye to Cycles?

Harvie Ramsay first published his influential theory on how participation was subject to cycles of control in the mid-1970s at the height of the debate about worker directors and around the time when the Bullock Committee of Inquiry reported its deliberations (Bullock 1977). As most readers will know, the Bullock Committee was set up by the Labour government, soon after Britain's accession to the European Union, to consider how – not whether – worker directors could be introduced on to the boards of UK companies. Most newspapers then felt the most significant feature of this form of participation would either be a fall in productivity as other board members struggled to explain the finer points of executive decision-making to shop stewards, or an opportunity for left-wing union leaders to undermine capitalism. Several cartoons featured union representatives in cloth caps bringing their sandwiches to board meetings, or asking what time the tea break was scheduled for, such was the seriousness with which the media took this important issue.

The Bullock Report (1977) comprised two parts, which in itself summed up the differences between trade unions and academics on the one hand, and employers on the other. The Majority Report recommended that an equal number of union and employer nominees (plus a group of independents) be appointed to the main board if sufficient employees voted in favour of the idea. By contrast, the Minority Report sought to restrict the influence of non-managerial staff on company affairs through their representation solely on supervisory boards. A subsequent White Paper and the election of a Conservative government two years later brought an end to any notion of worker directors and initiated a step-by-step dismantling of union rights through changes to the law. When the Ramsay piece was published, however, talk was still of evolution to a new era of industrial democracy, not only through institutions of power-sharing at corporate headquarters but also through job redesign to provide workers with more influence over their day-to-day working lives. One of the key points made by Harvie was that commentators should not be seduced by such an optimistic scenario, but instead appreciate that participation should be analysed within a sociological and historical perspective that demonstrated its cyclical nature. Referring to a quote by Daniel (1978: 49) – 'the tide (for participation) appears irresistible' – he noted wryly that 'the trouble with tides is that they are pulled by forces beyond direct observation: and they have a nasty habit of turning' (Ramsay 1983: 220).

Evidence was produced that indicated how interest in participation had waxed and waned since the mid-nineteenth century, taking on different forms in different periods. Briefly, there was evidence that profit-sharing grew in significance by several times during the late nineteenth century, and that joint consultation (variously through Whitley committees and joint production committees) had grown in importance during and just after the two world wars. For example, it was argued that there was a surge in profit-sharing schemes as employers became concerned about the threat of unionisation, especially from the general unions in the 1880s–1890s. In the three-year period 1889 to 1892, Ramsay (1977: 484) states that eighty-eight new schemes were implemented compared with forty during the previous fifteen years. Following this growth, the number of new schemes fell dramatically, and many of those that had started up fell into disuse. Similarly, it was stated that the number of workers covered by Whitley committees reached a peak of 3.5 million only to decline early in the 1920s; he notes (1977: 488) that 'this shows the magnitude of this participation wave compared with earlier ones . . . It also reveals its limits, for this peak lasted only a short time and covered areas not previously well organised.' Yet again, a similar pattern emerges with the third wave in the 1940s, with the number of JPCs reaching over 4,500 in 1944 only to decline to about 550 four years later. The most recent manifestation, during the 1960s and 1970s, incorporated a variety of developments, including productivity bargaining and worker directors, which merged into one. The fact that interest in participation seemed to appear in growth spurts and then decline almost as quickly led Harvie to conclude that, after initial enthusiasm, schemes tend to lose significance as managements come to realise that they offer very little. In short, he argued (Ramsay 1977: 496) that participation schemes:

(a) arose out of a managerial response to threats to its authority from labour;
(b) were designed to nullify the threat from labour through the offer of greater involvement (in whatever form) in the management or financial success of the enterprise;
(c) emphasised a consensual, unitary philosophy; and
(d) fell into disuse or were abandoned by management once the threat to its authority had been dissipated.

This 'cycles of control' thesis had its roots in a Marxist conflict analysis whereby the interests of capital and labour could never be accommodated without a fundamental change to the nature of ownership and employment. Within this perspective, participation schemes were to be treated with caution, if not disdain, because they offered employees the illusive and ultimately false opportunity to co-operate with employers for mutual gain. In a later publication (1983: 219), Harvie updated and refined the cycles thesis in the context of early 1980s Thatcherite industrial relations, arguing that the potential for industrial democracy had been 'swept under the carpet' through the new managerial offensive. He concluded that the cycles analysis had 'been more dramatically vindicated than could readily have been imagined in the mid-1970s' (Ramsay 1983: 219). It is notable that most books on participation published in the late 1970s and early 1980s (for example, Marchington 1980; Poole 1975, 1986; Brannen 1983) took the cycles analysis for granted, and it was reproduced routinely in leading industrial relations texts such as Farnham and Pimlott (1983).

Apart from some challenges to the data produced in support of the cycles analysis (for example, Bougen *et al.* 1988) to which we shall return later, it was only with the advent of the waves concept that a more serious and sustained alternative was unfurled. Broadly, it was argued (Ackers *et al.* 1992; Marchington *et al.* 1992; Marchington *et al.* 1993) that the cycles thesis could not account for growth in the number of employee involvement schemes from the mid-1980s onwards. Indeed, given that it was generally acknowledged that trade unions lacked power, and workers were unwilling to challenge management authority during this period, the cycles thesis would have predicted a decline in participation. Capital was not under any realistic threat from labour, and there was no move from the state to extend workers' collective rights – quite the contrary, in fact. Admittedly, the form that participation took at this time – and has tended to take since then – was dilute and managerially-motivated, but nevertheless it represented a new initiative by employers to seek co-operation from employees through various processes of information-sharing, consultation and financial involvement. Given that the Ramsay analysis had regarded profit-sharing as the first cycle, it was considered appropriate for other, in fact less dilute, forms of participation to be included in the discussion.

The detailed and longitudinal case studies on which the waves metaphor was based demonstrated clearly that, irrespective of broader developments, the dynamics of participation at workplace level were highly uneven. For example, some organisations utilised up to ten different schemes, several of which had operated for more than twenty years, while others were much newer. The importance of these schemes seemed to vary greatly, both between and within organisations, and there was evidence that different schemes had come to prominence at different times. Moreover, some had been revitalised while others had just slipped away quietly without anyone being that bothered about their demise. In other organisations, there were just one or two different techniques, they were of marginal interest to workers and managers, and their impact was minimal. Some patterns did emerge, largely because of organisational factors such as the age and size of establishments, their sector and degree of centralised decision-making – as well as trade union power – but *processes* were seen as being critically important. Interestingly, subsequent case study research by same team (Marchington *et al.* 2001) has confirmed that developments remain uneven, and that schemes recently introduced into one workplace may have been terminated in another. Additionally, although so-called new developments – such as partnerships – have become more extensive, they have been operating for years in some organisations under a different label, with the parties unaware that they were apparently at the forefront of contemporary employment relations. A key point to emerge from the waves concept was that, valuable though broad-brush and macro-level theories were, much more attention needed to be focused on the intricacies of workplace relations and the motives of all parties in order to analyse the dynamics of participation.

Rather than explaining the ebbs and flows of participation solely in terms of changes in power within capital–labour relations, the waves concept proposed that internal managerial relations was an equally important force at the organisational level (for a lengthier development of these ideas, see Marchington *et al.* 1993). Moreover, the waves research exposed the differences between management intentions and the practice of EI at workplace level with all its unintended consequences. The source of the impetus for new initiatives depended to some extent on organisational structures, with large, decentralised manufacturing firms being the most likely to implement participation schemes locally with a minimum of corporate involvement, and large centralised service sector organisations behaving in quite the opposite way. This had implications for the degree of ownership local managers felt for the schemes, and in some cases they went through the motions of operating the company-wide technique while promoting their own initiatives more vigorously. In all firms, however, the presence of champions was essential to bring about new developments and ensure that they were implemented at the workplace level. These people are often young managers on a fast-track promotion route through the organisation, keen to make an impression on more senior management by demonstrating their ability to introduce change. They also move within wider managerial and professional circles, perhaps through an MBA programme, so that they mix with colleagues from other organisations as well as their own and are tuned into the latest thinking on human resource management (HRM) and employment studies. Not only do they have the incentive to initiate new developments, but they are also able to interact with business-school professors, visiting speakers and management consultants.

There are three sets of reasons why participation schemes are such a fertile ground in which champions can sow their seeds. First, there has been continuing government interest, at least at a rhetorical level – through ideas of information, communication, consultation and partnership – for more open styles of management decision-making to be introduced on a voluntary basis. The most recent manifestation of this has been through the DTI Partnership Fund. Second, models of high-commitment HRM include specific reference to participation in one form or another, with a strong emphasis on the importance of employees feeling engaged with, and committed to, their organisations. In recent times, a particular focus has been on the impact of communication, team working and appraisal on aspects of organisational performance such as quality and productivity (for example, Guest *et al.* 2000, 2003) and even patient mortality (West *et al.* 2002). Neo-unitarist ideologies promote the idea that participation, especially of a direct and personalised nature, not only offers the potential to improve performance, but it is also a 'good' thing in principle (Wilkinson 2001). Finally, as Kanter (1985) suggests, in contrast to decisions about the implementation of new technology, there is little need for people who are championing participation techniques to have any great technical knowledge; this renders the field open to managers from a wide range of functional specialisms. Moreover, participation schemes are relatively cheap to design, theoretically straightforward to introduce, and the champion's efforts can soon reap rewards in terms of visibility – if not in impact.

If champions are largely responsible for the introduction of schemes in the first place, their mobility plays a major part in the subsequent decline or downgrading. It is apparent from a number of studies (for example, Marchington 1995; Edwards and Wright 1998; Marchington and Wilkinson 2000) that internal divisions within management, both between levels in the hierarchy and between functions, contribute significantly to the loss of impetus associated with any new initiative, including participation. There are three broad elements to this. First, as champions move on, other managers have the responsibility for maintaining commitment to a scheme over which they had no ownership or input. Not surprisingly, they show little interest in doing this, and are often content to allow the initiative to fade away. However, other upwardly mobile managers appear on the scene to promote their own ideas, often leading to a plethora of new practices that compete with one another (Ahlstrand 1990; Huczynski 1993). Second, the waves concept is built on an assumption that management is not cohesive, coherent and well-drilled, but instead is characterised by fragmentation, competition and instability. Given the ease with which participation schemes can be introduced, it is hardly surprising that different functional groupings see it as a good way to make an impression. In the original waves study (Marchington *et al.* 1992) there were a number of cases where conflict arose between functions about the best way to develop participation. As well as the human resource (HR) function, marketing also contributed to communications drives, operations management to total quality initiatives, and accountants to profit-sharing schemes. Similarly, proposals by senior managers often encounter resistance in the lower ranks, especially from supervisors, who regard any new idea as little more than the latest fad or the brainchild of young graduates who do not appreciate how sceptical workers really are. Finally, given that responsibility for implementing schemes resides with supervisors, participation often ranks low on their list of priorities in the face of competing production or service pressures. This is hardly surprising, when supervisors are appraised and rewarded on the basis of how well they meet operational goals rather than satisfying the less easily measurable needs of participation. In short, despite being ostensibly a device to encourage workers to contribute to organisational goals, participation at the workplace level often falls foul of divisions within management.

What Does Participation Really Mean?

One of the biggest problems with the literature on participation is the lack of a clear and unambiguous definition of its subject matter. More than twenty years ago, Harvie noted (Ramsay 1980: 46) that 'the literature on participation is vast. Yet, when the time comes to search for substance amid the wind, the results are sharply disappointing'. The situation is even more problematic at the start of the 2000s, with material referring to a multitude of different practices and approaches, often with little in common. For example, some would regard industrial democracy as the only true form of participation, since this offers workers an opportunity to take control of the organisations in which they are employed. Conversely, others would consider information-sharing as sufficient to be included in the definition because it is an example of management attempting to involve employees by providing data that was previously unavailable to them. Yet others would restrict their definition to financial participation, because this gives workers an opportunity not only to make a direct contribution to organisational success but also – and more importantly – to quite rightly take their fair share of company profits. Finally, some might feel that participation is only achievable when trade unions are able to protect workers' rights and channel their contributions through an independent body. In short, because participation is such an elastic term, greater precision is required if we are to analyse it properly. This task is made more problematic because the dominant terminology – workers' control, industrial democracy, workers' participation, employee involvement, empowerment, social partnership – has changed over time, to some extent reflecting different fads and fashions but also conveying contrasting motives. At one level, no one could possibly be 'against' workers participating in the organisations within which they are employed; after all, the alternative is autocracy and the unfettered exercise of managerial power, or indeed slavery. However, once we move beyond this simplistic dichotomy and start to analyse the nature and impact of participation, as well as the motives of those who propagate it, the picture becomes more complex and multi-faceted. In order to extend this discussion, the term needs to be deconstructed into degree, scope, level and form.

The *degree* of involvement indicates the extent to which workers – or their representatives – are able to influence management decisions. This can range from merely being provided with information, through two-way communication, consultation, co-determination and control. It is obvious that managers retain ultimate control over decisions until the final two categories in this list, and that, despite being accorded the right to be consulted about an issue, workers' views can be ignored if management sees fit. Yet, at the same time, it would be foolish of managers to discount strong and heartfelt opposition from workers even if they lack the power and resources to prevent action being taken. Unlike machines, workers have an independent will and they can make life tricky for managers by, for example, sticking rigidly to rules or working without enthusiasm. Such tactics are hard to counter unless there is a pool of equally-qualified labour available at short notice to replace those who are expressing discontent. At the same time, nobody would argue seriously that the right to be consulted carries anything like the same force as co-determination or control. The examples used in support of the cycles thesis were those where there was a rather limited degree of participation, ranging from virtually none (in the case of profit-sharing) through to consultation (in Whitleyism and JPCs), although the worker-director period offered the potential promise of co-determination. Ultimately, of course, this phase came to nothing and British trade unions are still fighting to get rights to information and consultation in line with their EU counterparts.

If the degree of participation is a vital aspect in any definition, then so too is the *scope* of the decisions that are open to involvement by workers. Scope relates to the type of subject matter dealt with in the participation arena, ranging from the trivial to the strategic. Examples of the former might include the venue and/or theme for the office Christmas party or the colour of the wallpaper in the office; among the list of supposedly trivial issues would normally be the allocation of car-parking spaces, but this often generates as much heat and discord as seemingly more important questions about the future direction of the organisation. Strategic issues would typically relate to broader questions of company objectives, plans for new products and services, and investment decisions, all of which can have major consequences for workers' current employment and future job prospects. These are the sorts of decisions that are routinely taken by senior managers alone, and at best workers are consulted before plans are finally approved or informed in advance of their coming into effect; though there have been cases when emails or text messages have been used to inform people they have been made redundant. The combination of scope and degree can lead to interesting situations, such as where employees are given extensive rights over trivial issues, or they are provided with little (or no) information about major changes. Of the participation practices examined in the original cycles thesis, the scope of issues considered by Whitley committees or by JPCs was principally production-related rather than being about strategic matters confronting the enterprise. However, it could be argued that 'local' decisions might be regarded as precisely the sorts of issues on which workers are best qualified and most keen to contribute.

It is also important to establish the *level* at which workers (or their representatives) are involved in management decisions. As with other dimensions of participation, this can vary quite substantially, ranging from workplace or departmental level through to establishment, division and headquarters. This is a useful distinction because it recognises explicitly the fact that management does not operate in a unified way and decisions taken at more senior levels – especially those by a foreign-owned multinational – are beyond the scope not only of shop-floor or office workers but also of local managers, and even governments in the host country. There is often a link between scope and level, in that the more trivial decisions tend to be made at workplace level, whereas the more strategic are taken at corporate headquarters without any employee involvement. Much of the management interest in participation, however, is focused at the lower levels, where it is felt workers are best placed to make a contribution to organisational goals and are able to apply their knowledge to improve quality, productivity and customer service.

Finally, participation takes quite different *forms*: it may be direct or face-to-face, as is the case with many of the recent employee-involvement initiatives, or it may be indirect – as occurs when trade unions represent workers on high-level consultative committees or works councils, or through collective bargaining. Some would argue that direct participation is covertly designed to weaken the collective will of workers by individualising their actions and getting them to identify with employer goals. As such, these forms of participation are often denigrated and ridiculed, and certainly not regarded as falling within the ambit of any meaningful definition. Yet an alternative perspective would suggest that workers are presented with a more direct route to managers if they do not have to funnel their views through representative channels where they can be subjected to distortion for other – albeit wider and possibly more beneficial – ends. Job redesign and self-management initiatives can offer workers opportunities to exert considerable control over their daily working lives, as various experiments have shown. However, the fact these are at workplace level may obscure the fact that control over day-to-day issues is meaningless if decisions taken further up the corporate hierarchy lead to plant closures.

It is therefore essential to classify different participation schemes according to this matrix of degree, scope, level and form. In the early part of the twenty-first century, there is little doubt that the most widely used forms of participation are concerned with communication and consultation, either at shop-floor or organisational level. Most – such as briefing groups, problem-solving groups and profit-sharing – are dilute on participation, and very few of the large number of team working initiatives offer any real opportunity for workers to manage themselves. There is little doubt that employers are now the main drivers of participation, and schemes are therefore likely to be designed with their objectives in mind. Even the champions that promote participation have to legitimise their ideas by explicit reference to managerial goals – such as improved quality and productivity, enhanced employee commitment and satisfaction, or reduced levels of absence or labour turnover – despite the fact they have more covert personal aims and objectives. However, even if schemes are set up to promote participation, this could backfire if workers treat management communications with suspicion. There is more evidence of consultation in the rest of Europe, and some limited degree of co-determination through works councils and worker directors, but in Britain this tends to be restricted to the major multinationals and a few firms where participation is offered through a mix of management benevolence and organisational traditions. Worker co-operatives are few and far between, despite continuing interest in them, so there is little evidence of more radical innovations except in some small firms with a strong ideological commitment to participation and democracy. It is clear, though, that most organisations, especially those that are larger and more established, operate with a mix of separate participation schemes, so it is more appropriate to conceive of participation in the plural rather than the singular. One scheme may fall into disrepute or collapse altogether, but others keep going, in some cases for many years.

The Breadth and Depth of Participation in Practice

Much of the research on participation has tended to focus on extensiveness, the proportion of organisations operating specific schemes, and their growth and decline over time (for example, MacInnes 1985; Cully *et al.* 1999). Ramsay's (1977) paper published in *Sociology* made use of secondary data to chart the ebbs and flows of participation in its different guises since the late nineteenth century. At one level, this is critically important as it provides an indication of coverage for each technique, and it allows an assessment of the popularity of particular methods of participation, not only in relation to each other but also to other employment practices such as collective bargaining. It also enables the results from case study analysis to be put into wider perspective and provides a benchmark for practitioners. There are dangers with quantitative data, however, particularly if it is open to alternative interpretation. Indeed, Bougen *et al.* (1988) critiqued the cycles thesis in relation to the data on profit-sharing, arguing that other material available for the late 1880s suggested that it had been introduced for reasons other than fighting off trade unions. Moreover, they argued (1988: 610–11) that, if profit-sharing had been used as the proxy for participation in the 1920s, instead of Whitley councils, it would have undermined the cycles thesis rather than substantiating it. Similar points were made in relation to the growth of profit-sharing post-1980. Of course, if we were to contend that profit-sharing is not a form of participation, and the original phase in the model were to be ignored, 'Cycles' might still contribute to an explanation for the dynamics of indirect participation.

We now know through the UK Workplace Employee Relations Survey (WERS) data in particular how the coverage of individual participation techniques has fared since 1980. For example, we find that joint consultation has declined marginally in extensiveness, but this is more a reflection of the changing nature of employment than to joint consultation's demise in particular workplaces: from 34 per cent in 1980 it went down to 29 per cent of workplaces employing twenty-five or more people by 1998. Compared with collective bargaining, joint consultation has held up reasonably well, albeit starting from a much lower base. By contrast, direct forms of participation have grown significantly since the 1980s, and now a large number of workplaces claim to practise these techniques. For example, at the time of the most recent WERS survey, teamworking was found in 65 per cent of workplaces (employing twenty-five or more people), team briefing in 61 per cent, attitude surveys in 45 per cent, and problem-solving groups in 42 per cent. Such detailed questions were not asked in the original WERS survey, itself an indicator of how this form of participation has assumed greater significance since the 1980s. Financial participation has also become more extensive, with over 50 per cent of workplaces offering profit sharing, employee share ownership or profit-related pay.

Incidentally, profit-related pay enjoyed short-run popularity, declining substantially relatively soon after it came to prominence. Its growth was related almost entirely to favourable governmental tax regimes, and its decline had nothing to do with capital–labour relations, but came about after the tax incentive was removed. This short episode reaffirms that participation is subject to variation over time, but it also adds weight to the argument that the cycles thesis needed to be extended beyond the capital–labour relationship if it was to be able to offer a more complete explanation for the dynamics of participation.

Relying on measures of extensiveness alone, however, is a very narrow way in which to evaluate the significance of particular techniques or participation in general, for a number of reasons. First, it assumes a level of specificity in definition that does not accord with practical realities, and that all respondents to surveys have the same understanding of a specific term. For example, it is quite possible that an organisation has a partnership arrangement, with all the usual characteristics, but it has always been called something else. While some respondents may choose to include this in the figures, others may not (Marchington *et al.* 2001). Equally, just because a particular name is used for a technique operating in a workplace, does this mean that it should be included irrespective of whether it conforms to the model? Second, relying on questions about absence or presence does not take into account *how* these schemes work in practice; for example, one firm may hold problem-solving groups every six months, while at another it happens every morning as a prelude to work, or every week to allow for staff training. Similarly, one briefing scheme may be a vehicle for supervisors to inform their staff about the latest developments in the organisation, with little or no chance for them to ask questions or engage in discussion, while in another it is designed specifically to allow an opportunity for debate. Third, asking questions about absence or presence, without any follow-up about the proportion of workers involved, overlooks the possibility that only a minority of those employed are able to take advantage of the scheme. This is recognised in WERS in relation to share-ownership arrangements, where schemes that only include a minority of staff – especially senior managers – are so fundamentally different from those for which staff from all grades are eligible. But the same principle applies to problem-solving groups or to team briefing that is only open to employees, rather than to agency workers or temporary staff – despite in some cases comprising the majority of those working at the site – who do not have access to participation machinery (Marchington *et al.* 2004). Finally, questions about extensiveness tell us nothing about the extent to which schemes are embedded within a workplace or an organisation. A particular technique may have been in operation for many years but be marginal to everything that occurs in the workplace; for example, a joint consultative committee (JCC) could be a tangential, albeit rather pleasant, talking shop or a briefing group only telling workers what they already know or in which they are not interested. Moreover, if more than one scheme is in operation, we are not able to determine which has the greater influence or importance in the organisation, nor are we able to assess how different stakeholders feel about participation at work. Similar questions arose repeatedly during the research project on which the original 'waves' concept was developed. Perhaps the most striking example was where a head office told us that team briefing was the flagship practice throughout the organisation, only for us to discover that at one branch we visited it had never operated (Marchington *et al*. 1992).

In order to address this problem, Cox *et al*. (2003) have developed two measures – breadth and depth – to assess the importance of particular partic-ipation techniques in the workplace. Breadth is a measure of how many different participation schemes operate in the workplace, implying that the more schemes there are, the greater the breadth. This makes the same assumption as has been applied to the 'bundles' debate in HRM, whereby combinations of practices within the high commitment paradigm are assumed to complement each other and provide a more rounded and inte-grated system of employment (Huselid 1995; Delery and Doty 1996). Indeed, Guest *et al*. (2000) indicate a clear link between the number of high commit-ment HR practices and positive employee attitudes. By contrast, a single scheme operating in isolation is unlikely to be central to the organisation, particularly if it occupies only a small amount of time (for example, an annual presentation to staff) and/or it has little in common with other HR practices in the workplace (for example, it is contained within an employ-ment regime that provides no job security, offers no training and is imple-mented by bullying supervisors). Participation in this context can easily be dismissed by workers as marginal to or out-of-line with their other experi-ences in the organisation, and the contradictions with hard-nosed HRM are all too apparent.

Depth measures how embedded each individual technique is within the workplace, assessing factors such as the regularity, significance and level of power accorded to employees in order to estimate the centrality of each tech-nique. While accepting that each of these factors assesses slightly different aspects of participation, they all measure depth, and we assume that partic-ipation practices occupying a more meaningful place within the workplace – in terms of covering a greater proportion of employees or being held at more frequent intervals – are likely to have a bigger impact on staff. Moreover, if they are also seen to offer opportunities for workers to have some say or influence over decisions – rather than being a cosmetic exercise or a blatant attempt to indoctrinate them – participation is likely to be seen as deeper and more genuine. Furthermore, if workers are able to choose their representatives for committees through election, without any manage-rial interference, as happens in some JCCs, participation techniques can be seen as being more meaningful. Cox *et al.* (2003) suggest that combining breadth and depth offers a better chance of evaluating participation in practice than does any attempt based on its absence or presence alone. Ideally, these indicators should be assessed through longitudinal case study work, but they are also amenable to measurement through the WERS management and employee databases.

Initial testing shows that breadth and depth are associated much more significantly with positive employee outcomes – such as commitment, satisfaction, loyalty, pride, fairness and shared values – than presence alone. The relationships are particularly strong for direct participation techniques, such as team briefing, where workers are more inclined to feel a sense of equity and fairness if briefings are conducted frequently and with a wide range of staff, and they are also given the opportunity to contribute their ideas to meetings. However, the associations between indirect participation and these sorts of employee outcomes are not significant (Cox *et al.* 2003). Given Harvie's very significant concern that many participation devices were 'phantom' and lacking in any real value, these findings about depth and breadth are of great interest.

Explanations Within and Beyond the Workplace

Perhaps the major difference between the cycles and waves concepts is the level at which analysis was focused. Cycles was unashamedly macro in orientation, seeking explanations that would account for general moves in interest – and not necessarily in extent – in participation. It was derived from Marxist underpinnings and thus saw employment relations as constituting a class struggle between capital and labour, in which the former would use any device at its disposal to regain control from the latter if its authority came under threat. Participation therefore offered a convenient – albeit phantom in Harvie's view – opportunity to convince workers that managers were in fact interested in their ideas. Once the threat fades away, according to this analysis, managers are free to return to their normal, autocratic behaviour. The waves concept, by contrast, was focused specifically on a micro and meso analysis at the organisation level, paying only limited attention to forces at a societal level. We were rather more interested in explaining patterns of diversity rather than similarity, and therefore located our investigation at the workplace level, seeking out reasons for differences not only in patterns of participation but also in the way that they ebbed and flowed in centrality and prominence. The waves analysis did not ignore capital–labour relations – far from it – but instead focused on how relations within management had a major impact on the schemes that were implemented, as well as on the processes that accompanied their growth and decline. By treating each technique individually, it became possible to chart the dynamics of participation over time in relation to the growth and decline of different schemes rather than as a whole.

In the exchange of views in the *Industrial Relations Journal*, both parties sought to defend their approach, and it was suggested that nothing was wrong with either concept, just that they were at cross-purposes. As Ackers *et al.* (1992: 281) noted, it could be argued that 'whilst we revel in micro-level complexity in a limited number of organisations for a given period, he [Harvie] soars high above, mapping out a macro-level theory of participation with a much greater temporal and spatial reach'. Harvie (Ramsay 1992: 79) responded by referring to a film (*Distant Thunder*) where people in an Indian village, ravaged by food shortages, have no understanding of why this is happening to them, nor why they hear aircraft engines far away. As he noted, 'their lives and their actions are nonetheless shaped by these things'. Just as the cycles analysis included specific examples of participation in companies, such as in John Lewis (Ramsay 1980) and elsewhere (Ramsay 1976), the waves study made reference to forces beyond the workplace – under the heading of political and institutional frameworks (Marchington *et al.* 1992: 53–4). This noted specifically how government attitudes to EI (including the law), the influence of popular management texts and consultants had promoted particular forms of participation.

In retrospect, I think we could have developed this much more and examined the interplay between a mix of forces beyond and within organisations, as well as the influence of foreign-owned multinationals on participation. Certainly, our subsequent research has attempted to enrich detailed workplace-level investigation with a more nuanced awareness of the influence of societal forces, particularly in our research on employee voice for the CIPD (Marchington *et al.* 2001). In addition, the analysis by Frobel (2001) showed how team-working practices and the attitudes of workers at two multinationals operating in Germany and the UK were influenced by a mix of host country characteristics (such as the legal and educational systems) and company-specific factors. Similarly, Galinos (2003) examined the ways in which the Greek system of industrial relations had an explicit, though far from complete and somewhat uneven, influence on partnership arrangements operating in different organisations depending on their traditions and structural characteristics. A study by Marchington *et al.* (2003) on the road haulage industry showed how, despite differences in the human resource practices adopted by individual firms, there were nevertheless substantial similarities in their approaches to managing employment because of industry-wide forces. Though each of these studies examined slightly different topics, they all demonstrated clearly that participation is influenced by a mix of forces – sometimes competing, sometimes complementary – both within and beyond the boundaries of the organisation. Other recent research conducted at UMIST (Rubery *et al.* 2003; Marchington *et al.* 2004) has

extended this yet further by analysing the way in which employment relations operates in multi-employer environments, where the combined influence of clients and employers can have major consequences for the workers
involved. This shows how difficult it is for marginal workers, such as agency
staff or sub-contracted labour, to attain an effective voice in situations where
they are operating beyond the boundaries of the organisation and no specific
arrangements are in place to involve them.

Conclusions

The legacy of Harvie Ramsay's research on participation has been immense,
not just his very early contribution on cycles of control but throughout his
entire career. His challenge to prevailing wisdom in the 1970s was important, and it needs to be appreciated within that time-frame as well as in
terms of its longer-standing influence on the study of participation since
then. Although the cycles analysis has been subject to detailed critique since
it was first published – in itself recognition of its value – it has not been
totally dismissed. The waves metaphor, with its focus on managerial relations as well as capital–labour relations, is probably best seen as a contribution to our understanding of participation at the level of the organisation,
whereas cycles provided one aspect of a macro-level thesis. Of course, both
are critically important if we are to extend our analysis, and it is the interplay of explicit and implicit forces at different levels that needs further
investigation. While the cycles analysis failed to predict the growth of direct
participation since the 1980s, it still helps to explain why indirect participation has declined as trade union power has reduced. Joint consultative
committees are less extensive than they were twenty-five years ago, and an
increasing number are now in non-union firms. Even though there has been
considerable interest in partnership, evidence of its incidence and impact
has been patchy despite the publicity. Moreover, this has been stimulated by
the threat of impending legislation and a desire on the part of employers to
find more co-operative ways of working, rather than by any attempt to 'head
off' a resurgent union backlash. Ultimately, however, if we are to understand better the patterns and dynamics of participation, we need to provide
a rather tighter definition and do more longitudinal research. For Harvie's
sake, let us make sure this happens.

Note

I am grateful to Peter Ackers, Annette Cox, Adrian Wilkinson and Stefan Zagelmeyer
for their comments on earlier drafts of this chapter.

References

Ackers, P., Marchington, M., Wilkinson, A. and Goodman, J. (1992) 'The Use of Cycles? Explaining Employee Involvement in the 1990s', *Industrial Relations Journal*, 23:4, 268–83.

Ahlstrand, B. (1990) *The Quest for Productivity* (Cambridge University Press).

Bougen, P., Ogden, S. and Outram, Q. (1988) 'Profit Sharing and the Cycle of Control', *Sociology*, 22:4 , 607–29.

Brannen, P. (1983) *Authority and Participation in Industry* (London: Batsford).

Bullock, Lord A. (1977) *Report of the Committee of Inquiry on Industrial Democracy*, London: HMSO.

Cox, A., Zagelmeyer, S. and Marchington, M. (2003) 'The Embeddedness of Employee Involvement and Participation (EIP) and Its Impact on Employee Outcomes – an Analysis of WERS 98', Paper presented at EGOS, Copenhagen.

Cully, M., Woodland, S., O'Reilly, A. and Dix, G. (1999) *Britain at Work* (London: Routledge).

Daniel, W.W. (1978) 'Industrial Democracy', in Torrington, D. (ed.) *Comparative Industrial Relations in Europe*, Westport, Conn.: Greenwood Press.

Delery, J. and Doty, D. (1996) Models of Theorising in Strategic HRM: Test of Universalistic Contingency and Configurational Perspectives', *Academy of Management Journal*, 39:4, 802–35.

Edwards, P. and Wright, M. (1998) 'HRM and Commitment: A Case Study of Team-working', in P. Sparrow and M. Marchington (eds), *Human Resource Management: The New Agenda* (London: Pitman).

Farnham, P. and Pimlott, J. (1983) *Understanding Industrial Relations*, 2nd edn (London: Cassell).

Frobel, P. (2001) 'Team Effectiveness: An International and Inter-Industry Perspective', Unpublished Ph.D. thesis, UMIST.

Galinos, E. (2003) 'The Form of Social Partnership on the Greek Context of Industrial Industrial', Unpublished Ph.D. thesis, UMIST.

Guest, D., Michie, J., Sheehan, M., Conway, N. and Metochi, M. (2000) *Effective People Management* (London: CIPD).

Guest, D., Michie, J., Sheehan, M. and Conway, N. (2003) 'Human Resource Management and Corporate Performance in the UK', *British Journal of Industrial Relations*, 41:2, 291–314.

Huczynski, A. (1993) *Management Gurus: What Makes Them and How to Become One* (London: Routledge).

Huselid, M. (1995) 'The Impact of Human Resource Management Practices on Turnover, Productivity and Corporate Financial Performance', *Academy of Management Journal*, 38:3, 635–72.

Kanter, R. (1985) *The Change Masters: Corporate Entrepreneurs at Work* (London: Unwin).

MacInnes, J. (1985) 'Conjuring Up Consultation: The Role and Extent of Joint Consultation in Post-war Private Manufacturing Industry', *British Journal of Industrial Relations*, 23:1, 93–113.

Marchington, M. (1980) *Responses to Participation at Work* (Farnborough: Gower).

Marchington, M. (1995) 'Fairy Tales and Magic Wands: New Employment Practices in Perspective', *Employee Relations*, 17:1, 51–66.

Marchington, M. and Wilkinson, A. (2000) 'Direct Participation', in S. Bach and K. Sisson (eds), *Personnel Management in Britain* (London: Blackwell).

Marchington, M., Carroll, M. and Boxall, P. (2003) 'Labour Scarcity and the Survival of Small Firms: A Resource-based View of the Road Haulage Industry', *Human Resource Management Journal*, 13:4, 5–22.

Marchington, M., Wilkinson, A., Ackers, P. and Goodman, J. (1993) 'The Influence of Managerial Relations on Waves of Employee Involvement', *British Journal of Industrial Relations*, 31:4, 543–76.

Marchington, M., Wilkinson, A., Ackers, P. and Dundon, T. (2001) *Management Choice and Employee Voice* (London: CIPD).

Marchington, M., Rubery, J., Grimshaw, D. and Willmott, H. (eds) (2004) *Fragmenting Work* (Oxford University Press).

Poole, M. (1975) *Workers' Participation in Industry* (London: Routledge & Kegan Paul).

Poole, M. (1986) *Towards a New Industrial Democracy: Workers' Participation in Industry* (London: Routledge & Kegan Paul).

Ramsay, H. (1976) 'Participation: The Shop Floor View', *British Journal of Industrial Relations*, 14:2, 128–41.

Ramsay, H. (1977) 'Cycles of Control: Worker Participation in Sociological and Historical Perspective', *Sociology*, 11:3, 481–506.

Ramsay, H. (1980) 'Phantom Participation: Patterns of Power and Conflict', *Industrial Relations Journal*, 11:3, 46–59.

Ramsay, H. (1983) 'Evolution or Cycle? Worker Participation in the 1970s and 1980s', in C. Crouch and F. Heller (eds), *Organizational Democracy and Political Processes* (Chichester: John Wiley), 203–25.

Ramsay, H. (1992) 'Recycled Waste? Debating the Analysis of Worker Participation: A Response to Ackers *et al.*', *Industrial Relations Journal*, 24:1, 76–80.

Rubery, J., Cooke, F.L., Earnshaw, J. and Marchington, M. (2003) 'Inter-organisational Relations and Employment in a Multi-employer Environment', *British Journal of Industrial Relations*, 41:2, 265–89.

West, M., Borrill, C., Dawson, J., Scully, J., Carter, M., Anelay, S., Patterson, M. and Waring, J. (2002) 'The Link Between the Management of Employees and Patient Mortality in Acute Hospitals', *International Journal of Human Resource Management*, 13:8, 1299–310.

Wilkinson, A. (2001) 'Empowerment', in M. Warner (ed.) *International Encyclopaedia of Business and Management* (London: International Thomson Business Press).

3
Hope or Hype? High-Performance Work Systems

Bill Harley

Introduction

Since the mid-1990s, a new discourse has emerged in the fields of human resource management (HRM), industrial relations and industrial sociology. This discourse proclaims the emergence of a genuinely new approach to organising work, in which organisations that 'empower' their staff by means of participative forms of work, buttressed with appropriate skill and reward practices, will reap performance gains at the same time as employees enjoy higher levels of autonomy in their jobs. The new approach to organising work – commonly labelled as 'high performance work systems' (HPWS)[1] – is, we are told, sweeping workplaces across the OECD.

The proclamation of 'the new' in the management of labour has a long pedigree, and the emphasis on what might be termed 'developmental humanism' in work organisation can be traced back at least to the human relations school in the 1930s. Since then, it has been repackaged repeatedly – in the 1950s, 1960s and 1970s by motivation theorists including Herzberg, Argyris and McGregor, as well as by theorists of socio-technical systems associated with the Tavistock Institute (Harley *et al.* 1999) and in the 1980s by 'post-Fordists' and advocates of 'soft' HRM (see Legge 1995).

The 1990s proved to be a particularly hype-ridden decade, with a marked increase in the speed at which new fashions emerged and then faded, as well as an increasing volume of literature devoted to each new panacea (Ramsay 1996; Kieser 1997). In the field of work organisation, HPWS was a particularly popular topic of discussion in the 1990s. Whether this will endure or, like earlier humanistic approaches to work organisation, be greeted with initial enthusiasm before fading in the face of the reality of managerial practice, remains to be seen. Since its emergence, however, HPWS has been subject to considerable empirical and theoretical scrutiny and debate. Central to the debates, and of course the concerns of this book, has been the role of employee participation and autonomy within HPWS. Advocates of HPWS argue that it is primarily through increasing employee autonomy that it yields gains in organisational performance.

This chapter aims to provide an overview of the debates and the evidence concerning HPWS, with a particular focus on participation and autonomy. It begins with a brief overview of the debates, which provides an agenda for the remainder of the chapter. Discussion then turns to the evidence concerning the extent of HPWS practices in workplaces, the association between practices and organisational performance, and between practices and employee outcomes, in particular autonomy. This includes a consideration of the putative role of employee outcomes in delivering organisational performance.

The chapter concludes by trying to make sense of HPWS. Should it be seen as 'old wine in new bottles', or is it qualitatively new and different? Will the changes associated with HPWS be enduring? Is it simply another attempt to win the compliance of workers or does it herald a new era of employee empowerment? It is argued that the claims that HPWS is qualitatively new, that it represents an enduring change and that it will enhance employee autonomy should be treated with caution.

High-performance Work Systems: The Debates

Management fads and fashions are nothing new, but since the 1980s it appears that there has been an increase in the rate at which new fashions come and go, as well as a general increase in the their impact (at least as measured by the volume of literature devoted to each new fashion) (Ramsay 1996; Kieser 1997). In the field of work organisation, a pervasive feature of recent fashions in work organisation has been the claim that they are 'empowering' (Harley 1999) or 'post-Taylorist' (Danford 1998: 41). This 'empowerment thesis' holds that inherent in the allegedly new approaches to management is some reversal of the separation of the conception and execution of production, and a corresponding increase in the control that employees have over their work (Harley 1999).

Since the early 1990s there has been an increasing emphasis by academics and other commentators on 'bundles' of labour management practices (see MacDuffie 1995). The advocacy of bundles is based on the argument that while individual practices – for example, self-managing teams, total quality management (TQM), performance-based pay systems – might be beneficial in their own right, suites of practices that are mutually consistent will deliver performance outcomes greater than the sum of the outcomes of the individual practices used (Purcell 1999: 27). The term 'bundles' has subsequently been replaced by 'systems' of human resource management (HRM), frequently discussed in terms of 'high-performance work systems' (HPWS).

An early appearance of the term 'high-performance work systems' is in Appelbaum and Batt's *The New American Workplace* (1994). The term is used by Appelbaum and Batt as a general label for a range of 'post-Taylorist' or 'post-Fordist' practices, including quality circles, worker participation schemes and autonomous work teams.

Since the mid-1990s, numerous other authors have written on approaches to work organisation and management, labelled variously as 'high performance' (Ramsay *et al.* 2000; Cappelli and Neumark 2001; Godard 2001), 'high commitment' (Wood and de Menezes 1998), and 'high involvement' (Pil and Macduffie 1996). Many more authors have published influential work in this area, but without specifically using any of the above terms (see Huselid 1995; Macduffie 1995; Ichniowski *et al.* 1996). In the context of a more general concern with demonstrating links between HRM and performance (see Legge 2001), HPWS has become a major topic of debate.

The precise features of a HPWS remain unclear, with different authors stressing different practices (Ramsay *et al.* 2000; Boxall and Purcell 2003: 20). According to Ramsay *et al.* in broad terms:

> the strategy entails managements ceding a degree of control to employees and introducing a range of progressive methods which increase employee welfare. These include measures such as involvement programmes, team-based work, enhanced training and development, forms of gain-sharing and high-wage reward systems (2000: 502).

Appelbaum (2002) identifies three components of HPWS. First, the heart of HPWS is a form of work organisation that enhances discretion (Giles 2002: 6). According to Appelbaum *et al.*:

> The core of a high performance work system . . . is that work is organised to permit front-line workers to participate in decisions that alter organisational routines . . . Workers in an HPWS experience greater autonomy over their job tasks and methods of work and have higher levels of communication about work matters with other workers, managers, experts (eg. engineers, accountants, maintenance and repair personnel), and, in some instances with vendors or customers. Work organisation practices in an HPWS require front-line workers to gather information, process it and act on it (2000: 7–8).

Work organisation that has these characteristics allows employees to 'use their initiative, creativity, and knowledge in the interests of the organisation' (Appelbaum 2002: 123). The specific aspects of work organisation that are commonly included in empirical studies of HPWS include such things as information sharing; staff briefings; management–employee meetings; employee surveys; suggestion schemes; consultative committees; employee consultation on organisational change; problem-solving groups; and formal teams (Ramsay *et al.* 2000).

In work organisations which involve a high level of employee discretion it is necessary to buttress this with two additional features. First, HPWS is characterised by workers having high levels of skill – basic, technical or occupation-specific, and social – which facilitate effective decision-making within the participative work organisation. More specifically, the practices might include sophisticated recruitment and selection to hire appropriately skilled staff; formal training schemes; and induction programmes (Ramsay *et al*. 2000). Second, if workers are to use their skills to improve production in an environment characterised by autonomy, it is necessary to find incentives that will encourage them to work effectively. Appelbaum (2002) argues that these should include intrinsic and extrinsic rewards as well as giving workers a long-term stake in the organisation. Intrinsic rewards are provided by high-discretion jobs and the use of skills that characterise HPWS, while extrinsic rewards might include performance-related pay (particularly on a group or team basis), profit-sharing schemes. and employee share-ownership programmes. The kinds of measures commonly identified as contributing to a long-term stake in the organisation for employees include job security, internal labour markets and family-friendly policies (Ramsay *et al*. 2000).

Within the broader literature on HPWS, it is possible to discern at least two 'sub-species', both of which emphasise enhanced employee autonomy. The first, usually characterised as 'high commitment management' (HCM), emphasises the capacity for progressive practices to contribute to enhanced employee commitment. This is said to take place chiefly by improving autonomy and intrinsic satisfaction, thereby contributing to superior organisational performance through improved motivation and effort, reduced need for managerial control and reduced turnover.

The second variant, 'high involvement management' (HIM), emphasises the capacity of HPWS to enhance employees' capacity to make decisions that improve production. In both cases, employee discretion is central. In HCM, the emphasis is on increased employee discretion as an antecedent to commitment, while in HIM the emphasis is on discretion as allowing organisations to harness the knowledge of employees in decision-making and improvements to production processes. In both cases, it is assumed that performance gains for organisations arise as a result of the positive impact of the practices on employees.

Critical scholars have subjected the dominant accounts of HPWS to considerable scrutiny. Of particular note here is Ramsay *et al*. (2000), in which the authors challenge the conventional accounts of HPWS as a 'win–win' approach, in which gains in organisational performance necessarily entail a positive transformation of work for employees. They construct an alternative 'neo-Fordist' account of HPWS which hypothesises that, while HPWS entails increased employee discretion, this can best be understood in terms of 'responsible autonomy' (Friedman 1977). That

is, management cedes control only as far as is necessary to win the compliance of employees and to tap into their creative capacities and tacit knowledge. The limited gains in discretion are outweighed by work
intensification and stress resulting chiefly from the increased levels of
responsibility.

The debates about the effectiveness of HPWS are far from being resolved.
To some extent, this reflects the divergent ideological and theoretical positions of those involved. It also reflects the fact that there remains only a
limited amount of rigorous research that would allow adjudication on the
competing claims of advocates and critics of HPWS. The remainder of this
chapter is an attempt to review the state of knowledge with respect to key
issues concerning HPWS – with a particular emphasis, of course, on
employee autonomy.

The key questions that need to be addressed, which provide an agenda
for the remainder of the chapter, are as follows. The first concerns the extent
to which HPWS can be said to exist outside the writings of management
scholars (see Kieser 1997). That is, does HPWS exist in a meaningful,
concrete sense as a coherent set of practices in workplaces? Second, does
HPWS work – do the practices associated with this model deliver performance outcomes – and, if so, how? In particular, is it the case that performance gains result from increased employee discretion? These questions
will be addressed via a review of the available evidence in the next part of
the chapter. In the final part of the chapter, attention will turn to the question of how we can best make sense of HPWS. Is it the case that HPWS represents a qualitatively new, and enduring, approach to work organisation? In
particular, is the promise of enhanced employee autonomy likely to be
realised, or is HPWS better understood as a managerial attempt to secure
worker consent as in Ramsay's (1977) 'cycles of control' thesis?

What Do We Know About HPWS? A Review of the Evidence

Before we can begin to make sense of HPWS, it is necessary to review the
state of our empirical knowledge of the phenomenon. As the section
unfolds, it will be increasingly clear that the evidence is partial at best, and
that this sets very real limits on our capacity to resolve key questions. None
the less, a number of significant inferences can be made, based on the available data, which inform the discussion in the final part of the chapter. This
section begins by asking to what extent we can say that HPWS exists 'out
there' in workplaces. Discussion then turns to the links between HPWS and
organisational performance, before looking at the outcomes of HPWS for
employees and the apparent role of these employee outcomes in generating
organisational outcomes.

The presence and diffusion of HPWS

Before we can begin to consider the outcomes of HPWS, though it is necessary to clarify the extent to which it can genuinely be said to exist. This remains a point of some contention. Of course, at one level at least, it is very evidently real. Clearly it exists as part of a discourse in the academic literature and to that extent, like many other concepts in management, it can be seen as having been talked or written into existence (see Guest 1987: 505). Even if there are doubts about the extent to which HPWS exists in terms of material practice, the dominance of a discourse which stresses the primacy of organisational performance is likely to have material outcomes in terms of legitimising particular managerial strategies (see Harley and Hardy 2004). To this extent, it is arguable that, regardless of material reality, 'HPWS' exists and its existence makes it worthy of serious academic attention.

Of course, the significance of HPWS is considerably greater if it can be shown to exist in the form of a coherent set of managerial practices being enacted in workplaces. It is difficult to gauge the extent of HPWS, for at least three reasons. First, there is a lack of agreement about the precise specification of HPWS, with the result that different studies have examined different sets of practices (Edwards *et al.* 2002: 73). Obviously, the practices one chooses will have implications for what one finds and the conclusions one draws. Many of the available studies – and this applies to almost all of those reported below – collect and analyse data on only a small sub-set of the suite of practices commonly associated with HPWS. This means that their conclusions about prevalence, as well as outcomes, tend to be based on a much narrower range of HPWS variables than would be considered ideal.

Second, there are few large-scale national surveys which allow quantification of the prevalence of HPWS, or even of its key components. Third, even where comprehensive survey-based data are available, there are various methodological problems that limit the utility of the resulting data. In particular, the measures used are somewhat 'blunt', resulting in a lack of detailed information; response rates are often low; and there are commonly problems of bias because innovative workplaces are often more willing to participate in surveys on innovation than other workplaces (Edwards *et al.* 2002: 80–1). Largely as a result of these three issues, the evidence on the diffusion of HPWS is limited and fragmentary, but it is none the less possible to piece together evidence which can inform an assessment of the extent to which HPWS is real.

In the USA, a number of nationally-based studies have reported a substantial take-up of individual practices associated with HPWS (Appelbaum *et al.* 2000: 11). Further, it seems clear that, in some organisations and some sectors, 'bundles' of practices associated with HPWS are quite prevalent. Osterman (2000) reviews the evidence in the USA – focusing on the core phenomena of TQM, teams, problem-solving groups and job rotation – and concludes that during the early 1990s HPWS practices were clearly diffusing and that this pattern continued through the late 1990s. None the less, it remains unclear whether *coherent systems* of practices are widespread (see Harley *et al.* 1999).

The evidence is also rather limited and fragmentary in Europe. Analysis of data from the British 1998 Workplace Employee Relations Survey (WERS98) shows that use of individual practices is widespread, but the take-up varies considerably across industry (Harley *et al.* 1999). Geary's (1999) research in the Republic of Ireland shows a very high take-up of teamwork and TQM. Edwards, Geary and Sisson review the evidence for France, Italy, Germany and Sweden, and report that the level of HPWS-style practices – though it must be made clear that, like Osterman (2000), they limit their analysis to 'core' aspects of work organisation – is generally significant, limitations of the data notwithstanding (Edwards *et al.* 2002: 88–92). They go on to report results from the ten-country EPOC study, which reinforce the view that there is significant experimentation with HPWS-style forms of participative work organisation, but a great deal of variation both within and between countries in Europe.

In Australia, evidence from the 1995 Australian Workplace Industrial Relations Survey suggests that the individual practices associated with HPWS tend to be taken up very unevenly across workplaces, industries and sectors (Harley *et al.* 1999). Perhaps more significantly, the individual practices appear to have been used in an opportunistic and *ad hoc* way rather than systematically (Harley 2002: 422).

Much as in earlier debates about whether HRM was 'real' (see Sisson 1995; Storey 1995), the lack of agreement about how to define HPWS and the lack of suitable data to measure its prevalence mean that we are unlikely to resolve the question of prevalence. None the less, it is clear that *some* of the practices associated with HPWS are widespread, and that there has been diffusion over time. Moreover, it seems likely that *some* organisations are using coherent systems of practice. It seems prudent, then, to regard HPWS more as an ideal type than as a description of empirical reality. If we adopt this approach, we can say that there is evidence of some shift towards this ideal type in many countries. But it would be extremely unwise to assume that HPWS is becoming the norm across the OECD.

HPWS and organisational performance

The central rationale for HPWS is that it improves organisational performance, and there is a growing body of empirical research in both the USA and the UK that supports this view. Among the more notable recent examples from the USA, Huselid's (1995) work has demonstrated positive associations between HPWS practices, productivity and financial performance, and a negative association with employee turnover, while Delaney and

Huselid's (1996) study found positive associations with financial performance and organisational effectiveness. In Britain, Ramsay *et al.* (2000)
found HPWS practices to be associated positively with labour productivity,
financial performance and product/service quality, but associated negatively with voluntary absenteeism and turnover. Overall, the evidence
suggests that HPWS contributes to superior performance.

The available evidence on HPWS and performance is drawn almost
universally from research involving analyses of cross-sectional data using
multivariate regression techniques to test hypotheses. This means that,
while in scientific terms the hypothesis that HPWS is associated with
performance has been tested and not disproved, the available evidence tells
us nothing about causal processes. Indeed, it is possible that, rather than
HPWS contributing to performance, organisations which enjoy high performance have the resources to implement HPWS.

A significant exception to the simple cross-sectional studies, Cappelli and
Neumark (2001) used a longitudinal design that allows somewhat more
confident inferences about causation. They conclude that HPWS practices
raise the cost of labour, that there is only weak evidence of improved
productivity, and that there is no evidence of improved labour efficiency as
measured by output per dollar spent on labour. This finding suggests that a
degree of caution should be exercised in accepting that HPWS results in
superior performance outcomes.

HPWS and employee outcomes

It has been common practice to assume that any performance gains from
HPWS would accrue by virtue of its positive impact on employees. While
the evidence of linkages between HPWS and performance has been demonstrated empirically, the processes leading to performance gains generally
have not. Recently, however, a number of studies have sought to look inside
the 'black box' (Ramsay *et al.* 2000) and explore the experience of employees
in HPWS. The available evidence suggests that, in general, the presence of
HPWS in organisations is associated with positive employee assessments of
a variety of facets of the experience of work. The evidence specifically
concerning the role of employee autonomy is, however, extremely limited
and at best equivocal.

For example, Appelbaum *et al.* (2000) analysed data from surveys of
manufacturing employees in the USA and found that the presence of HPWS
was associated with enhanced trust, commitment, intrinsic reward, job satisfaction and (less clearly) with reductions in stress. In this study, however,
employee autonomy was conceptualised as part of HPWS – that is, it was
one of the set of the independent variables used to operationalise HPWS –
rather than as an outcome (Appelbaum *et al.* 2000: 116–28). Further, the
analysis indicates that autonomy is often much more significant than the

more concrete elements of work organisation – for example, team member-ship – in associations with positive outcomes, suggesting that it is autonomy that matters, rather than work organisation (Danford 2003: 571). In view of other studies which have shown that employees who report high levels of autonomy also generally report positive experiences of other aspects of work (see Harley 2001a; 2001b), these results are not surprising, but they provide only limited support for the claim that HPWS *per se* contributes to positive employee outcomes.

Similarly, Guest argues that, in general, the available evidence shows 'that HR practices associated with high performance work practices, and centering around job design, are related to both superior performance, as rated by managers, and higher satisfaction and commitment as rated by workers' (Guest 2002: 343). It appears, however, that his analysis does not explore the associations involving HPWS practices and autonomy.

Perhaps surprisingly, given their generally critical perspective on HPWS, the work of Ramsay *et al.* (2000) provides some support for the claim that HPWS enhances employee autonomy. In their analysis of the WERS98 data, they found that HPWS practices were associated positively with employees' self-reported levels of discretion, relations with manage-ment, satisfaction with pay, and organisational commitment, but also with work effort (Ramsay *et al.* 2000: 514). Godard (2001), in his Canadian study, found that moderate adoption of HPWS practices was associated with a range of positive employee outcomes, including 'empowerment', but that high levels of implementation were negatively associated, possibly because of increased employee stress. Godard concludes that 'the implica-tions of alternative work practices associated with the high-performance model may be more complex than commonly assumed and . . . what many view as "best" practice for employers may not also be best practice for workers' (2001: 800).

A number of additional studies suggest that we should be cautious in accepting that HPWS is universally positive for employees. Harley's (1999) study in Australia found no links between TQM, QC (quality circles) or semi-autonomous teams and self-reported employee discretion. His analysis of the British WERS data also showed that team membership was not asso-ciated with self-reported discretion, satisfaction or commitment (Harley 2001a) and nor were characteristics of the team associated systematically with any of these outcomes (Harley 2001b).

Although our primary concern is with discretion and related subjective facets of employee experience of work, it is worth making a brief detour to consider some additional employee outcomes. Osterman (2000) explores layoffs and pay outcomes, and concludes that organisations with HPWS in place were more likely than others to lay staff off, and no more likely to pay high rates. On the basis of this he concludes that the promise of 'mutual gains' has not been fulfilled.

The evidence in all these studies is again derived from cross-sectional surveys, which means that causation cannot be imputed. Further, even if it is accepted that HPWS practices are associated systematically with positive employee experiences, it remains unclear whether, as *assumed* in much research, positive employee outcomes contribute to improved performance. Two studies which have attempted to delve into this are Ramsay *et al.* (2000) and Guest (2001). Ramsay *et al.* (2000) found little or no effect of employee experience on performance (depending on the specific variable in question) and concluded that the proposition that performance effects took place via positive employee responses was highly questionable (p. 521).

Guest (2001), while somewhat more circumspect, reports that his analysis provides some support for the view that the enhanced satisfaction and commitment arising from HPWS contribute to improved organisational performance. Of course, this says nothing of the role of autonomy, so any role for that factor must rely on assumption rather than demonstration in Guest's analysis. While both studies utilised data from WERS98, they employed quite different analytical strategies and utilised a different range of variables, which probably explains their slightly different results. In neither case was there strong support for the common assumption that HPWS works through employees to generate performance. On the basis of current knowledge we should be cautious about accepting the conventional wisdom, especially given the lack of empirical evidence that HPWS contributes to employee discretion.

The preceding discussion has explored some of the key empirical issues. Although we should be cautious in accepting the argument that HPWS is sweeping through workplaces in the OECD, none the less it is clear that key practices associated with this model of work organisation are widespread.

Consideration of the evidence concerning HPWS and organisational performance shows a consistent and positive association between them, on which basis we should provisionally accept the hypothesis that HPWS contributes to performance. This acceptance should be tempered by the lack of evidence concerning the processes and direction of causation. The evidence concerning employee outcomes is far from conclusive. While there is evidence that HPWS practices are associated with a range of positive employee outcomes, evidence specifically about autonomy is limited and equivocal. This, in conjunction with the almost total lack of evidence that performance gains are achieved via employee outcomes, suggests that we should regard the conventional accounts of HPWS with a measure of scepticism. This is not to suggest that HPWS never enhances autonomy, nor that they might in some cases generate performance gains via employees, but in the absence of compelling evidence we should remain wary.

Making Sense of High Performance Work Systems

In assessing the significance of HPWS, this section will address three questions. First, is HPWS just a fashionable term for the latest version of human relations, or is it something qualitatively new? Second, is there any reason to suppose that it represents an enduring change to the character of work organisation, or is it, like many other innovations at work, likely to fade as rapidly as it emerged? Finally, should we understand it as simply another attempt to win the compliance of workers without management genuinely ceding control of production and, if so, can we make sense of it in terms of Ramsay's 'cycles of control' thesis?

In a world riddled with managerial fads and a seemingly endless procession of gurus proclaiming fundamental change, it is prudent to be sceptical. As Thompson (2003) observes, noting the vested interest which academics, policy-makers and consultants have in celebrating the new: 'It is much harder to make a reputation or a splash in the ideas pool by arguing that nothing much has changed' (p. 359).

At one level, it is true that nothing has changed. The history of work organisation from the birth of the factory system up to the present is the history of managerial attempts to deal with the indeterminacy of labour and to exert control over the labour process. To this extent, there is nothing fundamentally new in work organisation. Moreover, virtually all supposedly new approaches to organising work owe a heavy debt to either Taylorism or human relations, and sometimes to both (see Waring 1991; Kanigel 1997).

On the other hand, to argue that, because the fundamentals of capitalist production remain unchanged nothing has changed is to risk trivialising the significant changes that have taken place in employment. There is a general consensus that there has been genuine change in work organisation, with the bone of contention being how we can make sense of the changes (Giles *et al.* 2002: 1–2). While clearly a degree of scepticism about the possibility of *fundamental* change is healthy, we still need to take seriously the possibility that there is something genuinely new about HPWS.

There are two main arguments claiming that HPWS is new and distinctive. The first is that it is the systematic nature of HPWS that distinguishes it from earlier approaches to work organisation. The theory underpinning HPWS emphasises the systematic nature of combinations of work organisation and supporting HRM practices, the internal coherence or 'fit' of practices, and the fit of HPWS with external factors such as competitive pressures and the need for flexibility of output (Danford 2003: 570). In the light of the available evidence, this argument seems difficult to sustain. The evidence is much more consistent with the proposition that HPWS practices are being used opportunistically and, for the most part, in an *ad hoc* way. Of course, as noted earlier, this might reflect a lack of appropriate data, but until more support is forthcoming we must remain cautious about accepting this argument.

The second argument that HPWS represents something qualitatively new and distinctive relates to the role of employee participation. Participative work organisation is at the core of HPWS (Appelbaum *et al.* 2000: 39–40). Belanger *et al.* (2002) argue that the emergence of HPWS reflects both a crisis in Fordist production and the subsequent need to develop new approaches to production to overcome this crisis. Similarly, Appelbaum and Batt (1994) present an account of changes in the economic environment and the emergence of new technologies as key drivers for workplace change that is similar to that of the authors associated with the post-Fordist school in the 1980s (see Piore and Sabel 1984; Mathews 1989).

The defining feature of work organisation under Fordist mass production, at least according to the conventional wisdom, was a lack of discretion. It is hardly surprising, then, that accounts that see the seeds of HPWS in the limits of Fordism should emphasise employee autonomy. It remains unclear, however, whether HPWS is the herald of a new world of high-autonomy work any more than were 'post-Fordism' or 'flexible specialisation'. Indeed, Belanger *et al.* (2002) are quite clear about the inherent contradictions of HPWS and the limits they set on participation. Moreover, the evidence on employee discretion presented earlier in this chapter, as well as the evidence about the limited take-up of HPWS practices, suggests that we should be very cautious in accepting that HPWS will lead to a generalised increase in employee autonomy. It is noteworthy that the recent UK Skills Survey shows a marked decline in discretion among UK workers since the 1980s (Felstead *et al.* 2002: 13).

We should also be wary of claims that HPWS represents enduring change. Appelbaum and Batt (1994) note the debt owed by HPWS to earlier attempts at work humanisation, notably human relations and the socio-technical systems school. They raise the possibility that, like its predecessors, HPWS will be characterised by initial enthusiasm, followed by disillusionment, as managerial practice fails to live up to the rhetoric (ibid. 1994: 5). Structural change in many OECD economies, in the form of massive growth of service sector employment and a corresponding decline in the manufacturing sector, might also set limits to the spread of HPWS. Appelbaum *et al.* (2000: 21–2) raise the possibility that while HPWS is an appropriate model for manufacturing settings, in the service sector the increasing segmentation of labour and the growth of low-complexity and low-value-added jobs might limit the potential for HPWS to spread, or even to be sustained.

Thompson (2003) also calls into question the viability and durability of the changes associated with HPWS. He challenges the claims of Appelbaum and Batt (1994), Belanger *et al.* (2002), and Boxall and Purcell (2003: 18–19) that changes in the political and economic environment associated with the crisis of Fordist mass production have led to the emergence of HPWS.

Rather, Thompson argues, the increasing dominance of capital markets in the economy, marked by downsizing and perpetual restructuring, makes it hard for managers to deliver either the employment stability or the investment in human capital necessary to sustain HPWS.

This leads to the final question for this part of the chapter – can we characterise HPWS as being simply a managerial strategy for gaining worker compliance without ceding significant control? More specifically, can it be explained by Ramsay's (1977) 'cycles of control' thesis?

On the first point, the allegedly empowering forms of work organisation that were characteristic of the period since the late 1980s were most commonly introduced by management, on management's terms (Procter and Mueller 2000: 7–8). They have been, to use Hyman and Mason's (1995) definition, characterised by 'involvement' rather than 'participation'. That is, as well as being managerially-driven, they have focused on task-based discretion rather than organisational decision-making. They have had as their primary aim the improvement of production processes and the establishment of managerial legitimacy by allowing limited employee discretion. These features explain in part the limited impact of many such practices on employee discretion (Harley 1999).

In spite of the claim that what distinguishes HPWS from earlier approaches is the genuine participation inherent in it, the literature canvassed in this chapter provides scant evidence that HPWS has had the effect of increasing employee autonomy. There is, however, somewhat more evidence of a positive association with satisfaction, commitment and orientation towards management.

It seems naïve to assume that the concern with commitment or 'social adhesion' (Giles *et al.* 2002: 5) does not reflect to some extent a managerial concern with eliciting co-operation from employees as a means of securing the benefit of their skills and effort. HPWS is, after all, a phenomenon associated with capitalist production and to this extent we should expect that the primary aim of any managerial innovation in work organisation will be to improve the bottom line. It would be a mistake to assume that the underlying relationships of power and control that characterise capitalism have simply disappeared (Giles *et al.* 2002: 6–7).

This leaves the question of the utility of the 'Cycles' thesis in making sense of HPWS. According to Ramsay's argument, participation is encouraged by managers at times when labour is strong and direct control strategies must give way to more subtle attempts to gain compliance. Edwards *et al.* (2002: 75–6) explicitly challenge this interpretation of HPWS. How can HPWS be understood in this way, they ask, when its emergence has coincided with a period during which labour has been in a relatively weak position across many OECD countries, particularly the Anglophone ones? Further, they argue, the 'Cycles' argument places too much emphasis on managers' rational and strategic attempts to control workers.

To deal with the latter argument first, Ramsay's later work (1985; 1991) on cycles went well beyond a crude deterministic view of managerial behaviour as simply rationally pursuing the needs of capitalism by exerting control. Moreover, he acknowledged the range of different motives behind particular approaches to participation and the many reasons that they fail to deliver, including limitations on managers' capacities to implement coherent control strategies. There appears to be no inconsistency between the view that labour management practices are constrained, limited, diverse and partial – which, in the case of HPWS appears to be supported by the empirical evidence – and the view that management commonly seeks to gain acquiescence via participation. Of course, the central rationale for HPWS is to improve performance in response to economic pressures. Even if this is the central rationale, the attempt to win employee consent can be understood as a partial means to this end. The argument that the 'Cycles' thesis fails to account for HPWS because it gives too much weight to rational managerial control strategies is questionable.

Turning to Edwards *et al.*'s (2002) first point, it is indeed the case that labour has been on the 'back foot' during the period in which HPWS has emerged, which calls into question the proposition that management has introduced HPWS to undermine organised labour. A possible response to this is that, in recent times at least, management might have seen the weakened position of labour as an opportunity to de-unionise their organisations. To put it another way, managers might be taking the opportunity to 'kick them when they're down', by utilising participation to gain employee compliance and reduce employee reliance on unions as a means of influencing outcomes.

An alternative explanation is suggested by the finding in both Britain and Australia that HPWS practices are positively associated with unionisation (Harley *et al.* 1999: 11). One interpretation of this finding is that management introduce these practices into workplaces where unions are present, possibly as a means of undermining their influence. Moreover, to the extent that HPWS is associated with autonomy, it appears to be limited to task discretion rather than employee influence over strategic or policy decisions, suggesting a relatively low-level kind of autonomy. The introduction of practices that might produce minor increases in discretion (although even this is questionable in light of the evidence) without challenging managerial prerogative is entirely consistent with the 'Cycles' view.

This is not to suggest that the 'Cycles' thesis provides a complete explanation of contemporary developments. Ramsay's (1985; 1991) development of the thesis indicates that he did not regard it as set in stone. None the less, there are insights from the thesis that have provided durable and are useful in making sense of HPWS. Fuller consideration of the currency of the 'Cycles' thesis is provided elsewhere in this volume.

How, then, should we make sense of HPWS? The available evidence is limited and thus any conclusions should be made with caution. None the less, the discussion in this chapter suggests that a good deal of scepticism is in order when assessing the key claims made about HPWS. HPWS does not appear to be the dominant approach to organising work across the advanced economies. There is, however, a growing body of credible research showing that it is associated positively with organisational performance outcomes. The evidence concerning employee outcomes is much more equivocal and suggests that we should be very wary of accepting that HPWS has consistently positive outcomes for employees, or that these employee outcomes feed into organisational performance. Thus, if our aim is to generalise about HPWS, the conclusion we are inevitably drawn to is that key theoretical claims are simply not supported by the evidence. Ultimately, HPWS stands or falls on the claim that it represents a potential 'win–win' approach to work organisation in which both employers and employees stand to gain from its implementation. On the basis of our current state of knowledge, this central claim remains questionable, as do the potential benefits, dissemination and longevity of HPWS.

Note

1   Hereafter, 'HPWS' is used in the singular, to refer to a general model.

References

Appelbaum, E. (2002) 'The Impact of New Forms of Work Organisation on Workers', in G. Murray, J. Bélanger, A. Giles and P. Lapointe (eds), *Work and Employment Relations in the High-Performance Workplace* (London: Continuum).

Appelbaum, E. and Batt, R. (1994) *The New American Workplace: Transforming Work Systems in the United States* (Ithaca, NY: ILR Press).

Appelbaum, E., Bailey, T., Berg, P. and Kalleberg, A. (2000) *Manufacturing Advantage: Why High-Performance Work Systems Pay Off* (Ithaca, NY: ILR Press).

Bélanger, J., Giles, A. and Murray, G. (2002) 'Towards a New Production Model: Potentialities, Tensions and Contradictions', in G. Murray, J. Bélanger, A. Giles and P. Lapointe (eds) *Work and Employment Relations in the High-Performance Workplace*, London: Continuum.

Boxall, P. and Purcell, J. (2003) *Strategy and Human Resource Management* (London: Palgrave).

Cappelli, P. and Neumark, D. (2001) 'Do "High Performance" Work Practices Improve Establishment-Level Outcomes?', *Industrial and Labor Relations Review*, 54, 737–75.

Danford, A. (1998) 'Work Organisation Inside Japanese Firms in South Wales: A Break from Taylorism?', in P. Thompson and C. Warhurst (eds), *Workplaces of the Future* (London: Macmillan), 40–64.

Danford, A. (2003) 'Review Essay: Workers, Unions and the High Performance Workplace', *Work, Employment and Society*, 17, 569–73.

Delaney, J. and Huselid, M. (1996) 'The Impact of Human Resource Management Practices on Perceptions of Organizational Performance', *Academy of Management Journal*, 39, 349–69.

Edwards, P., Geary, J. and Sisson, K. (2002) 'New Forms of Work Organisation in the Workplace: Transformative, Exploitative or Limited and Controlled?', in G. Murray, J. Bélanger, A. Giles and P. Lapointe (eds), *Work and Employment Relations in the High-Performance Workplace* (London: Continuum).

Felstead, A., Gallie, D. and Green, F. (2002) *Work Skills in Britain 1986–2001* (Nottingham: DFES).

Friedman, A. (1977) *Industry and Labour* (London: Macmillan).

Geary, J. (1999) 'The New Workplace: Change at Work in Ireland', *International Journal of Human Resource Management*, 10, 870–90.

Giles, A., Murray, G. and Bélanger, J. (2002) 'Introduction: Assessing the Prospects for the High Performance Workplace', in G. Murray, J. Bélanger, A. Giles and P. Lapointe (eds), *Work and Employment Relations in the High-Performance Workplace* (London: Continuum).

Godard, J. (2001) 'High Performance and the Transformation of Work? The Implications of Alternative Work Practices for the Experience and Outcomes of Work', *Industrial and Labor Relations Review*, 54, 776–805.

Guest, D. (1987) 'Human Resource Management and Industrial Relations', *Journal of Management Studies*, 24, 503–21.

Guest, D. (2001) 'Human Resource Management: When Theory Confronts Reality', *International Journal of Human Resource Management*, 12 1092–106.

Guest, D. (2002) 'Human Resource Management, Corporate Performance and Employee Well-Being: Building the Worker in to HRM', *Journal of Industrial Relations*, 44, 335–58.

Harley, B. (1999) 'The Myth of Empowerment: Work Organisation, Hierarchy and Employee Autonomy in Contemporary Australian Workplaces', *Work Employment and Society*, 13, 41–66.

Harley, B. (2001a) 'Team Membership and the Experience of Work in Britain: An Analysis of the WERS98 Data', *Work, Employment and Society*, 15, 721–42.

Harley, B. (2001b) 'The Impact of Team Characteristics on Individual Employees: An Analysis of the WERS98 Data', Paper presented to the Organisational Renewal: Challenging Human Resource Management Conference, Nijmegen Business School, Netherlands, 15 November.

Harley, B. (2002) 'Employee Responses to High Performance Work System Practices: An Analysis of the AWIRS95 Data', *The Journal of Industrial Relations*, 44, 418–34.

Harley, B. and Hardy, C. (2004) 'Firing Blanks? An Analysis of Discursive Struggle in HRM', *Journal of Management Studies*, 41, 377–400.

Harley, B., Ramsay, H. and Scholarios, D. (1999) *High Tide and Green Grass: Employee Experience in High Commitment Work Systems*, Paper presented to the Critical Management Studies Workshop, Academy of Management, Chicago, August.

Huselid, M. (1995) 'The Impact of Human Resource Management Practices on Turnover, Productivity and Corporate Financial Performance', *Academy of Management Journal*, 38, 635–72.

Hyman, J. and Mason, B. (1995) *Managing Employee Involvement and Participation* (London: Sage).

Ichniowski, C., Kochan, T., Levine, A., Olson, C. and Strauss, G. (1996) 'What Works at Work: Overview and Assessment', *Industrial Relations*, 35, 299–333.

Kanigel, M. (1997) *The One Best Way: Frederick Winslow Taylor and the Enigma of Efficiency* (New York: Penguin).

Kieser, A. (1997) 'Rhetoric and Myth in Management Fashion', *Organisation*, 4, 49–74.

Legge, K. (1995) *Human Resource Management: Rhetorics and Realities* (London: Macmillan).

Legge, K. (2001) 'Silver Bullet or Spent Round? Assessing the Meaning of the "High Commitment Management"/Performance Relationship', in J. Storey (ed.), *HRM – A Critical Text*, 2nd edn (London: Thompson Learning).

MacDuffie, J. (1995) 'Human Resource Bundles and Manufacturing Performance: Organisational Logic and Flexible Production Systems in the World Auto Industry', *Industrial and Labor Relations Review*, 48, 197–221.

Mathews, J. (1989) *Tools of Change: New Technology and the Democratisation of Work* (Sydney: Pluto Press).

Osterman, P. (2000) 'Work Reorganisation in an Era of Restructuring: Trends in Diffusion and Effects on Employee Welfare', *Industrial and Labor Relations Review*, 53, 179–96.

Pil, F. and MacDuffie, J. (1996) 'The Adoption of High-involvement Work Practices', *Industrial Relations*, 35, 423–55.

Piore, M. and Sabel, C. (1984) *The Second Industrial Divide: Possibilities for Prosperity* (New York: Basic).

Procter, S. and Mueller, F. (2000) 'Teamworking: Strategy, Structure, Systems and Culture', in S. Procter and F. Mueller (eds) *Teamworking* (London: Macmillan), 3–24.

Purcell, J. (1999) 'Best Practice and Best Fit: Chimera or Cul-de-Sac?', *Human Resource Management Journal*, 9, 26–41.

Ramsay, H. (1977) 'Cycles of Control: Worker Participation in Sociological and Historical Perspective', *Sociology*, 11, 481–506.

Ramsay, H. (1985) 'What is Participation For? A Critical Evaluation of "Labour Process" Analysis of Job Reform', in D. Knights, H. Willmott and D. Collinson (eds), *Job Redesign: Critical Perspectives on the Labour Process* (Aldershot: Gower).

Ramsay, H. (1991) 'Reinventing the Wheel? A Review of the Development and Performance of Employee Involvement', *Human Resource Management Journal*, 1, 1–22.

Ramsay, H. (1996) 'Managing Sceptically: A Critique of Organisational Fashion', in S. Clegg and G. Palmer (eds), *The Politics of Management Knowledge* (London: Sage), 155–72.

Ramsay, H., Scholarios, D. and Harley, B. 'Employees and High Performance Work Systems: Testing Inside the Black Box', *British Journal of Industrial Relations*, 38, 501–531.

Sisson, K. (1995) 'Human Resource Management and the Personnel Function', in J. Storey (ed.), *Human Resource Management: A Critical Text* (London: Routledge).

Storey, J. (1995) 'Human Resource Management: Still Marching On or Marching Out?', in J. Storey (ed.), *Human Resource Management: A Critical Text* (London: Routledge).

Thompson, P. (2003) 'Disconnected Capitalism: Or Why Employers Can't Keep Their Side of the Bargain', *Work, Employment and Society*, 17, 359–78.

Waring, S. (1991) *Taylorism Transformed: Scientific Management Theory Since 1945* (Chapel Hill, NC/London: University of North Carolina Press).

Wood, S. and de Menezes, L. (1998) 'High Commitment Management in the UK: Evidence from the Workplace Industrial Relations Survey and the Employers' Manpower and Skills Practices Survey', *Human Relations*, 51, 485–515.

4
Team Working:
A Tale of Partial Participation

Jos Benders

> We think that teams are here to stay, and that they constitute a funda-
> mental change in the way we go about work. We suspect the label and
> approach will evolve and perhaps pass – like all so-called fads – but the
> fundamental ways that teams do business will remain with us for a long
> time, mainly because teams are effective. (Manz and Sims 1993: 14)

This quote from the American academics Manz and Sims, from their book
*Business without Bosses: How Self-managing Teams are Building High Performance
Companies,* is typical of the confidence shown in some business literature in the
significance and sustainability of teams. For such confidence to be justified,
teams must receive and continue to enjoy broad support from various stakeholders. Teams have been claimed to be beneficial for employees and organizations alike. Enhanced employee participation is an important (although not
the only) explanation for these mutual gains. Organizations are seen to benefit, as they can react faster to changing circumstances if employees can make
decisions themselves rather than having to pass issues on to others. Employees
may benefit through a reduction of the stress associated with exclusion from
decision-making (Karasek 1979), as well as potentially higher wages and skills.
More broadly, participation can thus be seen as an instrument with which to
realize the goal of improving organizational performance, but also as a goal in
itself, freeing employees from strict directives which are held to be characteristic for the work organizations that team-based work replaces.

But it is open to question whether teams lead to increased employee
participation, and whether there is a balance of costs and benefits. Such
questions have been asked ever since teams have become a prominent topic
in the different literature. The chapter begins by discussing what teams are,
first in general terms and then by distinguishing forms of teams that are
central in the debates, and the types of participation emphasized in them.
Next, the limited degree of survey-based data on the incidence and character of the main forms of teamworking is presented. Team members' reactions to, and experiences of, such practices are then dealt with, before
concluding with a summary and suggestions for a way forward.

Teams: Defining Terms and Territories

There are two main problems with the kinds of definitions of teams found in mainstream managerial and organization behaviour literatures. First, they are set very broadly, such as an 'interdependent collection of individuals who share responsibility for specific outcomes of their organizations' (Sundstrom *et al.* 1990: 120). The problem with such definitions is that reference to a collection of individuals and responsibility for specific outcomes give few clues as to size and characteristics. There are many different types of team, from shop-floor units responsible for the ongoing work of the organization, to temporary project or top management teams. Given this book's focus on the issue of employee participation, the interest here is in shop-floor teams and the scope of their delegated responsibilities. Second, there tends to be an assumption that teams are associated inherently with high levels of autonomy. This can be seen in the term central to the title of Manz and Sims' (1993) book and many others – *self-managing* – though there are other similar ones such as autonomous, self-regulating, self-directing and semi-autonomous. At face value, these terms are logically contradictory, after all team members sell their labour capacity to the employing organization in exchange for wages. In other words, employees agree to work under the authority of managers who are appointed by their employing organizations. Thus the organization sets the boundaries within which any employee, thus also a team member, may act. Within these boundaries, employees may expect to be given directives. Full autonomy in the sense of complete freedom to act is thus an illusion for any employee. In Sundstrom *et al.*'s (1990) language, team members are expected to achieve 'specific outcomes' – in other words, they are assigned concrete goals to realize by managers acting in the interests of profit-seeking organizations. A first conclusion is, then, that team members' autonomy is constrained by each other's autonomy and by the fact that they are part of organizations and thus subject to organizational control.

This is not to say that the employment relationship within a market economy offers undifferentiated hierarchy and central direction. Among the tasks of research is to investigate the extent to which participation – through teams in this instance – is, or can be, used to modify traditional hierarchies and forms of work organization. This requires, first and foremost, that teams are not treated as a single type or generic category. Research has shown that there are many varieties of teams, many of whom are not necessarily highly participative, let alone self-managing (Benders and Van Hootegem 1999). Within this context, two kinds have been discussed prominently in the literature – socio-technical and lean teams – and this provides a framework for a more concrete examination of trends and evidence.

Socio-technical Teams

A very influential stream of literature originated at the London-based Tavistock Institute. This is widely regarded as the birthplace of 'socio-technical systems design' (STSD). Over the course of several decades, STSD developed into a set of sometimes conflicting views of how to design jobs, groups and organizations (van Eijnatten 1993). As far as teams are concerned, however, they share an emphasis on the importance of 'autonomy'. Initially, the favoured socio-technical term was 'autonomous work groups', or similar formulations that stressed the units' autonomous and collective character. During the 1980s and 1990s, this came to be replaced by 'self-managing teams', yet the core notions remained intact. To differentiate from the next form to be discussed, and to stress its origins, 'socio-technical teams' will be used in the remainder. A socio-technical team can be defined as:

> A group of employees, generally between 4 and 20 persons, responsible for a rounded-off part of the production process, and entitled to take certain decisions autonomously. (Benders and Van Hootegem 1999: 615)

Compared to the definition of Sundstrom *et al.* (1990), there is now more clarity about the size of the groups and, more importantly, autonomy – or at least delegation – is included. In addition, there is the component 'rounded-off part of the production process'. To understand the significance of 'autonomy' in a socio-technical understanding and of the phrase 'rounded-off part', some background information about the origin and development of STSD is useful.

Within the context of the growing influence of *Human Relations'* perspectives of the positive qualities of the small group, Trist and Bamforth (1951) published an article on the effects of mechanization in a coal mine. Before mechanization, small groups handled the entire production process autonomously, and Trist and Bamforth stressed the wholeness of the work process, the responsible autonomy of the group, and the multiplicity of skills of the individual group members. With the introduction of the 'longwall method of coal-getting', the existing work organization changed. The longwall production unit consisted of 40–50 men working three shifts, each of which specialized in a part of the production process. The interdependent nature of the tasks required close co-operation and intensive communication, yet the shift system and the underground working conditions led to numerous difficulties in the production process. Trist and Bamforth argued that such problems would be difficult to resolve without restoring responsible autonomy to primary groups throughout the system. Later, miners themselves came up with a solution along these lines called the 'composite short-wall'. Self-selected, multi-skilled and leaderless groups became responsible for the whole production process on a shift. Results were that productivity increased and absenteeism decreased (Buchanan 1994: 94).

After their start in the UK, socio-technical ideas and notions inspired developments in several countries (van Eijnatten 1993). Swedish reforms became particularly well-known. From 1966, the Swedish employers' association *Svenska Arbetsgivareföreningen* (SAF) started a long-term programme of organizational redesign. Job enrichment and semi-autonomous groups were seen and tried as solutions to problems attributed to fragmented, short-cyclic, monotonous and machine-paced jobs (Agurén and Edgren 1980). In practice, the SAF-induced projects shared socio-technical notions as 'joint optimization' and a belief in the possibilities of simultaneously achieving employees' and organizational goals. Yet the theoretical background to these projects does not seem to have been spelt out, but instead the projects were characterized by a pragmatic stance in which different experiments were conducted. Another characteristic is the involvement of engineers in these projects. Various alternatives to the traditional conveyor-driven line and to the functional workshop were tried at the well-known Volvo' Kalmar and Uddevalla plants (Engström *et al.* 1996).

Influenced by such Swedish work and various other lines of thought, the Dutch professor Ulbo de Sitter (1998) and his associates developed a socio-technical approach which stresses the importance of organizational design. Rather than seeing teams in isolation, this 'modern socio-technology' focuses on the organizational environment in which they function. By investigating interdependencies between operations (work tasks), it is possible to group together interdependent operations creating the 'rounded-off parts' mentioned in the definition of socio-technical teams. The operations are organized into a unit that is handled by a team. Regulating tasks that are necessary to manage the team's work are also assigned to the team. In this perspective, both production work and accompanying regulating tasks can, and should, be assigned to the team so that it can function autonomously. The allocation of these tasks is thus explicitly seen as a matter of organization design.

Job decision latitude

A key socio-technical understanding of the ambiguous idea of autonomy concerns 'job-decision latitude'. As noted earlier, Karasek (1979) demonstrated that particular illnesses occur less if people are able to solve the problems that occur in their work. Such illnesses are statistically related to stress that occurs when job-holders are faced with problems they are not authorised to solve. The obvious solution is to assign them the necessary decision rights. Optimal conditions are when people are (a) challenged in their work; and (b) are able to cope with those challenges. Karasek's stance fits well in the socio-technical conception of 'autonomy'. The normative implication of

Karasek's work is that jobs can and should be designed so that job-decision latitude and demands meet minimum criteria. This holds for individual jobs, but also at the team level. To map the variety of teams' autonomy, several dimensions need to be distinguished:

(i)   who decides;
(ii)   to what extent; and
(iii) about what aspects?

The first issue is related to questioning whether (a) a team has an internal horizontal division of labour, and (b) a team includes a hierarchical superior. The socio-technical preference for autonomy coincides with an anti-hierarchical stance, preferring the absence of team leaders. If there is one, the team leader is to act as 'facilitator', 'coach' or 'spokesperson', but not as someone who monopolises decision-making. If the team leader holds decision-making power, this is either seen as an interim stage on the route towards a 'real' team, or the presence of a team leader is accepted explicitly as a deviation from the ideal. In addition, one must realise that one member's decision latitude may constrain another member's freedom to act. For example, where group bonuses exist, team members are likely to exert pressure on each other to work harder so that the bonus may be awarded. Another example is where 'informal leaders' emerge within a group (Fröhlich 1983). These may easily resume an authoritarian stance.

Employee involvement in design

Apart from job-decision latitude, the notion of 'autonomy' in socio-technical reasoning also developed into the direction of participation in organization design. Various reasons have been put forward for this type of employee participation. The first reason is the claim that employees have a democratic right to influence their own working environment. The term 'industrial democracy' covers this. Influenced by the German philosopher Jürgen Habermas, who posited the ideal of power-free and open communication, scholars in Sweden and Australia began to stress the importance of employee and user participation in designing organisations. Instead of acting as engineers and architects, in their view, socio-technical consultants should 'facilitate' and guide design processes, ensuring that participants' opinions and views would be taken into account in the new organisation (see van Eijnatten 1993). In Australia, Fred Emery (1993) advocates 'Participative Design' and 'Search Conferences', and in the USA, participation also features high on the socio-technical agenda.

Second, a more pragmatic argument is that employees are more likely to accept working conditions that they helped to create. This reason is closely related to the first: using people's knowledge is likely to increase their willingness to use the system which they have helped to develop. A dilemma occurs when employees choose a non-socio-technical system: participative design is then at odds with the prescriptions of the socio-technical engineering school.

A third reason is knowledge utilization: being immersed daily in their work, employees are the experts at what they are doing. As early as 1776, Adam Smith (1950) stressed that workers are in a good position to come up with suggestions for improvements. Participative design might be a double-edged sword, however, as improvement measures might lead to work intensification and/or the elimination ('rationalization') of jobs. More efficient ways of working mean the same amount of work can be done with fewer staff. A counter-argument may be that using such knowledge is essential for a company's survival.

Lean Teams

For all the glib references to 'self-managing', some managers and business academics are uneasy about the promotion of forms of work organization associated with high degrees of employee autonomy, often couched in the language of rights and democracy. The increasing interest in Japanese models of work and employment led to an alternative model being developed that included the ideas of collaboration, interdependence and knowledge-sharing, but in a more constrained framework. The best-selling book, *The Machine That Changed the World* (Womack *et al.* 1990) was a eulogy on the way 'the Japanese' (or rather Toyota Motor Corporation) produced cars. The book led to the term 'lean production' becoming well known. This term was coined to stress the superior performance of Japanese producers compared to their American and European competitors. One explanation for lean production's achievements were teams:

> it is the dynamic work team that emerges as the heart of the lean factory. Building these efficient teams is not simple. First, workers need to be taught a wide variety of skills ... Workers then need to acquire many additional skills: simple machine repair, quality checking, housekeeping, and materials ordering. Then they need encouragement to think actively. (Womack *et al.* 1990: 99).

Apart from this description, Womack *et al.* gave little information about 'lean teams'. Yet Japanese work organizations and the significance of the small group had been studied long before (Cole 1971; Dore 1973). The additional element was the emergence of new production systems, and 'lean production' could be seen as a relabelling of the Toyota Production System into which 'Japanese teams' have been incorporated (Benders and van

Bijsterveld 2000). Morita (2001) conceptualizes these teams as having the following characteristics:

(i)   multi-skilled workers;
(ii)   programmes for continuous skill development;
(iii)   allocation of tasks to work units ('one task, one team') rather than to individuals; and
(iv)   strong work-unit leaders.

The first two issues are closely related. Japanese employees are considered first as members of their organization, irrespective of the particular post they happen to hold. Thus, traditionally, they are moved around among different tasks and jobs. The intensity of this rotation varies with individual capabilities and motivation, personnel policies and the level of the work. Organizations strive for multi-deployable employees, and may have extensive training programmes for their core operatives. which are tied to promotion and payment schemes.

Tasks are assigned to work units, known by a wide variety of names. At the lowest unit levels, they are often called 'han' or 'kumi', which has come to be translated into English as 'teams'. One characteristic is that the intra-unit allocation of tasks is done by the group or unit leader. Formal decision-making power for task allocation and a variety of production and personnel-related matters is concentrated with this leader, who is typically an experienced shop-floor worker and is considered to be a unit member rather than constituting a separate hierarchical layer. So far, the word 'participation' has not been mentioned. One reason for this absence is that, unlike socio-technical teams, autonomy as such was never a driving force behind the development of lean teams, but regardless of this, the lean team does embody a degree of participation.

This can be seen when considering the independent, but closely-related quality (control) circle (QC) – a practice that can essentially can be seen as Adam Smith's stress on using employees' knowledge rendered into organizational perfection. Lillrank and Kano (1989: 12–14) describe QCs as small groups of employees from the same organizational unit who, on a voluntary basis, use a set of tools and methods to realise a variety of improvements on a continuous basis. In Japanese practice, the QC often coincides with the shop-floor, team but various specialists may be added when needed. The term 'quality' in QC is slightly misleading, as the improvements are not necessarily aimed at developing a superior product or process quality, but may also concern other aspects such as safety, operational efficiency and ergonomic themes. A closely related notion is 'continuous improvement' (CI), or *kaizen* in Japanese (Imai 1986). CI is generally realised by means of 'standard operating procedures' (SOPs). These are descriptions detailing how specific tasks are to be conducted. Taiichi Ohno, an engineer who was the driving force behind the development of the Toyota Production System, claims that, when at Toyota Motor Corporation:

> The first thing I did was standardization of jobs. The shop floor of those days was controlled by foremen-craftsmen. Division managers and section managers could not control the shop floor, and they were always making excuse for production delay. So we first made manuals of standard operation procedures and posted them above the work stations so that supervisors could see if the workers were following the standard operations at a glance. Also, I told the shop floor operators to revise the standard operating procedures continuously. (Fujimoto 1999: 64)

The SOPs were gathered into handbooks, and some were displayed as posters above work-stations, so that every worker could see at a glance how a particular job had to be done. Ohno (1988) also stressed the importance of having employees write the procedures themselves as they were the specialists regarding their own work, and hence best capable of improving it. Once a particular way of working was established and laid down in a SOP, if a better way of working was sought and found, a new SOP would replace the old one.

Another issue with the lean team is that its leader's dominant role has been heavily criticised. Berggren's (1993: 48) expression 'platoon' for such teams, with its accompanying military associations, powerfully expresses the strong intra-team hierarchy against which many critics rail. In Japan, where lean teams originated, the team leader's role is supposed to be analogous with that of a traditional father: strict yet benevolent. Morita (2001: 182) distinguishes two functions: being a role model for team members, and an intermediary between workers and higher management. Fairris and Tohyama (2002) argue that such functions are typical in Japan, but not in the USA, where the team leader tends to act as the stereotypical 'traditional' authoritarian supervisor.

One should note that the literature on 'lean teams' is based on a typical production environment: assembly lines operating under a just-in-time regime with short cycle times, repetitive work and few opportunities to escape the line-paced rhythm. This production regime is generally applied in car plants, and it happened to be both a hallmark of Japanese productivity and a popular object of study for academics (see Berggren 1993; Murakami 1997). Consequently, a certain 'final car assembly bias' is reflected in the team debate. It is not always clear where general differences on issues of autonomy and participation have to be attributed to different production environments, or to contrasting models of work organization. This played a part in (sometimes heated) exchanges between defenders of lean production and its (predominantly European) critics concerning the pros and cons of using SOPs and the character of employee involvement within the process of continuous improvement (see Sandberg 1995). While critics focus on the constraints on autonomy and job satisfaction from the strong hierarchical control in the person of the team leader and standardization through CI, defenders emphasise that workers still have a say in improving production systems and their working conditions. Adler and Cole (1993) therefore introduce the term 'democratic Taylorism' to describe lean teams and argue that long job cycles and high autonomy are incompatible with efficient production in a contemporary market economy.

Even the critics pick up on the contradictory features of current arrangements. Drawing on case studies, Conti and Warner (1993: 39) argue that the 'labour process in the visited sites is contradictory, with employees working four hours a month in a very non-Taylorist manner to make their work for the rest of the month even more Taylor-like'. In other words, non-routine tasks make up only a small percentage of total working time, and with the effect that the remainder of the working time becomes even more routine. This kind of participative design, a form of employee participation, thus paradoxically has the effect of reducing operational autonomy. Former Daimler-Benz labour director, Ronald Springer (1999), coined the term 'participative rationalization'. This nicely captures participation's goal in this way of working: to improve organizational performance.

High-performance Work Teams

With declining attention to the theory and practice of 'Japanisation' of production and the spread of teams to service contexts, such debates have been partly transcended by a focus on high-performance work systems (HPWS). There was considerable continuity in evidence as some of the proponents of the new practices had been prominent promoters of lean production (Pil and MacDuffie 1996). Conscious, perhaps, of the association of that system with harsh working conditions, the traditional emphasis on the bottom-line performance benefits of team working was offset by its location within a bundle of progressive human resource practices. The argument is summarised by Batt and Doellgast:

> jobs require relatively high skills; work is organized to promote employee discretion, collaboration or teamwork; and employees are motivated by incentives and rewards such as investment in training, high pay plus some performance-based pay, and employment security. (2004: 146)

The associated research consists mainly of statistical comparisons between two groups of organisations, with one group scoring better on performance criteria than the other. The presence or absence of a number of work and HRM characteristics ('clusters'), including teams, is related to these performance criteria. This makes it impossible to isolate the effect of teams. An additional problem is that there is generally no distinction made between socio-techni-cal or lean teams in such debates. This may be because the HPWS literature is predominantly American, while the distinction between socio-technical and lean teams is part of an almost exclusively European discussion.

Given that there is extensive assessment of HPWS and the role of teams and participation elsewhere in this volume by Harley, as well as in Batt and Doellgast (2004), they are not dealt with more extensively here. Instead, evidence on the incidence of teamworking is considered.

The Incidence of Teamworking

Whereas teamwork has been discussed intensively from the 1980s onwards, hard evidence on its incidence is more limited. This is perhaps understand-able given the linguistic ambiguity surrounding teams, the difficulties in researching at the aggregate level of organizations, and the efforts and resources required to do such research. The available surveys have adopted a variety of methodological approaches, which all have their own draw-backs and this makes it hard to compare results. Thus the following simple questions are hard to answer:

(i)   Are there differences in the incidence of teamwork in different coun-tries?
(ii) Is the popularity of teamwork increasing?

Nevertheless, some studies do allow us to draw some cautious conclu-sions on the incidence of teamworking, if one keeps in mind a few of the problematic issues present in such survey-based research. The first problem is the difference between what one may call substantive and rhetorical understanding (Benders and van Bijsterveld 2000). In the substantive approach, neutral terms are used to describe the phenomenon and func-tional equivalents are sought; in the rhetorical approach, the phenomenon is more likely to be taken at face value according the labels ascribed to it. Concretely, asking about the presence of 'teams' without further qualifying their content runs the risk of getting answers based on a completely differ-ent understanding of what teams are. The second issue in organisation-level research concerns the 'coverage': over how large a part of individual orga-nization is the phenomenon adopted? Coverage can be assessed by gaining access at the establishment level, and asking how many employees work in teams. Unfortunately, many studies on HPWS, including some well-known and often-cited ones, have tended to adopt the rhetorical approach. Furthermore, coverage is not always taken into account, although this vari-able appears increasingly to be included.

In the 1990s, a broad research project was commissioned entitled 'Employee (direct) Participation in Organisational Chance' (EPOC), including a survey across ten European countries among establishments that used a substantive approach (Benders *et al.* 2002). To avoid confusion with Japanese-inspired teamwork and in line with German conventions, self-managed teams were called 'group work'. Its presence was assessed via two questions on the extent of group autonomy ('number of decision rights') and its coverage (within the establishments). To qualify as a 'group-based' establishment, two criteria had to be met:

(i)   at least four (out of a total of eight) decision rights are assigned to groups; and
(ii)   at least 70 per cent of core employees were working in groups.

In 462 establishments, at least 70 per cent of the core employees worked in some kind of group. Applying the first criterion to these 462 cases leaves 217 cases (about 4 per cent of a total response of 5,786 cases) to be used in analyses to characterise the 'group-based' establishments. These are split into three sub-categories:

- group-based organisations;
- weak group delegation (GD) (less than 30 per cent coverage and less than four decision rights); and
- medium GD (the intermediate group).

One consequence of this cautious attitude is that the data on the incidence of group work should be considered as minima.

Figure 4.1 contains the data for eight of the ten countries included in the EPOC survey (the Portuguese and Spanish responses were too low to be included). It follows from Figure 4.1 that group work is applied the most in Swedish establishments. The second-highest score is the Dutch one, but this is to a considerable extent because of the high score on medium GD. At the lower end of this group of eight is Italy. In between these extremes, there is a group of five countries between which the differences are small. In descending order, these are the United Kingdom, France, Germany, Denmark and Ireland.

EPOC's cross-national data can be complemented by those of the 'Nordflex'study. In 1996 and 1997, data was gathered about Nordic establishments – that is, covering Denmark, Finland, Norway and Sweden (NUTEK 1999). This choice is interesting, as it had been assumed that these countries have a long and well-established tradition of using socio-technical teams. As in the EPOC survey, Sweden has the highest score, with Denmark, Finland and Norway scoring about the same as each other.

% of group-based workplaces by sub-category

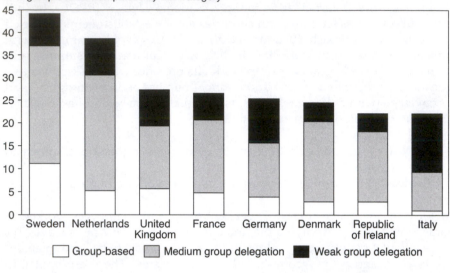

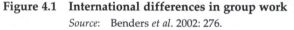

Figure 4.1   International differences in group work
Source: Benders *et al.* 2002: 276.

The low incidence of socio-technical teams in the EPOC study is consistent with findings of the 1998 UK Workplace Employee Relations Survey. Cully *et al.* report that the percentage of workplaces with team working drops with increasingly strict criteria. Where 65 per cent of their respondents claim that 'team working' applies to most of their employees in the largest occupational group, this drops to 62 per cent when joint work is taken into consideration, 54 per cent when responsibility for a specific product or service is added, to 35 per cent when 'joint decision-making' on 'how the work is to be done' is considered, and only 3 per cent when the final criterion, 'teams appoint their own team leaders', is considered (Cully *et al.* 1999: 40–2).

In contrast, longitudinal data (including the 1990s) is only available for two countries: Germany and the USA. Two German studies, using different samples (Antoni 1996; Kleinschmidt and Pekruhl 1994; Nordhause-Janz and Pekruhl 2000), suggest that the incidence of group work appears to be rather low but on the increase. The American data are more problematic to interpret: while an increase for large companies is reported for the period 1987–96, Osterman (1994; 1998) finds that, in contrast to the three other practices studied, teams do not increase. Gittleman *et al.* (1998) and Frazis *et al.* (2000) suggest a decrease based on other datasets. Lawler *et al.* (1998), however, suggest a steady increase in large US companies in the period 1987–96 (see Table 4.1).

Table 4.1 **'Self-managing work teams' in large US companies, 1987–96**

	At least some employees involved	*At least 40 per cent of employees involved*
1987	27	1
1990	47	1
1993	69	5
1996	78	9

Source: Lawler *et al.* (1998).

Mates versus Inmates: Team Member Interests and Experiences

Management literature tends to highlight the positive aspects of team working. Harley sums up the general findings of 'critical' qualitative research:

> The central argument put forward in many of the critical studies is that teamwork, while apparently empowering employees, generates new forms of control which assist management in extracting labour from employees via work intensification. ... Critical accounts almost invariably make employee experience of teamwork absolutely central to their analyses and explicitly question the unitarist assumption that positive employee experiences and improved organisational performance are necessarily natural partners. (2001: 725)

However, this research does not reproduce a simple managerial control and worker resistance model. The issue is more about what kind of control, and what kind of employee reaction? While participation via 'self-managing' teams has been advocated as a goal in itself, the phenomenon would probably have remained marginal if participation had not come to be seen primarily as an instrument for improving organisational performance. From a managerial perspective, an interesting and classic dilemma then emerges: the 'double bind of discretion' (Sewell 1998: 413). Those who are granted a certain autonomy are supposed to use this autonomy in the best interests of the organisation – to monitor, or even ensure, that managers maintain control over the teams. Teams (even the self-managing ones) are thus not a substitute for managerial control, but rather teams are controlled in other ways than via the direct control that is held to be typical for the 'Tayloristic' organisation. The forms of control are likely to be different, but the principle remains (as is implied within the constraints of the employment relationship).

Managerial concern with the team members' use of their autonomy is understandable. As early as the beginning of the twentieth century, the renowned German scholar Max Weber published a study (Weber 1908–9) on what he called 'braking': working less hard than would theoretically have been possible. Particularly in social psychology and organizational economics, 'social loafing', 'shirking' or 'the propensity to withhold effort' (Kidwell and Bennett 1993) is seen as an important reason why teamworking can lead to decreasing productivity (remarkably, loafing is virtually absent in the managerial literature on teams). As 'systematic soldiering', the phenomenon was the major concern for the American engineer Frederick Taylor (1911: 30). Through his extensive shop-floor experience, Taylor was very well aware that their '[social] relationships with other men' caused workers to restrain their output. Workers tended to be paid by the level of output in so-called 'piece rate systems'. If the norms above which bonuses were paid were to be increased because of the superior productivity of a few workers, everyone would have to work harder than previously. Consequently, those exceeding the norm were disciplined by their fellow workers. Output control is thus not an exclusive domain of management, but employees have vested interests in establishing and maintaining output norms and exerting pressure on each other to observe those norms. Although hardly ever discussed as such, this can be seen as employee participation *per se*.

A crucial issue is in what direction output norms develop. Management often tries to set high standards. A crude example comes from the nineteenth-century silk industry in Japan, where workers were commonly divided into teams. These 'were set against each other to see which one could produce the most and best silk. Sometimes the winners won small prizes ... And the losers could be made to pay for the winners' prizes' (Tsurumi 1991: 374). Such a zero-sum competition is nowadays unlikely to be felt acceptable. Agreements on what teams are to achieve, however, fit well with the socio-technical philosophy that teams should be controlled only (or at least primarily) on an output basis but are free as to how they realise that output. Contested, however, is to what extent such output goals should be coupled to performance-related pay. Team-member peer pressure tends to be particularly intensive when team working is combined with performance-related pay. Some socio-technical advocates therefore recommend small, and preferably symbolic rather than financial, bonuses (Van Amelsvoort and Scholtes 1993: 38–9), if any are given at all. However, this prescription is in stark contrast to much of the HPWS literature, where 'teams' and performance-related pay are typically both seen as constituting 'high-performance practices'.

Some in-depth case studies shed light on why group bonuses may be a bad idea from team members' perspectives. Sewell (1996) reports an example of management actively encouraging peer pressure within teams. Out of lack of confidence in British working attitudes, the managers of a Japanese transplant in the UK introduced an electronic surveillance system together with productivity bonuses. The latter gave team members the incentive to monitor each other, and the former enabled them to do so. Ezzamel and Willmott (1998) found other dynamics in an organization with group-based payments: experienced and highly productive team members work very hard to compensate for those with lower productivity levels. Rather than stimulating knowledge transfer from experienced workers to newcomers and generating mutual support, as management had intended and some managerial literature prescribes, employees came to work in a solitary way. Compared to the previous piece rate system, the most productive employees felt that they now not only had to work hard but also had to keep an eye on their team members. The result was hostility against socio-technical teams. Yet in the absence of a management directive regarding performance-related pay, team members may exert pressure to achieve high production levels. Barker (1993) presented a case in which team members' enthusiasm for self-managing teams evolved into increasingly high productivity norms and interpersonal control. Team members put high norms on each other, from which individuals could not escape. In this case, the pressured climate appears to have evolved without any stimulation from managers.

In general, such case studies illustrate that where 'team spirit' has positive connotations such as intra-team solidarity and mutual support, the same phenomenon has also been put in a totally different perspective. As team members often work in close physical proximity and are thus able to watch each other constantly, they are likely to exert strong pressure on each other to observe production (and other) norms, resulting in what has been called 'group terror' (Fröhlich 1983), 'tyranny' (Sinclair 1992) and, following the French philosopher Michel Foucault, a 'prison'. In the views of Foucauldians, such dense intra-team social relationships mean that team members are subjected to virtually inescapable omnipresent control of their fellows: their mates make them inmates. Here, employee participation results in mutual control.

These case studies illustrate that pressurised work climates may emerge spontaneously, but can also be created or consented to willingly. The methodological drawback, however, is that there are doubts whether the idea of teamwork as 'prison' and members as 'inmates' is representative of team-based organisations at large. Survey results reported by Harley (2001), as well as case studies in such varying settings as Scottish distilleries (see Findlay *et al*. 2000) and Dutch home care organisations (Schouteten 2004), point out that employees tend to experience teamwork as a mixed blessing. In general, employees seem to welcome an increased latitude of decision-making, yet have concerns about work intensification.

In other words, to the extent that peer pressure leads to higher productivity, labour process theorists will point to the exploitative effect of team working. On the other hand, they also stress that however tightly a control system is devised, complete control remains an illusion (Bain and Taylor 2000) and employees can always resist managerial control. In a broader perspective, like any social group, team members are perfectly capable of making their own judgements, based on their own preferences, experiences and circumstances. They are not passive recipients of a managerial concept, but rather are active constituents (Findlay *et al.* 2000). Whatever economic and social outcomes are realized, these are produced partly by the team members themselves. Team members will monitor each other, either to work harder or to work less hard.

Conclusions: Employee Participation Enhanced?

This chapter started by asking to what extent have teams led to increased employee participation, and are there any drawbacks to this? As usual, asking the question turned out to be easier than providing the answer. In effect, as must be clear from the discussions above, there are many answers. Some hold for all teams, while others are form-specific and/or depend on the perspective adopted. From a labour process perspective, for example, this means that increased employee participation leads to increased self-exploitation. In addition, team working involves dense social relationships through which team members try to influence each other's behaviour. The philosophy behind socio-technical teams stresses job decision latitude: employees ought to be free to manage their own jobs without exterior interference. The realisation of this idea appears to be limited, at least if judged by the relatively low incidence of socio-technical teams. Lean teams are contested much more than socio-technical teams, for one thing because team members' operational autonomy tends to be constrained by a strict hierarchy and the use of SOPs. However, employee participation *per se* was never a constituent for the development of lean teams. Whatever team form is applied, employee autonomy is also limited by the very nature of the employment relationship: the agreement to submit oneself to a hierarchical relationship in exchange for a wage.

The idea of team working is likely to remain influential for the foreseeable future. Apart from the intrinsic appeal of the notion, persistent publicity on the positive economic impacts of teams appears to have altered the view that teams are primarily, or even only, implemented to improve employees' conditions. Instead, many managers now seem convinced that teams are ultimately good for the bottom line. In terms of goals and instruments, this means that the early position, that employee participation should be a goal in itself, now hardly has any influence. Instead, employee participation has come to be seen as an instrument for achieving the goal of superior organisational performance.

Yet while teamworking in general may have the potential for the enhancement of productivity, this is not realised automatically, nor is it an unproblematical blessing. To the extent that team gurus paint a unilaterally positive picture, they run the risk of undermining their own recipe for success, as disappointment is likely to arise when the inevitable drawbacks surface. In a similar vein, those arguing against team working as being an inherently exploitative way of working run the risk that alternatives that are worse in terms of quality of working life will come to be favoured. Pointing to problematic issues in teamworking is legitimate and useful, but will not change the nature of the employment relationship in capitalist societies.

A way forward could be to bring potentially contested issues out into the open. Rather than stressing one-sidedly the economic and social benefits of team working, the reverse of the team coin might be emphasised as well. This holds in particular for the downsides that labour process theorists highlight: social control and the limits to decision latitude. Granting autonomy involves outlining which issues team members may make decisions about, and consequently, over which issues they have no legitimate influence. While the former is often brought into the open in prescriptive texts, its logical complement appears virtually to be ignored. Acknowledging this is a recognition that team working remains partial in participation.

Note

I am grateful to Jurriaan Nijholt, Marc Peeters and Paul Thompson, who provided useful comments on earlier drafts of this chapter. Of course, I retain responsibility for the content and opinions expressed.

References

Adler, P. S. and Cole, R.E. (1993) 'Designed for Learning; A Tale of Two Auto Plants', *Sloan Management Review*, 34:3, 85–94.

Agurén, S. and Edgren, J. (1980) *New Factories; Job Design through Factory Planning in Sweden* (Stockholm: SAF).

Antoni, C. H. (1996) 'Teilautonome Arbeitsgruppen – Eine Expertenbefragung zu Verbreitungsformen und Erfahrungen', *Angewandte Arbeitswissenschaften*, 147, 31–53.

Bain, P. and Taylor, P. (2000) 'Entrapped by the "Electronic Panopticon"? Worker Resistance in the Call Centre', *New Technology, Work and Employment*, 15:1, 2–18.

Barker, J. (1993) 'Tightening the Iron Cage: Concertive Control in Self-managing Teams', *Administrative Science Quarterly*, 38:3, 408–37.

Batt, R. and Doellgast, V. (2004) 'Groups, Teams and the Division of Labour: Interdisciplinary Perspectives on the Organization of Work', in S. Ackroyd, R. Batt, P. Thompson and P. Tolbert (eds), The *Handbook of Work and Organization* (Oxford University Press).

Benders, J. and van Bijsterveld, M. (2000) 'Leaning on Lean; The Reception of a Management Fashion in Germany', *New Technology, Work and Employment*, 15:1, 50–64.

Benders, J. and Van Hootegem, G. (1999) 'Teams and their Context; Moving the Team Discussion Beyond Existing Dichotomies', *Journal of Management Studies*, 36:5, 609–28.

Benders, J., Huijgen, F. and Pekruhl, U. (2002) 'What Do We Know About the Incidence of Group Work (If Anything)?', *Personnel Review*, 31:3, 371–85.

Berggren, C. (1993) *The Volvo Experience: Alternatives to Lean Production in the Swedish Auto Industry* (London: Macmillan).

Buchanan, D.A. (1994) 'Cellular Manufacture and the Role of Teams', in J. Storey, *New Wave Manufacturing Strategies* (London: Paul Chapman), 204–25.

Cole, R. E. (1971) *Japanese Blue Collar: The Changing Tradition*, (Berkeley/Los Angeles/London: University of California Press).

Conti, R. and Warner, M. (1993) 'Taylorism, New Technology and Just-in-time Systems in Japanese Manufacturing', *New Technology, Work and Employment*, 8:1, 31–42.

Cully, M., Woodland, S., O'Reilly, A. and Dix, G. (1999) *Britain at Work; As Depicted by the 1988 Workplace Employee Relations Survey* (London: Routledge).

de Sitter, L. U. (1998) *Synergetisch produceren; Human Resources Mobilisation in de produktie: een inleiding in de structuurbouw*, 2nd edn (Assen: van Gorcum).

Dore, R. (1973) *British Factory – Japanese Factory* (London: George Allen & Unwin).

Emery, F. (1993) 'Epilogue', in F. M. van Eijnatten, *The Paradigm That Changed the Work Place* (Stockholm/Assen: Arbetslivscentrum/van Gorcum), 192–7.

Engström, T., Jonsson, D. and Medbo, L. (1996) 'Production Model Discourse and Experiences from the Swedish Automotive Industry', *International Journal of Operations and Production Management*, 16:2, 141–58.

Ezzamel, M. and Willmott, H. (1998) 'Accounting for Teamwork: A Critical Study of Group-based Systems of Organizational Control', *Administrative Science Quarterly*, 38:3 , 358–96.

Fairris, D. and Tohyama, H. (2002) 'Productive Efficiency and the Lean Production System in Japan and the United States', *Economic and Industrial Democracy*, 23:5, 529–54.

Findlay, P., McKinlay, A., Marks, A. and Thompson, P. ' "Flexible When It Suits Them": The Use and Abuse of Teamwork Skills', in S. Procter and F. Mueller (eds), *Teamworking* (Basingstoke: Palgrave Macmillan, 2000), 222–43.

Frazis, H., Gittleman, M. and Joyce, M. (2000) 'Correlates of Training: An Analysis Using Employer and Employee Characteristics', *Industrial and Labor Relations Review*, 53:3, 443–62.

Fröhlich, D. (1983) 'Machtprobleme in teilautonomen Arbeitsgruppen', *Kölner Zeitschrift für Soziologie und Sozialpsychologie* (Special Issue 25), 532–51.

Fujimoto, T. (1999) *The Evolution of the Toyota Production System* (New York: Oxford University Press.

Gittleman, M., Horrigan, M. and Joyce, M. (1998) ' "Flexible" Workplace Practices: Evidence from a Nationally Representative Survey', *Industrial and Labor Relations Review*, 51:1, 99–115.

Harley, B. (2001) 'Team Membership and the Experience of Work in Britain: An Analysis of the WERS98 Data', *Work, Employment and Society*, 15:4, 721–42.

Imai, M. (1986) *KAIZEN – The Key to Japan's Competitive Success* (New York: McGraw-Hill).

Karasek, R. A. Jr. (1979) 'Job Demands, Job Decision Latitude, and Mental Strain: Implications for Job Redesign', *Administrative Science Quarterly*, 24:2, 285–308.

Kidwell, R. E. and Bennett, N. (1993) 'Employee Propensity to Withhold Effort: A Conceptual Model to Intersect Three Avenues of Research', *Academy of Management Review*, 18:3, 429–56.

Kleinschmidt, M. and Pekruhl, U. (1994) 'Kooperation, Partizipation und Autonomie: Gruppenarbeit in deutschen Betrieben', *Arbeit*, 4:2, 150–72.

Lawler, E. E., Albers Mohrman S. and Ledford, G. E. (1998) *Strategies for High Performance Organization; The CEO Report* (San Francisco: Jossey-Bass).

Lillrank, P. and Kano, N. (1989) *Continuous Improvement; Quality Control Circles in Japanese Industry* (Ann Arbor, Mich.: Center for Japanese Studies, University of Michigan).

Manz, C. C. and Sims, H. P. (1993) *Business Without Bosses; How Self-managing Teams Are Building High Performance Companies* (New York: Wiley).

Morita, M. (2001) 'Have the Seeds of Japanese Teamworking Taken Root Abroad?', *New Technology, Work and Employment*, 16:3, 178–90.

Murakami, T. (1997) 'The Autonomy of Teams in the Car Industry – A Cross National Comparison', *Work, Employment and Society*, 11:4, 749–58.

Nordhause-Janz, J. and Pekruhl, U. (2000) 'Managementmoden oder Zukunftskonzepte? Zur Entwicklung von Arbeitstrukturen und von Gruppenarbeit in Deutschland', in J. Nordhause-Janz and U. Pekruhl (eds), *Arbeiten in neuen Strukturen? Partizipation, Kooperation, Autonomie, und Gruppenarbeit in Deutschland* (Munich/Mering: Rainer Hampp Verlag), 13–68.

NUTEK (1999) *Flexibility Matters – The Flexible Enterprises in the Nordic Countries* (Stockholm: NUTEK).

Ohno, T. (1988) *Toyota Production System: Beyond Large-Scale Production* (Cambridge: Productivity Press).

Osterman, P. (1994) 'How Common Is Workplace Transformation and Who Adopts It?', *Industrial and Labor Relations Review*, 47:2, 173–88.

Osterman, P. (1998) 'Changing Work Organisation in America: What Has Happened and Who Has Benefited?', *Transfer*, 4:2, 246–63.

Pil, F. K. and MacDuffie, J. P. (1996) 'The Adoption of High-Involvement Work Practices', *Industrial Relations*, 35:3, 423–55.

Sandberg, A. (ed.) (1995) *Enriching Production* (Aldershot: Avebury).

Schouteten, R. (2004) 'Group Work in a Dutch Home Care Organization: Does it Improve the Quality of Working Life?', *International Journal of Health Planning and Management*, 19:2, 179–94.

Sewell, G. (1996) 'A Japanese "Cure" for a British "Disease"? Cultural Dimensions to the Development of Workplace Surveillance Technologies', *Information Technology and People*, 9:3, 19–29.

Sewell, G. (1998) 'The Discipline of Teams: The Control of Team-Based Industrial Work Through Electronic and Peer Surveillance', *Administrative Science Quarterly*, 43:2, 397–428.

Sinclair, A. (1992) 'The Tyranny of a Team Ideology', *Organization Studies*, 13:4, 611–26.

Smith, A. (1950) *An Inquiry into the Nature and Causes of the Wealth of Nations*, E. Cannan (ed.) (London: Methuen).

Springer, R. (1999) 'The End of New Production Concepts? Rationalization and Labour Policy in the German Auto Industry', *Economic and Industrial Democracy*, 20:1, 117–45.

Sundstrom, E., De Meuse, K. P. and Futrell, D. (1990) 'Work Teams. Applications and Effectiveness', *American Psychologist*, 45:2, 120–33.

Taylor, F. W. (1911) *Shop Management* (New York: Wiley).

Trist, E. A. and Bamforth, K. W. (1951) 'Some Social and Psychological Consequences of the Longwall Method of Coal-getting', *Human Relations*, 4:1, 3–38.

Tsurumi, E. P. (1991) 'Old Wine in New Bottles: Management Practices in Contemporary Japan', *Journal of Contemporary Asia*, 21:3), 371–8.

van Amelsvoort, P. and Scholtes, G. (1993) *Zelfsturende Teams: Ontwerpen, Invoeren en Begeleiden* (Vlijmen: ST-Groep).

van Eijnatten, F. M. (1993) *The Paradigm That Changed the Work Place* (Stockholm/Assen: Arbetslivscentrum/van Gorcum).

Weber, M. (1924) 'Zur Psychophysik der industriellen Arbeit', in *Gesammelte Aufsätze zur Soziologie und Sozialpolitik von Max Weber*, originally published 1908 (Tübingen: J. C. B. Mohr).

Womack, J. P., Jones, D. T. and Roos, D. (1990) *The Machine That Changed the World* (New York: Rawson Associates).

5
Employee Share Ownership, Employment Relationships and Corporate Governance

Andrew Pendleton

Introduction

A unifying characteristic of all bodies of theory on financial participation in the Anglo-American economies is a concern with the potential of profit-sharing, share ownership and share options to modify employee attitudes and behaviour. In the disciplines of economics and finance, principal–agent theory focuses on the potential for collective, performance-based reward systems to lower monitoring costs by aligning employee interests with those of the firm. Recent theory in corporate governance, deriving from transaction costs and human capital theories, suggests that share ownership facilitates human capital investments by employees where firms cannot guarantee 'traditional' returns (long-term employment, career advancement and so on) on these investments. In industrial relations, a long-standing perspective has been that financial participation is used both to weaken trade unions and ameliorate adversarial 'them and us' attitudes by promoting identification with the firm among employees. Since the late 1970s, this perspective has been associated particularly with Harvie Ramsay and his notion of 'cycles of control'.

In this chapter, we evaluate the 'cycles of control' perspective on financial participation by addressing the key questions to which his approach gives rise. These questions concern governmental and corporate motives for the use of financial participation, the effects of financial participation on employee attitudes, and the orientation and policies of trade unions towards financial participation. In some respects, our answers are similar to those provided by Ramsay, but in others they differ quite markedly. Our approach is essentially an institutional one: we see the character, practices and outcomes of financial participation as arising from the interplay of actor interests and behaviour in specific institutional contexts (where institutions are viewed as norms and rules, as well as formal organisations). As a result, we view financial participation as a more complex phenomenon than that of a simple, though possibly ineffective, instrument to achieve capitalist control by neutralising unions.

Cycles of Control

Harvie Ramsay's first, and perhaps most widely known, contribution to the industrial relations and sociology of work literature was published in 1977, and grew out of his doctoral studies at the University of Durham. In an influential paper in *Sociology* (1977a), he argued that managerial interest in employee participation occurred in 'Cycles'. Typically, widespread use of participation occurred at times of taut labour markets, when labour presented the strongest challenge to managerial interests and authority. However, the notion of common interests articulated by owners and managers during participation initiatives was ultimately untenable because of an underlying conflict of interests. Thus participation would descend into trivia, where this opposition of interests between labour and capital was not so salient, or would decay because of disillusion with the inability of participation to meet expectations (Ramsay, 1977b). Managerial calculation was also important: managers drop the charade of sharing control when they no longer need to manage the trade union challenge. Hence the notion of cycles of control: managerial interest in worker participation ebbs and flows according to the strength of organised labour and the challenges facing managers.

On this basis, Ramsay discerned five main cycles of employer activity in the UK. The first took place in the second half of the 1860s and was characterised by an interest in profit-sharing. Drawing on Church's work (1971), he noted how a ground-breaking experiment in profit-sharing at the Briggs colliery was motivated not by benevolence but by desperation. The profit-sharing scheme was aimed at detaching workers from trade unions. The second wave of interest – once again focused on profit-sharing – took place at the end of the 1880s, a time of substantial industrial militancy and the emergence of 'general unionism'. The third wave took the form of Whitleyism, being observed in the latter half of the 1920s, while the fourth took the form of Joint Production Committees during the Second World War. The most recent cycle emerged in the 1960s, in the shape of productivity bargaining and was a response to the growth of shop-floor power occasioned by taut labour and product markets. At the time he was writing (in the mid-1970s), Ramsay saw the material conditions for this as having subsided but the ideological 'superstructure' as lingering. Hence there was a great deal of interest at that time in various forms of worker participation, such as worker directors.

Ramsay studied the area of worker participation for the rest of his career, coming to focus more specifically on financial participation during the

1980s. In an article written jointly with Nigel Haworth (1984), he extended and deepened the analysis of financial participation found in the 'Cycles' papers. His earlier views on profit-sharing were reiterated: they argued that it has no potential to pass control to employees, and hence no potential to dilute the conflict between labour and capital. Instead, it usually takes the form of a simple wage bonus. Employee share ownership was viewed as having greater potential to bring about change because it modified the ownership relationship. However, it does so by making the worker a capitalist rather than by changing the capital–labour relationship fundamentally. In practice, though, the amount of ownership that capitalists and shareholders are willing to concede is too small to have any significant effect on employee attitudes and behaviour. For the most part, this analysis focused on profit-sharing, with share ownership plans largely conflated with profit-sharing. It was only later, in work conducted with colleagues at Glasgow University (Baddon *et al.* 1989), that Ramsay focused more specifically on employee share-ownership plans.

There are several features of the 'Cycles' approach that merit further elaboration and comment. A primary objective for Ramsay was to contest the often widely promulgated notion that there is a long-term, unfolding development of participation, arising from structural transformations of the nature of work and society coupled with the development of 'humanistic' forms of management (Ramsay 1977a; 1985; 1993). The underlying basis of participation cycles was the structural conflict of control between capital and labour, and this explains both the emergence and subsequent decline of interest in participation at particular times. However, he emphasised that the 'content' of cycles took different specific forms at different times, while the circumstances in which they arose would never be the same twice (Ramsay 1983).

A distinguishing feature of the 'Cycles' analysis was a focus on the 'macro' aspects of worker participation (Kelly 1998). Ramsay was interested in broad social trends in favour of participation, and the question of why participation was a dominant feature of the economic and industrial landscape at particular times. Although he used case studies of particular companies to illustrate his arguments, his view was that a cycle was more than the sum of all participation 'experiments' in operation at any one time. The general prominence of the ideology of participation characterised the upswing from the downswing of a cycle. In Ramsay's view, this emphasis on the macro aspects of participation distinguished his analysis of participation from those of others, such as Ackers *et al.* (1992) and Marchington *et al.* (1992). However, in his reply to criticisms of the 'Cycles' analysis by Ackers *et al.* (1992), Ramsay (1993) argued that the macro and micro aspects of participation are interdependent. His view was that the context in which organisations formulate participation initiatives was important, while at the same time we can only understand these wider dynamics by reference to how they are 'played out' in particular organisational contexts.

However, it is possible to discern tension between the micro and macro levels of analysis. In Ramsay's early writings, the failure of participation to give workers' effective 'voice' or to transform employment relationships is attributed primarily to the power relations in capitalism. As his work developed, he came to emphasise the role of the microdynamics of individual participation schemes, which occur to some extent independently of underlying property relations. In the original 'Cycles' formulation, management action reflected capitalist dynamics directly. By 1985, he was arguing against a 'vulgar Marxism' that saw management as rational strategists carrying out the will of capitalism, as the then fashionable Braverman perspective tended to imply. Instead, he emphasised the limits to consistent and rational behaviour among managers (Ramsay 1985). This type of analysis was taken further in the review of employee involvement published in *Human Resource Management Journal* (Ramsay 1991). Here, he drew attention to the diversity of motives behind the implementation of various schemes and the myriad ways that they fail to deliver. Managerial shortcomings (lack of understanding of participation, lack of preparation and so on) are a key contributor to the failure of employee involvement initiatives, and he recommended various actions that managers should take to bring about greater success, such as the development of clear objectives and the provision of clear support to schemes (Ramsay 1991).

Notwithstanding the evolution of Ramsay's views, the 'Cycles' thesis stands or falls on several key propositions. The first is that employer interest in worker participation is determined primarily by industrial relations considerations, and in particular the concern to avoid or undermine union representation. Employers aim to weaken unions at certain times by promoting employee identification with the firm, using mechanisms that appear to dilute managerial and employer control. The second is that periods of activity and interest in worker participation can be discerned clearly, at both macro and micro levels. The third is that the capacity of participation schemes to change employee attitudes and behaviour is limited by structural constraints in the capital–labour relationship. In the following sections we address these questions in relation to financial participation in the UK. We also examine the orientation of unions towards financial participation, since the use of participation to divert employee attachments from unions to their employer might be expected to be opposed by unions. Before we address these questions, we provide some summary details of the incidence of financial participation in the UK.

The Growth of Employee Financial Participation

The current 'cycle' or 'wave' of interest in financial participation in the UK has been a sustained one. Its beginning is usually taken to be 1978, when the

Callaghan Labour government introduced a share-based, profit-sharing scheme. Since then, there has been successive legislation establishing (and amending) tax and national insurance concessions for new financial participation plans. We focus on governmental objectives and legislation because research has shown that statutory frameworks and fiscal concessions are key determinants of the incidence of financial participation (Uvalic 1990; Pendleton *et al.* 2003). Furthermore, the overwhelming majority of employee financial participation plans in the UK (apart from plans restricted to top executives) are operated in accordance with statutory guidelines so as to benefit from tax concessions. Although government action is of primary importance, it should not simply be conflated with the 'macro' aspect of Ramsay's cycles as government action itself might reflect broader underlying social and economic forces. We consider the nature of these later.

The main 'approved' financial participation plans that have been used since 1978 are as follows.

Approved profit sharing (1978)

An all-employee plan providing for share distributions to employees financed out of profits. A variant (Buy-One-Get-One-Free or BOGOF) provided free shares for those purchasing shares. APS also provided the share distribution mechanism (in conjunction with Employee Benefit Trusts) in Employee Share Ownership Plans (ESOPs). This scheme was phased out by 2002, having been superseded by the Share Incentive Plan.

Save As You Earn ('Sharesave') (1980)

An all-employee share option scheme whereby employees save regular amounts, using a SAYE plan, to finance the exercise of options in three, five, or seven years' time.

Discretionary share options (1984)

Discretionary share option arrangements, without a savings plan. This plan was amended to become Company Share Options (CSOP) in 1996, with lower limits on the size of option grants that could be offered.

Profit-related pay (1987)

Profit-sharing arrangements by which employees received income tax relief on a portion of their pay classed as profit-related. The tax concessions were phased out by 2000.

Share incentive plan (2000)

A 'modular' share plan that enables employees to receive free shares or to purchase shares on very favourable terms (assisted by 'matching shares').

Enterprise management incentives (2000)

Share option arrangements targeted at smaller firms (initially those with gross assets of less than £15 million, at the time of writing, £30 million).

The core principle underlying these 'approved' share-based plans in the UK is that employee benefits are taxed as capital gains rather than as income, with the tax liability arising on the sale of the shares.[1] This contrasts with arrangements in several other European countries where tax liability (in share option plans) arises at either the date of grant of options or the date of exercise. Besides the specific schemes outlined above, the Blair Government has also further enhanced the tax concessions available to companies and participants. The capital gains tax regime for employee share plans is now the 'business assets taper relief system', whereby the tax liability decreases in line with the duration of shareholding. Companies now receive a statutory corporation tax deduction for the costs of operating share plans.

As of March 2001, there were just over 2,400 broad-based employee ownership schemes, supplemented by 5,500 selective stock option plans, operated in accordance with government legislation (Inland Revenue 2002). In total, about 1,750 firms now have at least one broad-based share-ownership scheme. Nearly all the firms in the FTSE 100[2] have an employee share-ownership scheme. It is estimated that about 2.75 million employees have received shares via approved profit-sharing schemes, and around 2 million employees received options under the savings-related share option scheme (Inland Revenue 2002).

Information from the Workplace Industrial/Employee Relations Surveys captures both the extent of financial participation in the UK and the trends over time. As Table 5.1 shows, there was very substantial growth in the use of profit-sharing (profit-related pay) from the second half of the 1980s. The incidence of share plans more than doubled during the 1980s, though it

Table 5.1   Percentage of workplaces with financial participation

	1980	1984	1990	1998
Profit-sharing	–	19	44	46
Share plans	13	22	30	24

Note: Base = All trading sector workplaces with 25 or more employees.

Source: Cully *et al.* (1999), 233.

subsequently stagnated somewhat in the 1990s. The new legislation in 2000 was designed to stimulate renewed growth of the use of share plans.

A Cycle of Control?

If the support for financial participation in the UK is conceived as a cycle, it has certainly been a long one. Government encouragement of share-owner-ship plans has, at the time of writing, extended for over twenty-five years and shows no signs of abating. The rationale for share plans displays conti-nuities throughout the period, though with some nuances. In the Thatcher years (1980s), share-ownership was portrayed as a key component of an 'enterprise culture', and as a useful mechanism for encouraging employee identification with their employer (Saunders and Harris 1990). The Blair Government has also emphasised the capacity of share plans to align employee interests with those of employers, thereby potentially leading to attitudinal and behavioural changes, and ultimately having an impact on corporate performance.

Given the Ramsay thesis, a key question is the extent to which these objec-tives are aimed at undermining trade union representation and activity. In the Thatcher era, it is indisputable that governments hoped that financial participation would undermine trade unions. The Secretary of State for Employment in the mid-1990s, Michael Portillo (1985), pointed out in an Employment Department publication that it was expected that there would be more employee shareholders than trade union members by the end of the twentieth century. While he did not connect one to the other explicitly, the message was nevertheless unmistakable. The government took the view that the promotion of an 'enterprise culture' would weaken employee attach-ment to unions and reduce 'them and us' feelings among employees. However, a clear problem for the Ramsay thesis is that the unions were in a position of weakness rather than strength at that time. They were losing members because of a combination of anti-union legislation, unemployment and government policy aimed at excluding unions from quasi-corporatist institutions and networks. Financial participation was an added ingredient in the assault on unions, but it was not the primary instrument. It was more about achieving a long-term reorientation in employee attitudes in order to complement the more immediate assaults on union power. However, in the Blair era, legislation has not been aimed at undermining union influence, though the emphasis on alignment of employee interests with those of the firm, and the encouragement of co-operation might be seen as incompatible with 'traditional' notions of industrial relations. Even so, there was no over-arching ideological anti-union stance accompanying new legislation, and elements of this legislation (the emphasis on fairness, for example) reflect trade union concerns.[3]

Turning to the corporate level, a key component of the 'Cycles' thesis is that corporate objectives focus on undermining trade unionism, either by removing part of the remuneration from collective bargaining or by undermining employee attachment to unions. So far, however, there is little evidence from the current wave of financial participation that this objective is important for the management of most companies. The most recent large-scale data comes from surveys conducted in the 1980s by Michael Poole (1988; 1989) and the Glasgow team, of which Ramsay was a member (Ramsay *et al.* 1990), but neither study included direct questions on the role of trade unionism as a factor in introducing financial participation. However, other data on unions in their surveys and accompanying case studies help to illuminate the role of industrial relations in the use of financial participation. Poole found that holding down wage claims is an unimportant objective for financial participation. He further showed that there is a positive relationship between trade union presence and financial participation. This could be viewed as supportive evidence for the 'Cycles' approach (that is, firms with strong unions adopt financial participation to weaken them), but Poole argued that the relationship is essentially indirect, with those firms entering into collective bargaining tending to be those that also use other forms of employee involvement. A positive relationship between trade union presence and financial participation has been found repeatedly in the WIRS/WERS surveys, though this relationship disappeared in the 1998 survey (see Gregg and Machin 1988; Pendleton 1997). Baddon *et al.* (1989) found that the most important objectives for financial participation were typically the promotion of identification with the company and the inducement of co-operation but, in the absence of explicit questions on unions, it is not possible to tell whether this was perceived to be at the expense of unions.

Earlier critiques of Ramsay's work have argued that management objectives for employee involvement are diverse in character and cannot be reduced to a uni-dimensional concern with trade unions and industrial relations. In their critique of the 'Cycles' thesis, based on a major study of employee involvement for the Department of Employment, Ackers *et al.* (1992) identify several aims: incorporation; HRM-inspired attempts to bypass or avoid unions; product market reasons; labour market reasons; philosophical reasons; and simple 'faddism'. This emphasis on diversity can be extended further by an appreciation that there might also be a diversity of actors involved in the introduction of employee involvement, both within management and externally. For example, in *Employee Ownership, Participation, and Governance* (Pendleton 2001), I showed that several groups of actors were involved in the creation of ESOPs in bus companies: local authorities; managers; financial institutions; unions; and workers. All had their own sets of motives and the final outcome was a function of the interplay of these objectives. Local authorities aimed to retain some degree of local control of service provision after privatisation, while unions, though wary of employee ownership, saw it as being preferable to ownership by large firms with reputations for reducing employment and wages. A key objective of managers was to retain their 'right to manage'. They saw union-led employee ownership as being preferable to workers' co-operatives, because the latter were more likely to generate unfettered employee 'interference' in management. The important lesson to draw from this example is the importance of context and the interplay of actors' interests. It is difficult to discern an underlying capitalist logic directly determining outcomes, though fundamental conflicts between capital and labour arising from property relations set parameters to what happened in specific cases.

The experience of the last twenty-five years or so of financial participation, then, is not supportive of the 'Cycles' perspective. The material conditions for the onset of cycles – taut product and labour markets plus union strength – have not been in evidence across the economy for much of the period. For the most part, anti-union objectives have not been a primary objective of companies, though they have been aims of successive governments for some of the time. Actor motives are heterogeneous, and government and corporate objectives are at best loosely coupled: companies take advantage of government initiatives but they do not necessarily share the same objectives. Furthermore, a multiplicity of actors might be involved in the generation of financial participation schemes, with the interplay of their objectives and policies within specific contexts leading to a multiplicity of outcomes. Although the 'Cycles' perspective is not incompatible with variation between actors and events within cycles (because underlying forces structure the cycle), extensive heterogeneity of practice suggests that the 'Cycles' analysis does not capture the complexity of employee participation initiatives.

Employee Attitudes and Behaviour

A key argument in Ramsay's thesis is that the underlying conflict between capital and labour will limit the extent to which employer initiatives can win the support of employees in the long term. Participation initiatives will either descend into trivia or else come up against the limits of what managements will allow, or both. Thus, the capacity of participation to transform employee attitudes and behaviour is decidedly limited. In the case of share-ownership plans, the small amounts of equity that owners and managers are willing to transfer to employees will limit the capacity of these plans to bring about significant changes in employee attitudes and behaviour (Ramsay and Haworth 1984).

These views on the limitations of financial participation to modify attitudes were largely borne out by the Glasgow study. Baddon *et al.* found that there was not a great deal of difference in attitudes to the company and views on management–employee relations between SAYE participants and non-participants, though the former were slightly more favourable (Baddon *et al*. 1989: 256; 1990: 191). They argue further that financial participation was viewed as a 'self-contained' aspect of employment, and that there was little 'carry-over' of attitudes from the share plan to a broader view of employee participation (1989: 267; 1990: 200–3). These findings have been echoed to a certain extent in other studies of employee shareholder attitudes, such as that by Dunn *et al*. (1991). They find little difference between participants and non-participants, and little change in attitudes over time (except among those who initially considered joining a plan but then decided against it). These findings are consistent with the 'cycles of control' perspective in that the stability of employee attitudes can be linked to the small proportion of equity held by employees and the associated lack of control or influence on corporate governance.

A critical test for Ramsay's perspective is what happens to employee attitudes in organisations where there is a substantial transfer of ownership and control to employees. In our study of bus company ESOPs (Pendleton *et al*. 1998) we found significant positive associations between share ownership and employee commitment in companies where significant portions of equity had been transferred to employees and some control had been passed to employee representatives. A key finding, at odds with earlier North American evidence (Klein 1987), was that the level of individual shareholding is associated positively with higher levels of commitment towards the company. However, consistent with the North American evidence (Long 1978; Klein 1987; Blasi *et al*. 2003), this study found that 'positive' attitudes to the firm are also more likely to occur where share ownership is accompanied by participation in decisions. Overall, these findings, taken in conjunction with the studies of other share plans, indicate that significant attitudinal change only occurs when there are substantial transfers of equity and control. The balance of the evidence is therefore consistent with Ramsay's views.

However, the reasons for the limited impact of share plans on employee attitudes might differ somewhat from the explanations provided by Ramsay and others. A critical assumption that underlies all the work on the attitudinal effects of employee financial participation is that ownership and involvement in governance is valued and sought after by employees. Yet if ownership and control is not especially salient to employees, share ownership plans are unlikely to bring about attitudinal change. Equally, if share plans are valued by employees for reasons other than ownership and governance, the plans could generate favourable employee attitudes even though their impact on the distribution of ownership and control is minimal. We must be careful not to assume that ownership and control are important to employees, or even that employees interpret financial participation in this way. A useful corrective to these assumptions can be found in a strand of Ramsay's early work that sits slightly uneasily with his work on cycles. In a paper published contemporaneously with the *Sociology* paper in 1977 (Ramsay 1977b), he found that the type of participation of most interest to employees is day-to-day involvement in decisions about their own job and work tasks rather than control of the direction of the company. Furthermore, greater participation was not a particularly important work goal of employees, though there was some demand for a greater say. Substantial majorities of employees liked the idea of profit-sharing and employee share ownership (though it is not clear why).

These findings, coupled with the observations above, can assist us in interpreting the complex and mixed findings from studies of employee attitudes. They help to explain the conjunction of favourable evaluations of share plans by employees and the limited attitudinal change or attitudinal differences between share plan participants and non-participants that is frequently found in the literature (for example, Baddon *et al.* 1989; Poole and Jenkins 1990). We should bear in mind too that employees might perceive that financial participation has a different purpose from the creation of ownership and transfer of control. SAYE schemes, for example, might be seen primarily as highly tax-advantageous, medium-term savings plans rather than mechanisms for acquiring a stake in the firm. A recent large-scale survey found that 96 per cent of employees joined a SAYE scheme to 'save for the future', compared with 45 per cent who joined to feel a 'greater sense of involvement in the company' (Pendleton, 2004). Any attitudinal effects might therefore derive not from the 'psychological ownership' of equity but rather from an appreciation of the provision of valuable benefits by the firm. Overall, the capacity for financial participation plans to generate employee consent is a function of employee perceptions of the purpose of the plan (which might be generated independently of governmental and managerial objectives), the extent to which these purposes are seen to be consistent with their own objectives and interests, and the extent to which the plan in fact meets these objectives and interests. The ability of employee share plans to affect employee attitudes therefore appears to be more complex than suggested by the 'cycles of control' thesis.

Trade Unions and Financial Participation

Finally, we examine the relationships between trade unions, industrial relations and financial participation. Our assumption here is that trade unions would be likely to oppose financial participation if it was seen clearly to be aimed at undermining unions and employee attachment to them. Historically, there is some support for this view in the UK, as unions have traditionally been wary and suspicious of financial participation and employee ownership (Bradley and Nejad 1989: 63–5). At the time of writing, in some European countries there is hostility to financial participation among unions or union confederations (for example, the CGT in France) on the grounds that there is a fundamental opposition of interests between labour and capital which financial participation undermines or muddies.

In the UK, union opposition to financial participation and employee share ownership derives from three potential effects of financial participation on unions (see Pendleton *et al.* 1995).[4] The first is that the development of new institutions associated with financial participation will lead to unions being bypassed. In the case of employee ownership, new institutions of employee-shareholder governance might supplant unions and collective bargaining institutions. In the case of profit-sharing, the 'automatic' linking of remuneration to profits might take some part of pay determination outside collective bargaining (though the formula or size of profit share might be bargained). The second argument is that, where unions continue to provide the main avenue of employee representation they will find themselves drawn into shareholder representation (where there is employee ownership), with the result that union functions become confused. Union activities might oscillate between the pursuit of (employee) owner interests (for example, maintaining profits) and employee interests (securing wage increases). This ambiguity of purpose can sap the legitimacy of unions from the perspective of their constituents (Hammer and Stern 1986). The history of the 'Benn co-operatives' in the 1970s is supportive of this view: Eccles (1981: 395–7) found that union involvement in strategic decisions contributed to employee cynicism that the unions could represent employees adequately in grievance cases. The third argument (discussed earlier) is that employees who become shareholders will develop new sets of values and attitudes that are less sympathetic to unions.

These arguments are best tested in contexts where there have been substantial transfers of equity to employees. In the 1990s, a sizeable part of the UK bus industry passed into employee ownership, using the ESOP mechanism, as a consequence of the privatisation of the industry. At the time, there was a great deal of ambivalence among the trade unions in the industry, for the reasons outlined above. The dominant union – the Transport and General Workers' Union (TGWU) – reluctantly accepted the case for employee ownership on the grounds that it provided some protection for employees against wage cuts and employment reductions.

Did employee ownership undermine union representation and activity in the way that has been suggested? On balance, the evidence suggests that it did not, and in some respects the union role was strengthened. To understand the impact of employee ownership on unions, we need to refer to the objectives of the main actors in the particular industrial relations context of the bus industry. Management were generally supportive of the strengthening of the unions' role in the new institutions of employee-shareholder representation and governance, on the grounds that representative democracy was preferable to the direct democracy that was seen to characterise workers' co-operatives. Managers believed their 'right to manage' would be better maintained by union-controlled representative democracy than by direct employee involvement in what hitherto were management decisions. Union representatives maintained the unions' distance from shareholder representation by establishing new institutions of employee-shareholder governance (worker directors, employee shareholder committees and so on) that were separate from collective bargaining and employee representative institutions. At the same time, the capacity of these new institutions to undermine union institutions was constrained by various mechanisms that subjected them to union control. For example, worker directors in most companies were required to provide regular reports to the local union branches. In some companies, 'shadow boards' composed of senior union representatives met regularly with the board of directors (see Pendleton *et al.* 1995; Pendleton 2001). This evidence suggests that any underlying structural imperatives arising from a fundamental conflict between labour and capital are not translated automatically into processes that reflect these contradictions. Instead, the interplay of actors' perceived interests in specific institutional contexts influences institutional outcomes. This evidence from the bus industry is therefore not only contrary to the specific predictions made by Ramsay but also to his insistence (in his early work at least) that underlying structural conditions will be the dominant influence on outcomes.

Most employee share-ownership plans in the UK are, however very different from these bus industry ESOPs in so far as the equity transferred to employees is typically maintained at less than 5 per cent, with ownership and control remaining with shareholders and managers. What are the relationships between employee share ownership and trade unions in these cases? The balance of evidence suggests that the introduction of employee share plans takes place independently of both collective bargaining and employee representation, even though share plans tended to be more prevalent in unionised workplaces, at least until recent times (see Gregg and Machin 1988; Pendleton 1997). In some cases, union representatives might have some involvement in the communication of information about share plans, but this is uncommon. A recent survey of fifty-six large listed firms (mainly drawn from the FTSE 100) found that in 91 per cent of cases there was no formal agreement with employees or their representatives to introduce financial participation. In 71 per cent of cases there was no employee involvement in the development of the plan, and in only 16 per cent of cases were employees or their representatives involved in the management and administration of the plan (see Kalmi *et al.* 2004). At the same time, employee share ownership is not accompanied by employee involvement in corporate governance. As the above results imply, it is rare for any institutions to be created to represent employee-shareholder interests, with the employee-shareholder association found in some companies in France notable by its absence. Any involvement in governance by employees in listed firms takes the form of attendance at the AGM, but this type of activity is ineffective (given the dominance of institutional shareholders) and uncommon. The vast majority of employee-shareholders do not attend: a recent survey of over 6,000 participants in employee share plans found that only 2.3 per cent of employees attend the AGM always or most years, while 92 per cent never attend (see Pendleton, 2004). There is a complex set of reasons for this: AGMs have not been a particularly important institution for governance, at least until recently; involvement in governance is not an important reason for share plan participation in most cases; and employers are usually reluctant to encourage employee involvement in governance.

This evidence suggests that union activities are neither undermined nor compromised by financial participation. Instead, financial participation occurs mainly independently of unions, union representation and collective bargaining. Managers have not in most cases actively sought to engage unions (even if they have not actively sought to exclude them). Equally, it is clear that many unions have failed to engage with financial participation in many cases, though some have welcomed the separation from collective bargaining. A recent study conducted for the European Foundation found that unions rarely have formal policies on this topic (see Pendleton *et al.* 2002). These findings are similar to those of some fifteen years earlier by Baddon *et al.* (1989) and Poole (1989). In a similar vein, a study by the Jim Conway Foundation (Allen *et al.* 1990) observed that trade unions are reliant on *ad hoc* initiatives, and lack a general framework for analysis and strategic policy development in the area of financial participation.

Earlier research suggested that trade union orientations to financial participation were a combination of lack of interest and mild opposition, described aptly in one study as 'bored hostility' (Incomes Data Services 1986). The main exceptions to this were the unions in the finance sector, where financial participation has been particularly prevalent. Three unions in this sector had formal policies in favour of financial participation in the late 1980s (see Baddon *et al.* 1989: 45). The evidence from our research suggests that trade union perceptions and views of financial participation have evolved to some extent. Financial participation is now regarded as 'a fact of life', as a large number of major employers operate schemes, and governments have invested considerable efforts in promoting participation. Union views are, in the main, neither strongly for nor against financial participation (with the TUC now describing its perspective as 'engaged scepticism'). Instead, unions respond pragmatically to the details of individual schemes in the small number of cases where they have some involvement. There are exceptions: in the European Foundation study mentioned above, one union was highly supportive of employee share ownership on social justice grounds. It was felt that members should share in the good times to counter the hardships faced in the bad times. There were a further two unions which, while they could not be viewed as ideological converts to financial participation, had supported share-ownership schemes on the grounds that they were a potentially attractive benefit to members and could provide useful additional bargaining levers.[5]

Discussion and Conclusions

The findings on trade unions and financial participation from the late 1980s onwards are not supportive of the 'Cycles' perspective, though equally they are not incompatible with aspects of it. There is little indication that unions have been undermined by financial participation (other measures achieved this end!) or that unions feel that financial participation poses a threat to them. The evidence suggests that companies introduce financial participation to promote employee identification and attachment, but that industrial relations considerations do not usually loom large in these rationales. A further observation is that share plans do not necessarily have a unitary meaning. Different sets of actors in different institutional contexts attach different meanings to financial participation. For some, it might be about ownership, for others it is about medium-term, low-risk savings. Within managements, some might aim to transform employment relationships, others might have more mundane objectives (retention of key employees, and so on). The interplay of actors' perceptions and objectives in specific contexts leads to context-specific institutions (broadly-defined) of financial participation. The logic of this is that, contrary to the implications of the 'Cycles' perspective, financial participation is not an off-the-shelf instrument. It does not have predictable, stable qualities and effects, that can be taken down, dusted off and put to work when circumstances dictate (even though statutory frameworks provide uniform core features).

Finally, an alternative explanation of 'cycles of control' might be advanced for the entrenched role of financial participation in the UK economy from the 1980s onwards. As others have remarked, the notion of cycles does not capture adequately the sustained interest in financial participation and other forms of employee involvement since the 1980s. Other formulations, such as that of 'waves' (Marchington *et al.* 1992) or 'favourable conjunctures' (Poole 1989) might well be preferable. Whatever formulation is preferred, a key consideration is that extensive financial participation can now be considered a long-term and entrenched feature of Anglo-American economies. The development of mass financial participation in the UK and US economies coincided, not with an upsurge of trade union power, but with the emergence of 'shareholder value' and the shift of corporate resources from labour to capital that has accompanied this (see Gospel and Pendleton 2005). In practical terms, this has meant less advantageous pension arrangements, and the disruption of internal labour markets and career opportunities in many cases. The major dilemma, which provides the context for financial participation, is how companies can engender the employee commitment seen increasingly as being necessary for a competitive advantage at the same time as the traditional supports for employee bonding are being removed by shareholder pressures to generate superior financial returns.

Share plans can be seen as a mechanism to generate commitment and a signal that employees will receive some returns, in a context where companies find it difficult to make long-term commitments to employees. Consideration of human capital investments makes this clear. As Margaret Blair (1995) has shown, corporate unwillingness to commit to employees threatens human capital investments because, even where firms bear the direct costs of these (firm-specific training), employees nevertheless bear opportunity costs. Share plans provide a signal to employees that managers and shareholders will not act opportunistically to capture all the gains from such training programmes, and hence can make it worthwhile for employees to undertake these co-specific investments. At the same time, share plans are a contingent commitment: if the company does not perform well, the cost to the company of this commitment can be negligible (as in the case of share option plans, where the benefit derives principally from an increase in share price). It is worth noting that recent evidence suggests a strong correlation between the level of training undertaken by companies and the presence of share plans, even when other relevant factors are controlled for (see Pendleton *et al.* 2001).

A further support for training provided by share plans can be located in the general nature of much of the human capital investment sponsored and financed by companies (contrary to the predictions of human capital theory). The context to this is the development of the 'knowledge economy' and the importance of general skills (for example, communication and listening skills) associated with this. Where initial vocational training is deficient, as is often said to be the case in the UK, continuing vocational training assumes a greater importance as a compensating device (see Green 1999). A dilemma for companies is how to deal with the free-rider potential associated with general skills training. Share plans help to resolve this by providing a medium-term lock-in of employees. Share plans typically provide deferred benefits, with these benefits being lost to the employee if they exit the firm 'prematurely'. For example, share options lapse if employees leave before vesting, while free or purchased shares are often required to be held for a certain period for tax benefits to be secured.[6]

In other economies, these issues and dilemmas have often been resolved in alternative ways. In Germany, for example, the works council and co-determination systems have provided institutions to articulate and balance the competing interests of labour and capital, with the result that 'shareholder value' has been a less-developed phenomenon than in the USA and the UK.[7] In the absence of similar governance institutions in the UK, coupled with a long-term decline in union presence and power, share plans have provided an alternative solution to governance problems. They have done so, not by facilitating employee involvement in corporate governance (which, as shown earlier, is negligible) but by providing some protection for workers' financial and economic interests. In relation to general skills development, the deferral and lock-in characteristics of share plans substitute for the pattern of employer regulation provided by employers' associations found in countries such as Germany.

Overall, then, our argument is that the recent development of mass financial participation in countries such as the UK and the USA is best understood not as a reaction to trade union power, as the Ramsay thesis suggests, but in the context of the development of shareholder value and the reliance on market-based rather than relationship-based forms of regulation and governance. Share plans help to engender commitment in contexts where it is difficult to generate by other means. This kind of explanation helps us to understand why financial participation has been particularly prevalent in economies such as the UK over the last twenty years or so, and why it has been less widespread in other European economies where unions have often been stronger and industrial relations issues more salient. The recent growth of 'shareholder value' ideologies and practices in other European economies helps to explain the expansion in employee financial participation in many instances (see Pendleton *et al.* 2001). The implication of this is that future research into employee share ownership should go beyond the parameters derived from 'traditional' industrial relations, and should engage with theory and concepts found in corporate governance and comparative political economy.

Notes

1 In the cash-based profit related pay scheme, the designated profit-share component of wages was free of income tax.
2 The 100 largest firms on the London Stock Exchange measured by market capitalisation.
3 The TUC had a nominee (Jeannie Drake of the Communication Workers' Union) on the advisory group that helped to design the new share plan legislation.
4 There are other arguments mounted by unions against financial participation. These relate to the inequities of transferring risk to employees with liquidity constraints and undiversified wealth portfolios.
5 It was recognised that the control rights associated with share ownership were in practice limited, but that share ownership gave moral 'clout' to unions' and workers' bargaining positions.
6 The new share incentive plan allows for forfeiture of free shares if employees leave (apart from 'good' reasons such as retirement).
7 The much smaller size of the listed company sector is also important.

References

Ackers, P., Marchington, M., Wilkinson, A. and Goodman, J. (1992) 'The Use of Cycles: Explaining Employee Involvement in the 1990s', *Industrial Relations Journal*, 23, 268–73.

Allen, C., Cunningham, I. and McArdle, L. (1990) 'Employee Participation and Involvement into the 1990s: Company Practice, Innovation and the Trade Union Role'. Stockton on Tees: Jim Conway Foundation.

Baddon, L., Hunter, L., Hyman, J., Leopold, J. and Ramsay, H. (1989) *Peoples' Capitalism? A Critical Analysis of Profit-Sharing and Employee Share Ownership* (London: Routledge).

Blair, M. (1995) *Ownership and Control: Rethinking Corporate Governance for the TwentyFirst Century* (Washington, DC: Brookings Institution).

Blasi, J., Kruse, D. and Berstein, A. (2003) *In the Company of Owners* (New York: Basic Books).

Bradley, K. and Nejad, A. (1989) *Managing Owners: The National Freight Company Buy-Out in Perspective* (Cambridge University Press).

Church, R. (1971) 'Profit Sharing and Labour Relations in the Nineteenth Century', *International Review of Social History*, 26, 2–16.

Cully, M., Woodland, S., O'Reilly, A. and Dix, G. (1999) *Britain at Work: As Depicted by the 1998 Workplace Employee Relations Survey* (London: Routledge).

Dunn, S., Richardson, R. and Dewe, P. (1991) 'The Impact of Employee Share Ownership on Worker Attitudes: A Longitudinal Case Study', *Human Resource Management Journal*, 1, 1–17.

Eccles, T. (1981) *Under New Management* (London: Pan).

Green, F. (1999) 'Training the Workers', in P. Gregg and J. Wadsworth (eds), *The State of Working Britain* (Manchester: Manchester University Press).

Gregg, P. and Machin, S. (1988) 'Unions and the Incidence of Performance-Linked Pay in Britain', *International Journal of Industrial Organisation*, 6, 91–109.

Gospel, H. and Pendleton, A. (2005) 'Corporate Governance and Labour Management: an International Comparison', Oxford: Oxford University Press.

Hammer, T. and Stern, R. 'A Yo-Yo Model of Co-operation: Union Participation at the Rath Packing Company', *Industrial and Labor Relations Review*, 39, 337–49.

Incomes Data Services (1986) *Profit Sharing and Employee Share Options* (London: IDS).

Inland Revenue (2002) *Inland Revenue Statistics 2001* (London: Inland Revenue).

Kalmi, P., Pendleton, A. and Poutsma, E. (2004) 'The Relationship Between Financial Participation and Other Forms of Participation: New Survey Evidence', Mimeo: Helsinki Center of Economic Research, Discussion Paper 3.

Kelly, J. (1998) *Rethinking Industrial Relations: Mobilisation, Collectivism and Long Waves* (London: Routledge).

Klein, K. (1987) 'Employee Stock Ownership and Employee Attitudes: A Test of Three Models', *Journal of Applied Psychology*, 72, 319–32.

Long, R. (1978) 'The Relative Effects of Share Ownership Versus Control on Job Attitudes in an Employee-Owned Company', *Human Relations*, 31, 753–63.

Marchington, M., Goodman, J., Wilkinson, A. and Ackers, P. (1992) *New Developments in Employee Involvement*, Employment Department Research Series Number 2.

Pendleton, A. (1997) 'Characteristics of Workplaces with Financial Participation: Evidence from the WIRS', *Industrial Relations Journal*, 28, 103–19.

Pendleton, A. (2001) *Employee Ownership, Participation, and Governance*, (London: Routledge).

Pendleton, A. (2004) 'Sellers or Keepers? Share retention in employee share option plans'. Manchester Metropolitan University, unpublished Mimeo.

Pendleton, A., Robinson, A. and Wilson, N. (1995) 'Does Employee Ownership Weaken Trade Unions? Recent Evidence from the UK Bus Industry', *Economic and Industrial Democracy*, 16, 577–605.

Pendleton, A., Wilson, N. and Wright, M. (1998) 'The Perception and Effects of Share Ownership: Evidence from Employee Buy-Outs', *British Journal of Industrial Relations*, 36, 99–124.

Pendleton, A., Poutsma, E., van Ommeren, J. and Brewster, C. (2001) *Profit Sharing and Employee Share Ownership in the European Union* (Dublin: European Foundation).

Pendleton, A., Rigby, M., Smith, R. and Brewster, C. (2002) *The Policies and Views of Peak Organisations towards Financial Participation: United Kingdom* (Dublin: European Foundation).

Pendleton, A., Poutsma, E., van Ommeren, J. and Brewster, C. (2003) 'The Incidence and Determinants of Employee Share Ownership and Profit Sharing in Europe', in T. Kato and J. Pliskin (eds), *The Determinants of the Incidence and the Effects of Participatory Organisations: Advances in the Economic Analysis of Participatory and Labor-Managed Firms*, Vol. 7 (Oxford: Elsevier).

Poole, M. (1988) 'Factors Affecting the Development of Employee Financial Participation in Contemporary Britain: Evidence from a National Survey', *British Journal of Industrial Relations*, 26, 21–36.

Poole, M. (1989) *The Origins of Economic Democracy: Profit-Sharing and Employee Shareholding Schemes* (London: Routledge).

Poole, M. and Jenkins, G. (1990) *The Impact of Economic Democracy* (London: Routledge).

Portillo, M. (1985) 'The competitive edge', Department of Employment Gazette, July, 271.

Ramsay, H. (1977a) 'Cycles of Control: Worker Participation in Sociological and Historical Perspective', *Sociology*, 11, 481–506.

Ramsay, H. (1977b) 'Participation: The Shop Floor View', *British Journal of Industrial Relations*, 14, 128–41.

Ramsay, H. (1980) 'Phantom Participation: Patterns of Power and Conflict', *Industrial Relations Journal*, 11, 46–59.

Ramsay, H. (1983) 'Evolution or Cycle? Worker Participation in the 1970s and 1980s', in C. Crouch and F. Heller (eds), *International Yearbook of Organisational Democracy: Organisational Democracy and Political Processes* (Chichester: Wiley).

Ramsay, H. (1985) 'What is Participation For? A Critical Evaluation of "Labour Process" Analyses of Job Reform', in D. Knights, H. Willmott and D. Collinson (eds), *Job Redesign: Critical Perspectives on the Labour Process* (Aldershot: Gower).

Ramsay, H. (1991) 'Reinventing the Wheel? A Review of the Development and Performance of Employee Involvement', *Human Resource Management Journal*, 1, 1–22.

Ramsay, H. (1993) 'Recycled Waste? Debating the Analysis of Worker Participation: A Response to Ackers et al.', *Industrial Relations Journal*, 24, 76–80.

Ramsay, H. and Haworth, N. (1984) 'Worker Capitalism? Profit-Sharing, Capital-Sharing and Juridicial Forms of Socialism', *Economic and Industrial Democracy*, 5, 295–324.

Ramsay, H., Hyman, J., Baddon, L., Hunter, L. and Leopold, J. (1990) 'Options for Workers: Owner or Employee?', in G. Jenkins and M. Poole (eds), *New Forms of Ownership, Management, and Employment* (London: Routledge).

Saunders, P. and Harris, C. (1990) 'Privatisation and the Consumer', *Sociology*, 24, 37–76.

Uvalic, M. (1990) 'Social Europe–The PEPPER Report' Brussels and Florence Commission of the European Communities.

6
In the Name of the Customer: Service Work and Participation[1]

Andrew Sturdy and Marek Korczynski

Introduction

Much of what has been written – traditional and modern, mainstream and critical – on participation assumes a manufacturing context. However, within Western economies, service work has become the norm and, it is typically claimed, service is quite different from manufacturing. While service work is now prominent, if not dominant, in the literature on paid employment, there are relatively few studies focusing on participation within this specific context. However, the distinctions between the sectors are often overdrawn. First, intra-sector variations can be more significant – compare cleaning, call centres and consultancy, for example. Indeed, one aim of this chapter is to explore some key variations within much service work. Second, core attributes of the capitalist employment relationship remain shared. This means that long-standing debates on participation being based on managerial concerns with labour productivity, compliance and organisation (that is, control) rather than humanisation, as well as persistent differences in perspectives on the extent of participation desired and experienced (Ramsay 1977) both remain relevant. Third, many apparent differences between manufacturing and service work have been obscured in recent years by the importation of 'the customer' into manufacturing and its analysis in terms of managerial concerns with quality, supply chains, internal customers and culture management, for example (Sturdy 2001).

This is not to deny that (while not being wholly distinctive) there are varying characteristics in service contexts that can make an important contribution to wider debates on participation and control, and it is these that form the focus of this chapter. In particular, the simultaneity and relative intangibility of service/consumption combined with the more explicit and multifarious role of the customer present particular challenges for the manageability or control of work and labour. Furthermore, there are tensions and contradictions within service work organisation and its accompanying and powerful managerial rhetoric that warrant critical scrutiny. Within both service and manufacturing, but especially service sectors, employee participation is increasingly justified, not so much in relation to familiar ideals of work humanisation or democratisation, or to the more prosaic notions of job satisfaction, employee retention or organisational effectiveness, but in the name of the customer. However, we shall argue that the intrusion of the customer, and therefore forms and levels of task-based participation, varies between different types of service work. The chapter is organised in the following way. First, the varying managerial rationales for increased employee participation in service work and competing pressures for rationalisation are explored, with a particular emphasis on the ideology of the sovereign consumer alongside employee responses and initiatives. This draws attention to different bases of variability in participation in practice, in terms of its form and extent – which is then systematically developed through a focus on categories of service work organisation, and roles in terms of sales and service, and 'front-office' and 'back-office' work.

Participation Rationales and Rhetorics – from Employee Commitment to Customer Satisfaction and Relationships?

Service work or, for some, servitude, has a long and continuing history, whether as paid or unpaid (for example, domestic) work (see Glenn 1996), a commercial/professional activity and/or a 'public service' (Pratchett and Wingfield 1996). Most service jobs attract low pay, status and prospects and, relatedly, are performed mainly by women and/or minority groups (see MacDonald and Sirianni 1996; Thompson *et al.* 2000). Furthermore, much service work has increasingly become standardised through the application of Tayloristic and/or bureaucratic principles (Mills 1951; Braverman 1974; Ritzer 1993) as well as an associated requirement to perform emotional and aesthetic labour (Hochschild 1983; Nickson *et al.* 2001). At the same time, service work includes more privileged or, at least autonomous, occupations by virtue of labour market and related professional power or, in a minority of cases, ownership structure ideologies such as in the case of mutual and co-operative organisations (for example, the John Lewis Partnership and the Cooperative Society). However, these issues and (control–engage) dynamics are not peculiar to service work. What we are concerned with in this section is to explore the contemporary pressures and rationales for employee task participation practices that are more distinctive as well as countervailing forces such as alternative managerial options and employees' negotiation and translation of job autonomy.

It seems hardly necessary to assert that an ideology of customer (public or professional) service has permeated all areas of work, especially in service occupations (du Gay and Salaman 1992; Sturdy *et al.* 2001). It is based on the fundamentally flawed, but powerful, neo-liberal concept and universalist assumption of the *sovereign consumer combined with free markets*. Consumers know what they want and are all-powerful in being able to choose and switch suppliers. Therefore, in order to succeed or survive in increasingly competitive markets, organisations, it is argued, must identify customer needs and direct their activities towards addressing them (profitably) (see Knights *et al.* 1994). Part of this can be achieved by seeking efficiencies in costs and service delivery (that is, service speed and price) but the immediacy and intangibility of most services – produced and consumed at the same time – combined with the necessarily active involvement and relative unpredictability of consumers means that discretion is required from service workers. Moreover, it is held that, given that other factors can be duplicated more readily in certain markets (for example, IS systems, product design, delivery channels and organisational structures), the quality of service – how well it fits or exceeds customer expectations – is seen as a key differentiating factor in securing competitive advantage. Furthermore, in recent years, this has led to a shift in managerial emphasis from service transactions to securing longer term 'customer relationships' (CRM).

While human behaviour is inherently unpredictable, this apparent imperative for varied or tailored (for example, fast and/or friendly) service has been intensified or reinforced, becoming almost a self-fulfilling prophecy. For example, the more service quality is promoted by organisations, the greater customers' expectations become (as well as their willingness to switch suppliers) and therefore the more flexibility is required in order to respond to them. Similarly, social changes in consumer societies, including those promoted by the marketing of notionally diverse or 'niche' products or services reinforce the likely variability of customer wants. If such changes are not forthcoming, then policy bodies, including governments, seek to encourage greater 'sophistication' or active consumption from consumers through education and de/re-regulation, for example. In short, we are being empowered (and entrapped) as customers (Hodgson 2001).

The above developments, then, have provided a new impetus and rationale to management participation initiatives – to better 'personalise' or tailor services to consumers. This is reflected in numerous accounts of organisations in prescriptive and popular business texts as well as other literature (for example, Bowen and Lawler 1992). Such initiatives are not, however, wholly divorced from the established managerial rationale claimed of securing employee commitment or co-operation. For example, Rucci *et al.* (1997) set out the idea of 'The Employee–Customer–Profit Chain' from a case study of Sears in the USA, although the notion has become more widespread, to include non-retail sectors in the UK (Sturdy and Terzi 2001). Here, it is claimed that there is a *causal link* between 'looking after' employees (including through task participation), their commitment to the organisation – 'the best place to work' – and to the customer and organisational profitability (for a review of the empirical evidence on this, see Korczynski 2002). More sophisticated accounts would suggest that commitment to customer service is more complex in its outcomes and antecedents, but it would still include a measure of 'empowerment', comprising job autonomy, supervisory support and low routinisation, for example (Peccei and Rosenthal 1997). Other accounts point to changing structures and reward systems by ascribing customer contact with higher status and rewards such as in parts of UK retail banking where new, albeit limited or capped and gendered, career paths are emerging for some employees (Morgan and Sturdy 2000). Elsewhere, in cases long cited by customer service protagonists (for example, FedEx and Scandinavian Airlines), organisational structures are flattened and notionally inverted with the customer at the top (see Ritzer and Stillman 2001).

Such grand and somewhat opaque claims, can be contrasted with more modest or even token forms of participation, interesting, however, by virtue of the fact that they are often heralded as significant. For example, in an article in *People Management*, the case of the hotel chain, Travel Inn was discussed in terms of the customer retention (that is, relationship) benefits of empowering 'low level' employees to encourage customer complaints and provide refunds, compensation and their own solutions to problems without approval from above (Crabb 2002). Similarly, a number of participation programmes and practices emerge in response to perceived customer wants, such as their antipathy to rationalised forms of service and communication. For example, some initiatives seek to encourage employees to draw on their own personal characteristics such as appearance, feelings and personality – be 'themselves' (Nickson *et al.* 2001). In a call centre context, talk is obviously a central part of most work tasks and of service quality – 'verbal labour'. In one reported case, the traditional employee scripts were modified and employees were encouraged to develop their 'own' vocabulary of 'sexy words' albeit with a set conversation structure geared towards sales and cross-selling – that is, selling products that are related to the main product or service being delivered (Sturdy and Fleming 2003).

Complexities and contradictions

Through such, albeit limited, managerial interventions, but also more generally through market surveys and focus groups, customers also participate, indirectly, in the design of work tasks. Indeed, it has been claimed that a 'new' third party has been introduced to the traditional employer–employee relationship that problematises both the practice and theorising of control in the labour process (Leidner 1993; see Weatherley and Tansik 1993). For example, MacDonald and Sirianni (1996a) note how, in theory, management influences customers through employees, but in practice management may join with employees to manipulate consumers (Leidner 1996), albeit sometimes for different ends (see Burawoy 1979), or with customers to supervise employees, most obviously through 'mystery shoppers' (Fuller and Smith

1991). As we shall see, workers too may use their understanding of customers and the enhanced legitimacy of service (that is, 'customer first') ideology to influence management. Also, customers may oversee or even override/replace management (Lopez 1996). Of course, management may also use others, through the development and use of technologies, to control customers remotely via telephone data entry, the internet ('electronic virtual assistants') or service tills, for example (see Baldry *et al.* 1998; *Financial Times* 2000). In this sense, customers do not so much participate in employees' tasks as replace them – with self-service.

These complexities are not simply a case of role conflict (see Weatherley and Tansik 1993), but arise from, or are reflected in, the triangular nature of the service labour process and are compounded by fundamental flaws in the broader assumptions of customer service. The concept of the 'sovereign', knowledgeable and mobile/active consumer obscures producer power, in distribution and advertising, for example, and presents a view of consumers as undersocialised and yet omniscient (see Keat *et al.* 1994). Equally, there is a tension between serving, or relating to, the customer flexibly in a 'person-alised' way (for example, through 'empowerment') and managerial concerns over costs, sales, profitability and the control/standardisation of labour – a customer may want to talk for hours when making a one-off purchase of a 'low margin' product, for example. This tension can be managed, albeit precariously, in different ways with implications for patterns of employee participation.

First, and following the marketing logic of segmentation, some customers (and/or services) are 'selected out' as being insufficiently profitable. This is evident in retail financial services (for example, personal banking) in partic-ular, where favoured (that is, profitable) customers are granted their own 'personal bankers', who have greater status, prospects, rewards, autonomy and flexibility for informality than do general call centre staff say. At the same time and as intimated above, other customers are 'pushed' into self-service and automated telephone services or, in the case of the poor, virtu-ally excluded from using banks (Sturdy and Knights 1996). Similarly, standardised services may be presented *as if* they are personalised – mass marketing to units (niches) of one. Indeed, this has been common practice for some time (Smith 1956). Second, cost control and maintaining levels of service can be sought through drawing on cheaper sources of labour, in areas of high unemployment, for example, and, as in the well-publicised cases of graduates in Indian call centres for UK-based services, low wages. Similarly, at the heart of the rise of CRM is not so much competitive concern to exceed customer expectations as an opportunity to cut the costs of customer turnover, and using 'relationships' to sell-on connected services to existing customers (Fitchett and McDonagh 2001). Third, task-based partici-pation schemes may be substituted (as well as reinforced) by selective recruitment. Here, the first stage of the 'employee – customer – profit' chain does not so much comprise schemes to energise employees and elicit their commitment through empowerment as to appropriate their already acquired personal characteristics. Thus, stereotyped and stratified character- istics of gender, sexuality, race, class, age and 'beauty' may be employed and reinforced in recruitment and advertising, (see for example, Filby 1992; Denzin 1999; Tyler and Taylor 2001). In this way, the risks of 'participation' theoretically are reduced, but also skills are devalued, long-standing inequalities are reinforced and new divisions emerge. Service becomes segregation.

These managerial approaches to resolving the tensions in service between 'Tailorism and/or Taylorism' (Korczynski 2001) in many respects mirror those associated with 'responsible autonomy' and 'direct control' (Friedman 1977) and the distribution of these forms of control in different contexts. In both cases, there are further dynamics and complexities. Although we have noted how employer-led participation may arise from *consumer* resistance to rationalised service, *employee* resistance remains important (Ramsay 1977). Here, however, the explicit focus may not be so much about job autonomy and participation, nor scepticism at the hollowness of managerial rhetoric (see Ramsay 1996). Rather, the concerns may also be associated with notions of 'personal authenticity', as symbolised by 'smile strikes' (see Fuller and Smith 1991; Sturdy and Fineman 2001) or heterosexual/'masculine' male perceptions of service requirements as being feminine (Pierce 1996; Wray- Bliss 2001).

Such resistance may also emerge from, or lead to, what might be seen as an alternative ethics of service such as that associated with public service (Boyne *et al.* 1999) as well as other 'ethics of care' (Tyler and Taylor 2001). These may arise from a rejection of managerial service practices directed at sales and efficiency *at the expense of the customer* and reflect moves to greater participation, not only in the practice of service work, but also the construc- tion of its ideology. They may be organised, as in the case of unions seeking to redefine and/or negotiate the meaning of 'quality service' (Martinez 1995; Holtgrewe 2000) and achieve a 'dignified and self respecting position' for employees (Eaton 1996: 305; see also Cobble 1996). While such organised efforts may be rather muted in the face of the onslaught of the neo-liberal conception of service and competition, the power of this ideology, paradox- ically, also serves as a basis for employees to reassert control and participa- tion in work. In the same way as managerial product quality concerns legitimate a role for employee participation in manufacturing, the rhetoric of service intangibility and the unpredictability and variability of customer demands and their legitimacy within organisations opens a space for employee participation – in the name of the customer (Heery 1993). This space is limited, however, by the contradictory requirement for profitability or cost control and, as we shall see in the following section, other ways in which the intrusion of 'the customer' varies in particular work settings.

Disaggregating Service Work

We have seen how there are a range of dynamics and tensions informing the rationale for, and emergence of, task-based participation, some of which are particularly pronounced in the context of service work and its accompanying rhetoric. Implicitly, this gives rise to a complex and varied picture of service work organisation. For example, service or segment profitability, available technological alternatives, consumer regulation, managerial ideology, labour markets and characteristics, and employee resistance/organisation may all inform the *intrusion* of the customer and related level of participation. Without losing sight of some of the core dynamics and contradictions as well as the importance of critique, asserting this variability is important, as universalistic accounts of service work remain common. They tend to reflect two perspectives that are illustrated in the portrayal of call centres – post-Fordist 'empowered' workplaces or 'bright satanic offices' (for example, Baldry *et al.* 1999; see Kinnie *et al.* 1998). While an increasing number of studies now focus on complexities and variability (for example, Rosenthal *et al.* 1997; Wilkinson *et al.* 1997; Edwards *et al.* 1998; Frenkel *et al.* 1999), there is a danger of becoming lost in a mass of contingencies. Therefore, we seek here to provide some focus by developing an analysis of different types of service work which, although not objective, nor independent of other influences, appear to have their own patterns and dynamics: front line sales work, front line service work and back-office sales/service work. Underlying this classification is the idea that the level of task-based participation is informed by the degree and nature of the worker–customer relationship or 'intrusion' of the customer. Reviewing relevant theoretical analyses and empirical research, we argue that there tends to be a descending level of participation in these three types of service work.

Front-line sales work

Front-line sales work involves workers in actively stimulating demand, encouraging customers to purchase goods or services. Examples include the sales assistants in the mobile phone shop or in the high-value goods section of a department store, the itinerant financial services worker selling insurance or mortgage products, and the car salesperson. Sales workers already comprise a significant proportion of the labour force in many advanced economies, and estimates show that the growth in the numbers of people employed in sales work is set to continue (Castells and Aoyama 1994; Rothman 1998: 152). In the banking industry, for example, a major international study concluded that there is a significant movement 'From Tellers to Sellers' (Regini *et al.* 1999).[2]

Despite the numerical and, arguably, economic importance of sales work, it tends to be an under-studied and, particularly, under-theorised area.

Biggart (1988) and Frenkel *et al.* (1999) provide the main sustained attempts to conceptualise the overall nature of work organisation within sales work. Each puts forward a theoretical 'ideal type'. In Biggart's case, it is of a direct sales organisation, as an explicit alternative to Weber's model of bureaucracy, while Frenkel *et al.* present an ideal type of an 'entrepreneurial form of work organisation'. In each of these models there is a high degree of task participation for sales workers. For Biggart, workers 'have almost no rules, and ... few managers' (Biggart, 1988: 7). For Frenkel *et al.* (1999) sales worker 'discretion' is 'high regarding the work process'. That is to say, although sales workers are required by management to make sales, *how* they make them is left largely in the hands of the workers (and, sometimes, the regulators).

Unfortunately, neither Biggart nor Frenkel *et al.* draw out explicitly *why* they view task participation as being high in sales work. Two points are relevant in addressing this issue. One is that in sales work the management emphasis on cost minimisation – which is frequently translated into restrictions on task participation by the establishment of tight procedures governing the labour process – is tempered by the emphasis on revenue generation as a key aim of sales work. Second, task participation may be conceptualised as high in sales work because of the 'unmanageable' (Gabriel and Lang 1995) nature of customers in sales interactions. As noted earlier, 'unmanageable' in this sense refers to the difficulty of predicting and controlling individual customer behaviour and perceptions, not least because the reasons for buying a product can vary significantly. As Baudrillard (1970/1988) argues, goods and services have both a use-value, relating to the practical utility of a good, and a sign-value, relating to the good's symbolic meaning. The use-value of a car, for example, relates to travelling from A to B, but its sign-value may involve a range of connotations – for example, sexiness or chic-ness. Further, the sign-value of a good is highly indeterminate and can be subject to considerable reappropriation by customers (de Certeau 1984). Therefore it becomes particularly problematic for management to set down a pre-designed mode of selling for sales workers to follow. High task participation for sales workers flows from this, either by default or design.

This theorising tends to be borne out by the empirical studies of sales work (House 1977; Prus 1989; Knights and Morgan 1990; Oakes 1990; Clarke *et al.* 1994; Frenkel *et al.* 1999; Clarke 2000; Lawson 2000; Hodgson 2003; Korczynski and Ott forthcoming). Browne's (1973) examination of car-sales work, for example, shows that the smiling façade of the sales worker during interactions with customers is in fact partly informed by the challenge that their autonomy over the work process gives them. Howton and Rosenberg (1965: 298) also cite the material basis of high task participation for the way in which sales workers glorify the entrepreneurial, self-dependent, ethic and the way that this constitutes an escape from bureaucracy. Clearly, some front-line sales work remains highly prescribed, especially in conditions of high visibility to superordinates or through the use of technology. A counter-example of a lower level of task participation in sales workers, for example, is given in Leidner's (1993) study of life assurance sales workers. Even here, however, where management attempted to impose a strict sales script for workers to follow, there was considerable evidence of workers systematically departing from it when they worked 'in the field'.

While there are theoretical and empirical grounds for stating that task participation tends to be high for sales workers, there are also grounds for pointing to the very low levels of participation beyond the task level – in setting objectives, for example. Furthermore, in Frenkel *et al.*'s (1999) model, sales workers are conceptualised effectively as existing at arm's length from the employing organisation. This is echoed in Hodson and Sullivan's (1995: 355) summary overview of the status of sales workers in the USA: 'in effect, [some sales] workers are independent contractors who are offered a desk in the firm but who have few of the other characteristics of steady employment'. The (contested) opportunity to participate in decisions beyond the task level tends to be one of these characteristics.

Front-line service work

Front-line service work also involves a worker in interacting directly with a customer as a key part of the job. Service work can be differentiated from sales work, however, because the *central* aim of the former does not involve the active encouragement of a customer to make a purchase, although clearly in practice this distinction is often not clear-cut. Nevertheless, we can focus here on service work in mass-customised market segments. Examples include much hospitality work, retail work, nursing and care work, and financial service work. While the application of Taylorist principles, and its creation of jobs with minimal discretion continues in mass-production service sectors such as fast food (Ritzer 2000), a growing wave of theoretical arguments and empirical research suggests that in the mass-customised sectors there are difficulties involved in the simple application of Taylorist principles of work organisation to jobs involving direct customer contact (Herzenberg *et al.* 1998). This by no means suggests that Taylorism is dead in service work generally, nor that it does not have limits or contradictions in fast-food services, as elsewhere. Rather, there are significant and particular tensions in its application in the above contexts.[3] Offe's (1985) work can be seen as prefiguring these theoretical approaches. He argued that it was difficult simply to bureaucratise front-line work because:

> On the one hand, the particularity, individuality, contingency and variability (of the situations and needs of clients . . .) must be preserved . . . On the other hand, service labour must ultimately bring about a state of affairs which conforms to certain general rules. The definition of service

labour . . . draws attention to the processes of individuation and differentiation on the one hand and coordination and standardization requirement on the other. Service labour can be deemed successful if it effects a balance between these two aspects. (pp. 105–6)

We have explored these tensions elsewhere, both generally and in the context of work organization (see, for example, Sturdy 1998; 2001). In particular, Offe's work has been developed by arguing that much contemporary service work is best analysed in terms of an ideal-type of 'customer-oriented bureaucracy' (Korczynski 2001; 2002) (see Table 6.1). Here, dual and potentially contradictory logics of rationalisation and customer orientation coexist – out of which management attempts to fashion a fragile social order. This approach suggests an organisation of front-line service work in which the nature of task participation is structured by the rationalising imperative of imposing rigid, repeatable procedures and the customer-orientation imperative of allowing scope for worker discretion to alter tasks in accordance with variable customer behaviour and perceptions although, as we have noted, customers are by no means immune from being managed, nor are they uninterested in some of the outcomes of bureaucracy control (for example, cost/price control).

Another way of conceptualising the duality in front-line work is put forward by Kerst and Holtgrewe (2001). Drawing on the work of Thompson (1967), they argue that front-line service work can be thought of as acting in a boundary-spanning role. Front-line service work, in this approach, acts as a buffer between the relatively rationalised sphere of back-office service production and the relatively unrationalised sphere of consumption. In this boundary-spanning role, front-line service work is organised systematically to take on elements of both the sphere of production and the sphere of consumption.

These approaches sit well with recent studies suggesting front-line service workers have more discretion in their jobs than in the recent past at

Table 6.1 Features of customer-oriented bureaucracy

Dimension	Customer-oriented bureaucracy
Dominant organising principle	Rationalisation and customer orientation
Basis of division of labour	Efficient task completion and customer relationship
Basis of authority	Rules and customer
Form of control	Imperfect (bureaucratic) measurement of performance and normative role for customers
Affectivity	Rationalised emotional labour to the customer

Source: Korczynski (2001).

least (see Mills 1951). This evidence comes from a range of settings – hospitality (Jones *et al.* 1997; Lashley 1997); retail (du Gay 1996; Rosenthal *et al.* 1997); airlines (Wouters 1989); and public welfare workers (Foster and Hoggett 1999). Lashley's discussion of task empowerment in the hospitality context brings out aspects common to many of these instances of increased discretion:

> Empowerment is largely related to attempts to generate improved service quality by improving responsiveness of front-line employees in the immediate service situation. Empowerment consists chiefly of authority to operate within prescribed boundaries. This could be a cash value to be given to the guest as a refund for a complaint, a reduction on the bill, a free meal, a complementary drink or bottle of wine . . . In the main this form of empowerment consists of empowering employees to provide extra service . . . The employee takes ownership of the service encounter and provides a level of service not normally given without reference to a supervisor or manager. (Lashley 1997: 47)

Our analysis should not, however, get carried away by highlighting the moves to greater task participation. Notwithstanding the importance of limiting our scope here to employee task participation and its management, and of variability in perspectives on empowerment (Ramsay 1977), two specific caveats need to be raised. First, although there is widespread evidence that discretion has increased, it must be borne in mind that, in many cases, increases came from a very low starting position, suggesting that the levels of discretion remain circumscribed to an important degree. Rosenthal *et al.*'s (1997) careful study of a large UK supermarket chain is a case in point. The authors note on the one hand that, 'discretion and responsibility have increased noticeably at Shopco' (p. 491), but, on the other hand, they state that previously there had been a 'virtual absence of discretion under the old regime' (p. 492). They conclude, therefore, that 'we would assess this empowerment as being fairly limited' (p. 492). The second caveat is that many of the cases of task empowerment concentrate on the 'service recovery' (Bowen and Lawler 1995) aspect of the job, such as resolving a customer's complaint or taking 'ownership' of a particular customer's problem. The rise in discretion and latitude tends to be concentrated in these areas. A key question, not properly addressed in studies so far, is therefore how far has discretion risen in the original 'service offer', rather than in the service recovery aspect of the job.

Back-office sales/service work

Back-office service work here is taken to mean work connected to front-line service or sales work but which itself does not involve direct, especially face-to-face, contact with customers. Examples include administrative, processing and checking jobs. Earlier rafts of research on back-office service work established that much of this work had been organised in a highly bureaucratic manner with very little opportunity for task participation (Crozier 1971; Blau 1972; Crompton and Jones 1984; Coomb and Jonsson 1991; Sturdy 1992). The limited amount of recent research into this area does little to discredit this finding. For example, Poynter (1999) studied the back-office processing of credit card transactions and found that this work was organised as a 'white-collar factory'. He highlights the continued routinisation of this work, with the only recent significant change in work organisation involving a strengthening of bureaucratisation through the introduction of more detailed measurement of work processes for control purposes. Further, Batt's (2000) survey research on call-centre work in the USA found that the back-office work was organised predominantly along the lines of the bureaucratic 'classic mass production' (p. 540) model. Moreover, Korczynski (forthcoming) examined a range of back-office functions in financial service industries and found that the jobs had lower task participation than the jobs in the front-line areas studied by Frenkel *et al.* (1999); see also Terzi and Sturdy (2001).

The continued finding of low task participation in back-office service work is not surprising given that the arguments concerning service work as a customer-oriented bureaucracy do not translate theoretically to the back-office environment. The existence of customer interaction within the labour process is the central point from which Offe's ideas and the idea of the customer-oriented bureaucracy are extrapolated. Although variations in work organisation are clearly not restricted to this (see Friedman 1977; Edwards 1979; Child 1981), without customer interaction the logic of these arguments falls away. The arguments rest on the assumption that consumption and production occur simultaneously within the labour process of the service interaction, and that the simple bureaucratisation of production therefore becomes highly problematic without the rigorous bureaucratisation of consumption. The argument continues that rigorously bureaucratised consumption is increasingly difficult to achieve with service quality and (growing) consumer expectations entering the terrain of competition between service firms. If, however, as is the case with back-office service work, there is no simultaneous consumption and production within the labour process, then this particular essential problematic for the bureaucratisation of production is removed.

The threefold schema of types of service work is analytical in intent, and, as already noted, it must be recognised that it may not be possible to draw an easy dividing line between the types of service work. In practice, there are a number of important forms of service jobs where there is a blurring between the three types of work examined above. For example, the mixing of service and sales elements in front-line jobs is becoming more widespread, both in terms of practices and labels. Some sales jobs are beginning to encompass service elements (Clarke *et al.* 1994), and many service jobs are having active sales aims added to them (Regini *et al.* 1999). Most notably, as firms move to capitalise from the strength of brands (Klein 2000) as well seeking to secure longer-term customer 'relationships', so it is more likely that the front-line roles in these firms will involve cross-selling. Task participation in these hybrid forms of jobs is also therefore likely to be of a hybrid form. Overall, however, the existence of hybrid forms of work should not detract from the analytical purchase that the threefold schema offers the examination of participation in service work in practice.

Discussion

In this chapter, we have sought to explore task-based participation in service work. In particular, we have focused on some of the more distinctive features and dynamics of service work, both generally and in its different forms. While this has given rise to a wide range of issues, two themes lie at the heart of our analysis. The first is that of the 'intrusion of the customer' in terms of recent rhetoric and rationales, an 'additional' labour process actor and service work practices and roles. The second is that of ideational and material tensions and contradictions which inform the varying, fragile and sometimes contested outcomes of work organisation, and participation in particular. We have, then, sought to provide an analysis that is sensitive to empirical data, complexity and variability and yet based on a number of core theoretical parameters. In doing so, however, some complexity has been lost. For example, in our threefold schema of service work, it is possible that, despite the underlying logic of customer interaction as a function of particular tasks, participation is introduced at all levels, including the back-office. This may be the result of managerial commitment to the ideology of participation or service in toto – the 'internal customer', for example – or a response to employee demands for service flexibility or quality. Indeed, this is evident in many manufacturing jobs, which are comparable to back-office functions. Equally, the schema and analysis is somewhat ahistorical and static. The organisation of work into front- and back-offices is clearly no neutral act, but a rationalised form of production and consumption that emerged over time and in contrasting competitive and ideological conditions (see Mills 1951). There is considerable scope, therefore, to explore participation in service historically. For example, the 'hybrid' forms of work discussed in the previous section may well come to be the norm, such that the intrusion of the customer becomes so complete as to be invisible.

   This is not to argue that service work and ideas will become monolithic because, as our attention to contradictions and tensions demonstrates, arrangements are necessarily fragile, context-dependent and negotiated. Equally, there are other potentially competing logics for participation, such as those associated with organisational learning, which have not been explored here (see Senge 1990, for example). Moreover, although there are some parallels between our analysis and contingency views of organisational (and work) structures (see, for example, Child 1981), we are certainly not claiming that the ways in which service work and participation are organised are the most effective for organisations. Rather, and as we have already intimated, there is a need for a wider ideological and policy debate over the nature, role and ethics of service – the 'kind of servants we want' (Cobble 1996). This needs to include those calls for ways of achieving greater 'dignity' (for example, participation) for employees in comparison with customers and employers (for example, see Korczynski's (2002) argument that trade unions can usefully seek to develop an ideology of simultaneous civilising production and consumption in their attempts to organise service workers). However, and as Ramsay noted in relation to the issue of democratic control of industry, 'proposals for achieving this remain facile if they view it as an isolated reform within the existing structure of relationships' (Ramsay 1977: 498). Similarly, in relation to contemporary service, is not simply a zero-sum, three-party relationship where customers' interests and participation are placed above those of employees. Within variations of neoliberalism (and other regimes), some customers and employees (for example, profitable, Western) are 'served' at the expense of others.

Notes

1 Short extracts from this chapter are revised versions of part of Sturdy (2001) and Korczynski (2002), although the chapter as a whole has not been published elsewhere.
2 This shift is sometimes disguised by the promotion by companies with a service, rather than a sales, emphasis (see Morgan and Sturdy 2000, for a detailed discussion of the relationship between these).
3 Further note the detailed workplace-based research which indicate that even where highly standardised procedures existed on paper, the necessary variability of front line work meant that these procedures were not followed in practice. This is true for rigid paper procedures in restaurants (Paules 1991), the tight scripting of interaction in call centres (Frenkel *et al.* 1999), and rigid medical protocols in health care work (Bolton 2000). See also Adler's (1986) more detailed discussion of this in relation to bank work.

References

Adler, P. (1986) 'New Technologies, New Skills', *California Management Review*, Fall, 9–28.
Baldry, C., Bain, P. and Taylor, P. (1998) 'Bright Satanic Offices – Intensification, Control and Team Taylorism', in Thompson, P. and Warhurst, C. (eds) *Workplaces of the Future*, London: Macmillan.

Batt, R. (2000) 'Strategic Segmentation in Front-line Services', *International Journal of Human Resource Management*, 11:3, 540–61.

Baudrillard, J. (1970/1988) 'Consumer Society', in M. Poster (ed.), *Jean Baudrillard: Selected Writings* (Cambridge: Polity Press).

Bauman, Z. (1998) *Work, Consumerism and the New Poor* (Milton Keynes: Open University Press).

Biggart, N. (1988) *Charismatic Capitalism* (Chicago: University of Chicago Press).

Blau, P. (1972) *The Dynamics of Bureaucracy* (Chicago: University of Chicago Press).

Bolton, S. (2000) 'Who's Controlling Who? NHS Hospital Nurses and "New" Management', Paper presented at the Labour Process Conference, University of Strathclyde, April.

Bowen, D. and Lawler, F. (1992) 'The Empowerment of Service Workers', *Sloan Management Review* (Spring), 31–39.

Bowen, D. and Lawler, E. (1995) 'Organising for Service: Empowerment or Production Line?', in W. Glynn and J. Barnes (eds), *Understanding Service Management* (John Wiley), 269–94.

Boyne, G., Jenkins, G. and Poole, M. (1999) 'Human resource management in the public and private sectors: an empirical comparison', *Public Administration*, 77 (2): 407–20.

Braverman, H. (1974) *Labour and Monopoly Capital* (New York: Monthly Review Press).

Browne, J. (1973) *The Used Car Game* (Lexington KY: Lexington Books).

Burawoy, M. (1979) *Manufacturing Consent*, London: University of Chicago Press.

Castells, M. and Aoyama, Y. (1994) 'Paths Towards the Information Society', *International Labour Review*, 133:1, 5–33.

Child, J. (1981) *The Challenge of Management Control* (London: Kogan Page).

Clarke, M. (2000) *Citizens' Financial Futures* (Aldershot: Ashgate).

Clarke, M., Smith, D. and McConville, M. (1994) *Slippery Customers: Estate Agents, the Public and Regulation* (London: Blackstone).

Cobble, D. S. (1996) 'The Prospects for Unionism in a Service Society', in C. L. MacDonald and C. Sirianni (eds), *Working in the Service Society* (Philadelphia: Temple University Press).

Coombs, R. and Jonsson, O. (1991) 'New Technology and Management in a Non-market Environment', in C. Smith, D. Knights and H. Willmott (eds). *White-Collar Work* (London: Macmillan, 89–108).

Crabb, S. (2002) 'Sleep Easy', *People Management*, 7 November, 36–8.

Crompton, R. and Jones, G. (1984) *White Collar Proletariat* (London: Macmillan).

Crozier, M. (1971) *The World of the Office Worker* (Chicago: University of Chicago Press).

de Certeau, M. (1984) *The Practice of Everyday Life* (Berkeley, Calif.: University of California Press).

Denzin, N. K. (1999) 'Dennis Hopper, McDonald's and Nike', in Smart, B. (ed.) *Resisting MacDonaldization*, London: Sage.

du Gay, P. (1996) *Consumption and Identity at Work* (London: Sage).

du Gay, P. and Salaman, G. (1992) 'The Cult(ure) of the Customer', *Journal of Management Studies*, 29:5, 615–33.

Eaton, S. C. (1996) ' "The Customer Is Always Interesting" – Unionised Harvard Clericals Renegotiate Work Relationships', in C. L. MacDonald and C. Sirianni (eds), *Working in the Service Society* (Philadelphia: Temple University Press).

Edwards, P., Collinson, M. and Rees, C. (1998) 'The Determinants of Employee Responses to TQM: Six Cases Studies', *Organization Studies*, 19 (3): 449–42.

Edwards, R. (1979) *Contested Terrain* (New York: Basic Books).

Filby, M. P. (1992) 'The Figures, The Personality and The Bums: Service Work and Sexuality', *Work, Employment and Society*, 6:1, 23–42.

Financial Times (2000) 'Dawn of the Cyberbabes', August 17th, 20.

Fitchett, J. and McDonagh, P. (2001) 'Relationship Marketing, E-Commerce and the Emancipation of the Consumer', in Sturdy, A. J., Grugulis, I. and Willmott, H. (eds) *Customer Service – Empowerment and Entrapment*, Basingstoke: Palgrave Macmillan.

Foster, D. and Hoggett, P. (1999) 'Change in the Benefits Agency: Empowering the Exhausted Worker?', *Work, Employment and Society*, 13, 19–39.

Frenkel, S., Korczynski, M., Shire, K. and Tam, M. (1999) *On the Front Line: Work Orgnization in the Service Economy* (Ithaca, NY: ILR/Cornell University Press).

Friedman, A. L. (1977) *Industry and Labour*, London: Macmillan.

Fuller, L. and Smith, V. (1991) 'Consumers' Reports: Management by Customers in a Changing Economy', *Work, Employment and Society*, 5:1, 1–16.

Gabriel, Y. and Lang, T. (1995) *The Unmanageable Consumer: Contemporary Consumption and its Fragmentations* (London: Sage).

Glenn, E. N. (1996) 'From Servitude to Service Work – Historical Continuities in the Racial Division of Paid Reproductive Labor', in C. L. MacDonald and C. Sirianni (eds), *Working in the Service Society* (Philadelphia: Temple University Press).

Heery, E. (1993) 'Industrial Relations and the Customer', *Industrial Relations Journal*, 24:4, 284–95.

Herzenberg, S., Alic, J. and Wial, H. (1998) *New Rules for a New Economy* (Ithaca, NY: Cornell University Press).

Hochschild, A. R. (1983) *The Managed Heart: Commercialization of Human Feeling*, London: University of California Press.

Hodgson, D. (2003) 'Taking it like a man': Masculinity, Subjection and Resistance in the Selling of Life Assurance, *Gender, Work and Organization* 10, 1, 1–21.

Hodgson, D. (2001) ' "Empowering Customers Through Eduation" Or Governing without Goverment?', in Sturdy, A. J., Grugulis, I. and Willmott, H. (eds) *Customer Service – Empowerment and Entrapment*, Basingstoke: Palgrave Macmillan.

Hodson, R. and Sullivan, T. (1995) *The Social Organization of Work* (Washington, DC: Wadsworth).

Holtgrewe, U. (2000) 'Recognition, Inter-subjectivity and Service Work – Beyond Subjectivity and Control', Paper presented at the 18th Annual International Labour Process Conference, University of Strathclyde, 25–27 April.

House, J. (1977) *Contemporary Entrepreneurs: The Sociology of Residential Real Estate Agents* (London: Greenwood Press).

Howton, F. and Rosenberg, B. (1965) 'The Salesman: Ideology and Self-imagery in a Prototypic Occupation', *Social Research*, 32, 277–98.

Jones, C., Taylor, G. and Nickson, D. (1997) 'Whatever It Takes? Managing "Empowered" Employees and the Service Encounter in an International Hotel Chain', *Work, Employment and Society*, 11:3, 541–54.

Keat, R., Abercrombie, N. and Whiteley, N. (1994) *The Authority of the Consumer*. (London: Routledge).

Kerst, C. and Holtgrewe, U. (2001) 'Flexibility and Customer Orientation: Where Does the Slack Come From?', Paper presented at Work, Employment and Society conference, University of Nottingham, September.

Kinnie, N., Hutchinson, S. and Purcell, J. (1998) 'Fun and Surveillance – The Paradox of High Commitment Management in Call Centres', WERC Research Paper, University of Bath.

Klein, N. (2000) *No Logo* (London: Flamingo).

Knights, D. and Morgan, G. (1990) 'Management Control in Sales Forces', *Work, Employment and Society*, 4:3, 369–89.

Knights, D., Sturdy, A. J. and Morgan, G. (1994) 'The Consumer Rules? The Rhetoric and Reality of Marketing in Financial Services', *European Journal of Marketing*, 28:3, 42–54.

Korczynski, M. (2001) 'The Contradictions of Service Work: Call Centre as Customer-oriented Bureaucracy', in A. Sturdy, I. Grugulis and H. Willmott (eds), *Customer Service* (Basingstoke: Palgrave Macmillan).

Korczynski, M. (2002) *Human Resource Management in Service Work* (Basingstoke: Palgrave).

Korczynski, M. (forthcoming) 'Back-office Service Work', *Work, Employment and Society*.

Korczynski, M. and Ott, U. (forthcoming) 'Sales Work Under Marketization: The Social Relations of the Cash Nexus?', *Organization Studies*.

Lashley, C. (1997) *Empowering Service Excellence* (London: Cassell).

Lawson, H. (2000) *Ladies on the Lot: Women, Car Sales and the Pursuit of the American Dream* (New York: Rowman and Littlefield).

Leidner, R. (1993) *Fast Food, Fast Talk* (Berkeley, Calif.: University of California Press).

Leidner, R. (1996) 'Rethinking Questions of Control – Lessons from McDonalds' in C. L. MacDonald and C. Sirianni (eds), *Working in the Service Society* (Philadelphia: Temple University Press).

Lopez, S. H. (1996) 'The Politics of Service Production – Route Sales Work in the Potato-Chip Industry', in MacDonald, C. L. and Sirianni, C. (eds), *Working in the Service Society*, Philadelphia: Temple University Press.

MacDonald, C. L. and Sirianni, C. (eds) (1991) *Working in the Service Society* (Philadelphia: Temple University Press).

Martinez, Lucio, M. (1995) 'Quality and "New Industrial Relations" – The Case of Royal Mail' in Kirkpatrick, I. and Lucio, M. M. (eds) *The Politics of Quality*, London: Routledge.

Mills, C. Wright (1951) *White Collar – The American Middle Classes* (New York: Oxford University Press).

Morgan, G. and Sturdy, A. J. (2000) *Beyond Organisational Change – Discourse, Structure and Power in UK Financial Services* (Basingstoke: Palgrave Macmillan).

Nickson, D., Warhurst, C., Witz, A. and Cullen, A. M. (2001) 'The Importance of Being Aesthetic: Work, Employment and Service Organization', in Sturdy, A. J., Grugulis, I. and Willmott, H. (eds), *Customer Service – Empowerment and Entrapment*, Basingstoke: Palgrave Macmillan.

Oakes, G. (1990) *The Soul of the Salesman: The Moral Ethos of Personal Sales* (London: Humanities Press International).

Offe, C. (1985) *Disorganised Capitalism* (Cambridge: Polity Press).

Paules, G. F. (1991) *Dishing It Out* (Philadelphia: Temple University Press).

Paules, G. F. (1996) 'Resisting the Symbolism of Service among Waitresses', in C. L. MacDonald and C. Sirianni (eds), *Working in the Service Society* (Philadelphia: Temple University Press).

Pierce, J. L. (1996) 'Reproducing Gender Relations in Large Law Firms' in MacDonald, C. L. and Sirianni, C. (eds), *Working in the Service Society* (Philadelphia: Temple University Press).

Poynter, G. (1999) *Restructuring in the Service Industries* (London: Mansell).

Pratchett, L. and Wingfield, M. (1996) 'Petty Bureaucracy and Woolly-minded Liberalism? The Changing Ethos of Local Government Officers', *Public Administration*, 74, 639–56.

Prus, R. (1989) *Making Sales* (London: Sage).

Ramsay, H. (1977) 'Cycles of Control', *Sociology*, 11:3, 481–506.

Ramsay, H. (1996) 'Managing Sceptically: A Critique of Organisational Fashion', in

S. R. Clegg and G. Palmer (eds), *The Politics of Management Knowledge* (London: Sage).

Regini, M., Kitay, J. and Baethge, M. (eds) (1999) *From Tellers to Sellers* (Cambridge, MA: MIT Press).

Ritzer, G. (1993) *The McDonaldization of Society* (Thousand Oaks, CA: Pine Forge).

Ritzer, G. and Stillman, T. (2001) 'From Person-Oriented To System-Oriented Service', in Sturdy, A. J., Grugulis, J. and Willmott, H. (eds) *Customer Service – Empowerment and Entrapment*, Basingstoke: Palgrave Macmillan.

Peccei, R. and Rosenthal, P. (1997) 'The Antecedents of Employee Commitment to Customer Service – Evidence from a UK Service Context', *The International Journal of HRM*, 8, 1, 66–86.

Rosenthal, P., Hill, S. and Peccei, R. (1997) 'Checking Out Service: Evaluating Excellence, HRM and TQM in Retailing', *Work, Employment and Society*, 11(3), 481–503.

Rothman, R. (1998) *Working: Sociological Perspective* (London: Prentice-Hall).

Rucci, A. J., Kirn, S. P. and Quinn, R. T. (1997) 'The Employee–Customer–Profit Chain at Sears', *Harvard Business Review* (January–February) 83–97.

Senge, P. M. (1990) *The Fifth Discipline* (New York: Doubleday).

Smart, B. (ed.) (1999) *Resisting McDonaldization* (London: Sage).

Smith W. R. (1956) 'Product differentiation and market segmentation as alternative strategies' *Journal of Marketing* July, 3–8 reprinted in Ennis, B. and Cox, K. K. (eds) (1988) Marketing Classics 6th edition (London: Allyn & Bacon).

Sturdy, A. (1992) 'Clerical Consent', in A. Sturdy, D. Knights and H. Willmott (eds), *Skill and Consent* (London: Routledge).

Sturdy, A. J. (1998) 'Customer Care in a Consumer Society', *Organization*, 5:1, 27–53.

Sturdy, A. J. (2001) 'Servicing Societies? – Colonisation, Control, Contradiction and Contestation', in A. J. Sturdy, I. Grugulis and H. Willmott (eds), *Customer Service – Empowerment and Entrapment* (Basingstoke: Palgrave Macmillan).

Sturdy, A. J. and Fleming, P. (2003) 'Talk as Technique – A Critique of the Words and Deeds Distinction in the Diffusion of Customer Service Cultures', *Journal of Management Studies*, 40:5, 753–73.

Sturdy, A. J. and Knights, D. (1996) 'The Subjectivity of Segmentation and the Segmentation of Subjectivity', in S. R. Clegg and G. Palmer (eds), *Constituting Management: Markets, Meanings and Identities* (Berlin: De Gruyter).

Sturdy, A. J. and Fineman, S. (2001) 'Struggles for the Control of Affect – Resistance as Politics and Emotion', in Sturdy, A. J., Grugulis, I. and Willmott, H. (eds), *Customer Service – Empowerment and Entrapment*, Basingstoke: Palgrave Macmillan.

Sturdy, A. J., Grugulis, I. and Willmott, H. (eds), (2001) *Customer Service – Empowerment and Entrapment* (Basingstoke: Palgrave Macmillan).

Sturdy, A. J. and Terzi, K. A. (2001) 'The *Odyssey* of Customer-Facing Employees within an Environment of Continuous Organisational Change', Paper presented at the 17th European Group for Organizational Studies Colloquium, Lyon, France, July 5–7.

Thompson, J. (1967) *Organizations in Action* (New York: McGraw-Hill).

Thompson, P., Warhurst, C. and Callaghan, G. (2000) 'Human Capital or Capitalising on Humanity? Knowledge, Skills and Competencies in Interactive Service Work', in Prichard, C. et al. (eds), *Manging Knowledge* (London: Macmillan).

Tyler, M. and Taylor, S. (2001) 'Juggling Justice and Care: Gendered Customer Service in the Contemporary Airline Industry', in Sturdy, A. J., Grugulis, I. and Willmott, H. (eds), *Customer Service – Empowerment and Entrapment*, Basingstoke: Palgrave Macmillan.

Weatherly, K. A. and Tansik, D. A. (1993) 'Tactics Used by Customer-Contact

Workers: Effects of Role Stress, Boundary Spanning and Control', *International Journal of Service Industry Management* 4 (3): 4–17.

Wilkinson, A., Godfrey, G. and Marchington, M. (1997) 'Bouquets, Brickbats and Blinkers – TQM and Employee Involvement in Practice', *Organization Studies*, 18 (5): 799–819.

Wouters, C. (1989) 'The Sociology of Emotions and Flight Attendants', *Theory, Culture and Society*, 6, 95–123.

Wray-Bliss, E. (2001) 'Representing Customer Service: Telephones and Texts', in Sturdy, A. J., Grugulis, I. and Willmott, H. (eds), *Customer Service – Empowerment and Entrapment* (Basingstoke: Palgrave Macmillan).

7
Organisational Participation and Women: An Attitude Problem?

Harvie Ramsay and Dora Scholarios

Introduction

For all that has been written on the subject of worker participation, there has been remarkably little consideration of how the prospects of exerting influence and control vary across the 'worker' group. The tendency in theoretical discussions is to treat the workforce as a homogeneous group (Acker and van Houten 1974), and empirical investigations have made almost no effort to correct this. Once made explicit, it is evident that this position is untenable. A concern for democratisation should attend to any factors that: (a) divide the disadvantaged and so weaken the pressure for progressive change; and (b) might entail any advances applying to some only. This chapter will examine aspects of this issue, as it applies to gender disadvantage in particular.

As the literature on gender inequalities has developed, numerous aspects of disadvantage have been explored. Many of these have evident implications for the issue of democratic control, but the connections have rarely been addressed directly (notable exceptions include Pateman (1983) and Phillips (1991)), and the consideration of evidence to refine our understanding of the question has been minimal and fragmentary. This is true particularly of work organisation, where attempts to address the way that gender inequalities have an impact on women's attitudes to industrial democracy are about as common as paperless offices (see Kaul and Lie (1982), Baldwin and Walpole (1986) and Maddock (1994) for exceptions). Yet most of us would be aware of competing, if largely unspoken, assumptions. For example, do women feel relatively excluded from influence over decisions at work? If so, is this despite a desire equivalent to men's for participation? Or is it a consequence of a relative lack of interest in work and workplace decisions? And if the latter, is that lack of interest a false consciousness, a result of socialisation within a patriarchal system, or an expression of more fundamentally different priorities and attitudes? To take the highly controversial

113

claims of Hakim (1995) at face value, for example, could lead by extrapola-
tion to the view that women are less likely to want to participate in decisions, or to be involved at work.

The lack of focus on such questions is likely to be debilitating in itself, in
that power inequalities are themselves barriers to progress, and constitute a
key variable in the disadvantaging of women as well as in their experience
of disadvantage. However, there may be as much of a risk in *presuming*
gender to be *the* variable as in ignoring it, since this both takes difference for
granted (rather than similarity in the usual gender-blind discussions) and
homogenises afresh, this time within genders, rather than examining the
differential impact of other variables such as age, ethnicity or occupation. As
such it may potentially encourage managerial stereotypes of women as
being passive and uninterested in participation *en bloc*, for example.

This chapter makes only an initial foray into this issue. It begins with a
consideration of different emphases in explanations of inequality, distinguishing a focus on attitude differences from those which attribute greater
importance to structural conditions and processes. The empirical analysis
uses a secondary dataset based on a large-scale survey to test for gender
differences in employee work attitudes, perceptions of control, perceptions
of participation mechanisms, and issues of communication, consultation and
representation. The findings from the attitude survey make a case for avoiding homogenisation of employees in discussions of organisational participation, and challenge the various stereotypes of female employees which are
prevalent in much management thinking and practice. Factors such as age,
occupational position, hours worked, relations with one's manager, and
union membership have all emerged as significant variables explaining
differences in responses at various points in the analysis. Thus this chapter
emphasises the danger of oversimplified generalisations about responses
within as well as between genders, and considers the implications of these
results for more subtle analyses of gender and participation.

Organisational Participation and Gendered Inequality

The question of workplace democracy and power is arguably an indivisible
one in principle, with everything affecting everything else, and control
analysed as both process and structure. Thus payment systems, skills grading, performance assessment and competency measurement systems, selection and recruitment, training and development, and all aspects of
employment practice could be seen as having an impact on opportunities
and the perceived capacity to participate in decisions at different levels. It
has been established that levels of education or recognised skill influence
people's feeling of efficacy and levels of participative activity, for example
(Wall and Lischerson 1977).

If anything that has an impact on workplace inequality has possible implications for democracy and control, as argued above, it follows that the analysis of gendered disadvantage quickly dissolves the presumption that only
factors within the employment relationship itself should be the subject of
study. We would have to consider socialisation in the family, domestic
responsibilities and pressures, and wider patriarchal relations in society in
order to make sense of what happens with regard to worker participation.
Perhaps the discomfort this creates by challenging the closure of industrial
democracy debates helps to explain the reluctance of writers in the field to
tackle the gender question – or, potentially, race, age and wider class issues,
it might be added. In many ways it was Pateman's (1970) exposure of the
political/industrial democracy link that opened up this issue, though few
have explored it, possibly diverted by the fact that Pateman's initial primary
interest was in the link *from* work *to* the wider socio-political sphere rather
than the reverse. Her later self-correction (Pateman 1983) introduced gender,
and in the process considered the importance of the link in the other direction.

While one of the most significant and consistent findings of research on
gendered disadvantage is the mutually conditioning and reinforcing nature
of different aspects of disadvantage, it is possible to characterise different
emphases in explanations of inequality. The empirical work presented in
this chapter provides a test of *attitude differences*. From this viewpoint
women's own attitudes are important to their being disadvantaged. Women,
or at least a significant proportion of them, are seen as preferring and priori-
tising homebuilding, child raising and various domestic roles over other
work. They may work outside the home only reluctantly, or they may
choose to work part-time and take maternity career breaks in an attempt to
balance competing claims on their time. This fits human capital or orthodox
dual labour market approaches which suggest that women's disadvantages
lie in their own decisions about investing in training and seeking jobs, for
example (Mincer 1966; Polachek 1981). This viewpoint rests, among other
things, on an assumption that women do have distinct attitudes to work in
general and to participation in particular.

Alternative explanations emphasise different primary sources of disadvantage and imply different responses to achieving greater democratisation.
Hegemonic patriarchy emphasises the process by which gendered attitudes
are formed positing a hegemony of masculine values in socialisation
concerning work roles (that is, on a kind of female false consciousness). As
long as opportunities are provided, reluctance on the part of women to
become democratically involved should be taken at face value and
respected. Other perspectives are less accepting of attitudinal, individual-
level explanation. The presence of masculine organisational cultures, for
example, imply disadvantaging structures that shape women's actions and
act as powerful sub-texts to organisational decision-making and interaction.

Patriarchal management practices may restrict women's access to influential or skilled positions through implicit stereotyping and discrimination, resulting in more deliberate and visible prejudices and actions, and the segmentation of labour markets. Similarly, patriarchal practices among workers may produce intra-class divisions through gender bias by unions, other representative bodies, or powerful groups of male employees – for example, in monopolising training in the use of new technology, or in the grading of jobs. And explanations based on domestic patriarchy and material constraint stress the domestic division of household and childcare labour and the power distribution in the domestic sphere (control of money, decisions, task allocation) as shaping the 'decision' to work outside the home or not, and whether to become involved in unions or participation channels.

None of these alternatives predict particularly different attitudes by gender. Rather, the process of democratisation requires a challenge to male hegemony over socialising institutions and values, the exposure of masculine, undemocratic organisation itself, or practical reforms such as proper support and benefits/taxation for single mothers, childcare facilities, and training access and support. Patriarchal practices imply that women feel at a greater distance from decision-making and therefore powerlessness, while explanations based on domestic patriarchy suggest that union membership may not correct, or may even exacerbate, any perceived power differentials between men and women.

The Evidence

The empirical analysis in this chapter focuses on testing the proposed distinctiveness of women's attitudes using a large-scale survey. We recognise the limited discriminatory power of attitude surveys, particularly as the one used here was not designed for the purpose at hand and cannot provide a test of the alternative perspectives outlined above. The beginning of explanation is nevertheless better than continued neglect, the findings are of sufficient interest to guide future research, and can in the meantime challenge some powerful presumptions on the issues under examination. We, therefore, first outline the empirical findings before returning to consider the implications of these for the alternative explanations of inequality presented above.

The dataset was made available by the Department of Trade and Industry and compiled from a large survey of employees' experience of employee involvement. An earlier summary of some of the findings may be found in Tillsley (1994). Unlike many such surveys, numbers are large enough for both sexes (799 women and 721 men) to allow analyses to be conducted with acceptable levels of statistical confidence.[1] The original survey was in fact larger than this, but it was decided to focus on employees for the purposes of the analysis here, and we have excluded those who are classified as self-employed (15 per cent of the original sample) or on government-sponsored training schemes (2 per cent). In addition, the chapter refers to evidence drawn from a variety of fragmentary sources on the relationship between gender, work attitudes and participation (see Ramsay (1996) for a detailed review). These other findings, when drawn together, can clarify the consistency or variation in patterns of observations from available research, and also fill certain gaps in the DTI survey data.

Table 7.1 summarises the characteristics of the respondent sample. Although 77 per cent of respondents worked more than 30 hours per week, 42 per cent of women and 3 per cent of men worked less than 30 hours per week. Males were significantly more likely to have managerial or supervisory responsibility, and longer tenure. A trade union or staff association existed in 40 per cent of organisations, and within these, 10 per cent more men than women reported being union members. The sample was evenly distributed by age and there was no difference in male versus female participation in share ownership schemes.

With respect to the characteristics of the organisations employing these respondents, Table 7.2 shows that the sample is broadly spread across sectors and different sized organisations, and across types of work. This helps to a degree in getting around one of the perennial problems in assessing differences of work-related attitudes between men and women: that almost a half of all jobs are effectively gender-segregated. This is apparent also from this survey: some occupational classifications are dominated by women – for example, clerical/secretarial (74 per cent female), and personal and protective service occupations (75 per cent), while craft and related occupations, and plant and machine operatives, are predominantly male (93 per cent and 78 per cent, respectively). Sectorally, women were also particularly prevalent in local government, health and charities, which together represented 30 per cent of the female sample. Sectoral and occupational variables may well affect work control and experience, but such differences might themselves be traced back to gender assumptions and have an impact on gendered cultures in different loci. This chapter therefore avoids the presumption that an analysis such as that presented here fully comprehends the impact of gender as a variable.

Work Attitudes and Perceptions of Control

Work orientations

The salience of democratic control at work may be expected to be lower to the extent that the work itself is of less importance than other activities in an individual's priorities and identity. If objectives are primarily monetary,

Table 7.1 Employee characteristics by gender

Variables	Total sample		Men		Women		χ^2	
	N'	%	n	%	n	%		
Total sample	1520	100.0	721	47.4	799	52.6	–	
Occupational classifications[a]								
Managerial/professional	413	29.1	214	32.9	199	25.9		
Clerical/secretarial	366	23.7	86	13.2	250	32.6		
Personal/protection	261	18.4	64	9.8	197	25.7		
Plant and machine operatives	177	12.5	139	21.4	38	5.0		
Craft and related	119	8.4	111	17.1	8	1.0		
Sales	111	7.8	36	5.5	75	9.8	307.3	***
Hours worked/week								
0–7 hours	29	1.9	2	0.3	27	3.4		
8–15 hours	109	7.2	6	0.8	103	12.9		
16–30 hours	217	14.3	16	2.2	201	25.2		
>30 hours	1162	76.6	696	96.7	466	58.5	23.6	***
Level of job responsibility								
Managerial	364	23.9	213	29.5	151	18.9		
Supervisory	227	14.9	118	16.4	109	13.6		
Neither	929	61.1	390		539	67.5		
Years with present employer								
5 years or less	781	54.2	327	49.2	454	58.4		
More than 5 years	661	45.8	338	50.8	323	41.6	12.4	**
Trade union/staff association								
Member	520	70.1	285	74.2	235	65.6		
Non-member	222	29.9	99	25.8	123	34.4	6.5	*

							χ²	
Share ownership scheme								
Participant	120	46.7	84	50.3	36	40.0	2.5	ns
Non-participant	137	53.3	83	49.7	54	60.0		
Age [b]							5.1	*
15–24	232	15.3	121	16.8	111	13.9		
25–34	439	28.9	211	29.3	228	28.5		
35–44	374	24.6	165	22.9	209	26.2		
45–54	308	20.3	131	18.2	177	22.2		
Over 54	167	11.0	93	12.9	74	9.2		

Notes: [a]Only the most common standard occupational classifications are shown in the table. Managerial/professional includes managers/administrators, professional and associate professional occupations. The higher proportion of males in management/professional occupations is significantly different from the higher proportion of females in clerical/secretarial ($\chi^2(1) = 53.05$, $p < 0.0001$), personal/protective ($\chi^2(1) = 49.17$, $p < 0.0001$) and sales ($\chi^2(1) = 13.18$, $p < 0.005$). These occupations with more females also form a statistically different group from those with more males (craft and related, and plant and machine operatives ($\chi^2(1) = 287.67$, $p < 0.0001$).
[b]The χ^2 for age represents contrasts between males and females aged 15–34 or 35–54; 53% of females as opposed to 46% of males comprised the older age band.
* $p < 0.05$; ** $p < 0.01$; *** $p < 0.001$; *ns* = not significant.

Table 7.2 Organisation characteristics by gender

Variables	Total sample		Men		Women	
	N'	%	n	%	n	%
Total sample	1520	100.0	721	47.4	799	52.6
Type of organisation[a]						
Public limited company	447	29.5	257	35.6	190	24.0
Other private firms	537	35.5	275	38.1	262	33.0
Local government	220	14.5	67	9.3	153	19.3
Health authority	109	7.2	20	2.8	89	11.2
Central government	60	4.0	26	3.6	34	4.3
Nationalised industry	51	3.4	43	6.0	8	1.0
Other[b]	90	5.9	33	4.6	57	7.2
Major SIC groups[c]						
General service sector	572	38.2	168	23.6	404	51.5
Distribution/hotels	276	18.4	118	16.6	158	20.1
General manufacturing	195	13.0	121	17.0	74	9.4
Banking and finance	154	10.3	66	9.3	88	11.2
Metal goods/engineering	122	8.1	98	13.8	24	3.1
Transport/communications	89	5.9	69	9.7	20	2.5
Size (number of employees)						
1–9	251	17.0	86	12.1	165	21.4
10–24	241	16.3	92	13.0	149	19.3
25–99	365	24.7	185	26.1	180	23.3
100–499	340	23.0	188	26.6	152	19.7
500 or more	283	19.0	157	22.2	126	16.3
Ownership (private company)	664	43.7	349	74.3	315	84.2
Wholly UK	104	6.8	69	14.7	35	9.4
Partly UK/partly foreign	76	5.0	52	11.1	24	6.4
Wholly foreign						
Existence of:						
Trade union/association	742	48.8	384	54.7	358	47.8
Share acquisition scheme	257	16.9	167	36.9	90	24.1
Profit-related pay scheme	93	6.1	68	16.0	25	6.9

Notes: [a]Overall, a greater proportion of women (40% compared to 20% of men) were employed in public sector organisations, including central and local government, health authorities and universities.
[b]'Other' types of organisation include higher education, charity and voluntary organisations.
[c]Overall, a greater proportion of women (50% compared to 29% of men) were employed in the service sector than in any other SIC.

social or security-oriented, for example, participation might be expected to be viewed instrumentally or marginalised. Similarly, if a person's priorities are outside their paid work, most obviously in the home with their family, one might again expect workplace influence to be less important to them, though if they do work outside the home they might place greater emphasis on some aspects of workplace relations. Stereotypes would suggest that work outside the home is less central to women's lives, and they are more likely to prioritise convenience of work (in allowing them to meet domestic needs), peer relations and relations with management. Meanwhile, men, it may be argued, will be more work-centred in their identity and focus, and at the same time, as 'breadwinners', will tend to be more economistic.

The supposed marginality of work content to women has been criticised by Feldberg and Glenn (1979) as applying a 'gender' model to women's employment, while a 'job' model is applied to men. They are scornful of this essentialist assumption, and argue that women, too, are affected by job content and rewards. Yet Hakim's (1995) recent intervention appears to tip the argument back towards expectations that the priorities of at least a large proportion of women will be dictated by other factors than those related to paid employment.

Evidence suggests that women are less different to men in their priorities at work than stereotypes would suggest (Whirlpool Foundation 1995, 1996; Clark 1997; Sloane and Williams 2000); but this in turn is countered by other sources, including findings from the Workplace Employee Relations Survey series, showing generally more positive attitudes among women except at the highest skill levels (Beynon and Blackburn 1972; Gallie and White 1993; Rose 2000).

The DTI study asked respondents to identify the single most important factor influencing them in taking their present jobs. As shown in Table 7.3, women most often cited convenient working hours, interesting work making use of their skills, and job security; while men cited interesting work, job security and no other available job, respectively, with few men mentioning convenient hours. The relative figures for hours and job security seem to confirm women's emphasis on non-work commitments. Further analysis of the female sub-sample showed that this was particularly so for those working less than 30 hours a week, of whom 75 per cent selected convenient hours, compared to just 12 per cent of full-time working women (χ^2 (2) = 154.61, $p < 0.001$) and in occupations such as clerical/secretarial, personal/protective and sales, which tended to be female-dominated.

However, this does not tell us whether the priority is seen as a matter of practicality or a preferred role. Other results in Table 7.3 seem to deny as much as to confirm stereotypical notions, with women at least as likely to be concerned with job content as men, for example. Exploring this further, a logistic regression of the likelihood of choosing interesting work rather than any of the other factors in Table 7.3 entered all the variables and their interactions

Table 7.3 Most important reason for taking present job: men and women

Reasons in order of overall popularity	Total		Men		Women	
	N	% of total	n	% of males	n	% of females
Interesting work/makes use of skills	398	26.2	185	25.7	213	26.7
Convenient working hours	251	16.5	19	2.6	232	29.0
Job security	249	16.4	163	22.6	86	10.8
No other job available	170	11.2	116	16.1	54	6.8
Good rates of pay	140	9.2	84	11.7	56	7.0
Location	69	4.5	35	4.9	34	4.3
Opportunity to work in own way	58	3.8	30	4.2	28	3.5
Possibility of promotion	52	3.4	30	4.2	22	2.8
Good fringe benefits	28	1.8	17	2.4	11	1.4
Friends worked there	20	1.3	11	1.5	9	1.1
Clean/pleasant working conditions	14	0.9	6	0.8	8	1.0
Total	1449	100.0	696	47.4	753	52.6

Note: All χ^2 tests conducted on the basis of 2×2 contingency tables with all other responses.
$**p < 0.01$; $***p < 0.001$; *ns* = not significant.

with gender into the equation, excluding hours worked because of the few part-time males. Gender did not enter as a significant variable, either on its own or in interaction with other variables. For both men and women, as more responsibility was gained at work, if they were in managerial/ professional occupations, and if they were employed in the public rather than the private sector, interest in the job became more prominent. This tends to confirm the similarities in orientation among working men and women observed in other studies, although it leaves open the possibility that the number of hours worked reflects a key division of attitudes among women, as Hakim argues. This point is examined later in the chapter.

Satisfaction, commitment and management relations

Table 7.4 summarises several attitude variables by gender, and shows that women reported a slightly higher level of satisfaction with the job factor most important to them. The analysis of covariance (ANCOVA) F-test in this table also indicates that gender differences that are significant in the one-way ANOVA remain when the effects of other personal and organisational covariates are controlled for; in this case, age, job level, hours worked, tenure, organisation size, organisation type (public or private sector), and trade union membership.

Some versions of stereotypical gender images would predict that women will be more co-operative with management and less likely by nature to take a conflictual position. However, the countervailing notion that women are less tied to employment than are men makes hypotheses concerning their organisational commitment less clearly derivable from such a portrait. Marsden *et al.* (1993) suggest that organisational commitment is slightly higher among men, but that this can largely be accounted for by the less attractive nature of women's jobs. Other evidence (see Cohen and Lowenberg 1990; Mathieu and Zajac 1990) suggests little or no difference in organisational loyalty between men and women, apparently disposing of both versions of the difference thesis. Age has been found to be more important, with commitment increasing over time, and particularly steeply, for women (Gallie and White 1993).

The results in Table 7.4 show that women tended to be more positive than men about relations with their boss, and that this gender difference survives the analysis of covariance. In a review of evidence from a number of European countries, good relations with management were found to be positively correlated with job satisfaction, this applying equally to part-time and full-time male and female workers (Curtice 1993). The table also shows, however, that men and women exhibit almost indistinguishable reported levels of commitment to the success of their employing unit, whether defined as a department or across the whole organisation. Generally, commitment to the department is higher than to the organisation as a whole.

Table 7.4 Attitudes and perceptions of personal control: men and women

Variables[a]	Total sample			Men			Women			ANOVA F	ANCOVA F
	N	Mean	S.D.	n	Mean	S.D.	n	Mean	S.D.		
Overall job satisfaction	1437	4.11	1.04	688	3.95	1.08	749	4.24	0.98	28.47***	12.65***
Commitment to organisation's success	1474	3.39	0.70	704	3.36	0.70	770	3.41	0.69	1.74	
Commitment to department's success	1471	3.51	0.66	703	3.51	0.67	768	3.50	0.65	0.01	
Perceived control/job	1520	2.80	1.01	721	2.89	1.02	799	2.72	1.01	10.02**	0.06
Perceived control/working conditions	1520	2.34	0.99	721	2.44	1.01	799	2.25	0.98	13.71***	0.62
Perceived control/department	1520	2.22	1.05	721	2.31	1.06	799	2.15	1.03	7.98**	1.01
Perceived control/organisation	1520	1.82	0.90	721	1.88	0.92	799	1.76	0.89	7.12**	0.35
Relations with boss	1485	4.39	0.84	699	4.32	0.89	786	4.45	0.79	9.69**	4.21**

Notes: [a]Overall job satisfaction and relations with boss were rated on a 5-point Likert scale. All other variables were rated on a 4-point Likert scale. The higher the rating, the greater intensity of feeling.
*$p < 0.05$; **$p < 0.01$; ***$p < 0.001$.

Explanations of commitment were explored further in two multiple regressions. The results in Table 7.5 confirm that different variables influence commitment for men and women. Only good relations with one's boss was a significant predictor of both types of commitment for both sexes. For men, commitment to the organisation increased with tenure and personal control in the job or department, while commitment to the department increased with level of responsibility and the same personal control variables. For women, commitment to organisational success also increased with age, and as perceived control at organisational levels increased, but enhanced feelings of control in the job did not seem to transfer to organisational commitment as they did for men. In addition, working in the public sector, which encompasses a large proportion of women in this sample, was also likely to be associated with increased levels of organisational commitment. Job level did not predict increased commitment to the department for women as much as it did for men. In other words, female managers do not have much more commitment to their own department's success than other female employees unless some other factor, such as good relations with their boss, enables them to have increased feelings of job control. Finally, the effect of age on organisational commitment is significant only for women, and persists regardless of the number of hours worked. This may reflect different life-cycles, especially for those in the older age groups, for whom it has been less typical for women to work almost throughout their adult lives, so unfettered escape from the home may mean more to the oldest group.

The reciprocal of good relations with management and organisational commitment is arguably attachment to a union or degree of militancy. Notwithstanding possibilities of dual commitment (Angle and Perry 1986; Guest and Dewe 1991), the extent to which men and women differ on these issues does offer possible insights reflecting on images of female quiescence and submission to authority. It also relates to the question of worker patriarchy raised above, which adds a complicating twist to possible interpretations. While unionisation and shop-floor militancy are often associated with traditional male-dominated industries, this might not be because of gender itself, although employment relations history and gender cultures are connected in some way. Case studies suggest that women are no less 'unionate' than men, nor less willing to act where required, but they also demonstrate that unions themselves are often felt to be unresponsive to women either as individuals or to women's particular demands (for example, Pollert 1981; Cavendish 1982; Cockburn 1983; Wajcman 1983; Findlay 1989).

In the DTI sample, union membership was markedly higher (70.1 per cent) than it is known to be for the working population as a whole; this reflects the disproportionate numbers of larger companies in the sample, and our focus on employees. Women in the sample were less likely to be union members than were men (65.6 per cent as against 74.2 per cent), a finding consistent with known differentials in propensity to join unions, but

Table 7.5 Standardised regression estimates for prediction of commitment: men and women

Variables	Commitment to organisational success				Commitment to department/area			
	Men (n = 320)		Women (n = 310)		Men (n = 320)		Women (n = 310)	
	b	SE(b)	b	SE(b)	b	SE(b)	b	SE(b)
Intercept	1.79***	0.28	2.06***	0.29	1.96***	0.26	2.20***	0.27
Level of job responsibility	0.04	0.05	0.05	0.05	0.13**	0.05	0.04	0.04
Hours worked/week	—	—	0.03	0.05	—	—	0.05	0.05
Years with present employer	0.12	0.09	-0.03	0.08	0.01	0.09	0.07	0.08
Age	0.01	0.04	0.07*	0.04	0.02	0.03	0.03	0.03
Organization size	-0.01	0.4	-0.02	0.02	0.002	0.03	-0.004	0.03
Organization type (1=public sector)	-0.06	0.09	0.03	0.03	-0.06	0.09	0.08	0.07
Perceived control/job	0.02	0.05	0.18***	0.07	0.11*	0.05	0.018***	0.05
Perceived control/conditions	0.05	0.05	0.03	0.05	-0.03	0.05	0.02	0.05
Perceived control/department	0.08	0.06	-0.07	0.05	0.05	0.06	-0.04	0.05
Perceived control/organisation	0.12	0.07	0.014*	0.06	0.08	0.087	0.09	0.06
Relations with boss	0.18***	0.04	0.10*	0.05	0.19***	0.04	0.08	0.04
Trade union membership (yes = 1)	-0.003	0.09	0.04	0.08	0.13	0.09	-0.07	0.07
Equation characteristics								
R²	0.021		0.19		0.23		0.21	
Adjusted R²	0.17		0.15		0.20		0.17	
F	6.48***		5.50***		7.35***		6.22***	

Notes: Hours worked, occupation and participation in company schemes were excluded from these regressions because of restricted sample sizes.
*$p < 0.05$; **$p < 0.01$; ***$p < 0.001$.

largely explicable in terms of the different employment settings and circum-stances of the two genders (Sinclair 1995).

Beyond this, the DTI study affords only limited leverage in an examina-tion of militancy or critical/conflictual attitudes to the company. It does confirm the need for caution in assuming that trade unionism entails less support for the employing unit, however, as shown by the non-significant coefficients in Table 7.5 for both men and women.

Perceived personal control

The DTI study focused on perceived personal influence on decisions at four levels of participation:

(i)   the job;
(ii) immediate physical working conditions;
(iii) department or branch operation; and
(iv) the overall organisation.

Respondents were invited to locate their position on a four-point scale rang-ing from 'none at all' to 'a great deal'. Previous studies (for example, Ramsay 1976; Wall and Lischerson 1977) suggest that perceived personal control should decline as respondents work through this list from job-level to organ-isational-level decisions. So it proves to be also with the DTI sample. At the job level, 67 per cent report a great deal or quite a lot of control; for work conditions, the figure is 46 per cent; at departmental level, 40 per cent; and for the organisation as a whole, 22 per cent. This pattern was evident across all occupational groups, and for both men and women.[2] Those with manage-rial responsibility were far more likely than those without to report the top two levels of control on all four types of decision, and both males and females in managerial or administrative posts reported higher feelings of personal control in their jobs relative to other occupations, both male- and female-dominated. Intriguingly, however, females in managerial and super-visory positions were markedly more likely to be disadvantaged relative to males at their own level in terms of personal control than were other groups of women. This could be consistent with Wajcman's (1996) finding that management were more, and not less, prone to sex-role stereotyping, and that women felt forced to adopt male styles in order to succeed. The relative enhancement of perceived control afforded by managerial and supervisory status was markedly greater than the gender differentials, though. Women supervisors report almost identical control to their male counterparts, and their differential over female non-supervisory staff was particularly sharp at this level (2.53 to 1.87 mean score).

Separate multiple regression analyses for men and women predicting perceptions of control at different levels of decisions are shown in Table 7.6

Table 7.6 Standardised regression estimates for prediction of perceived personal control: men and women

| | a) Job | | | | b) Physical /working conditions | | | |
| | Men | | Women | | Men | | Women | |
Variable	b	SE(b)	b	SE(b)	b	SE(b)	b	SE(b)
Intercept	1.20*	0.36	0.31	0.40	1.67*	0.38	0.47	0.41
Level of job responsibility	0.29*	0.06	0.34*	0.06	0.20*	0.07	0.23*	0.06
Hours worked/week	–*	–	0.28*	0.08	–*	0.29	0.34*	0.08
Years with present employer	0.03*	0.12	0.10*	0.11	0.16	0.13	–0.03*	0.11
Age	–0.04*	0.05	–0.002*	0.05	–0.06	0.05	0.04*	0.05
Organisation size	0.05	0.05	–0.03*	0.04	–0.03	0.05	–0.002*	0.04
Organisation type (1 = public sector)	0.07*	0.12	0.27*	0.10	–0.04	0.13	0.05*	0.10
Relations with boss	0.23	0.06	0.29	0.06	0.15	0.06	0.14	0.06
Trade union membership (yes = 1)	–0.21	0.12	–0.04	0.11	–0.12*	0.13	–0.04	0.11
Equation characteristics								
R^2	0.18		0.24		0.07		0.14	
Adjusted R^2	0.16		0.21		0.05		0.12	
F	8.88***		11.72***		3.25***		6.15***	

Variable	c) Department				d) Organisation			
	Men		Women		Men		Women	
	b	SE(b)	b	SE(b)	b	SE(b)	b	SE(b)
Intercept	0.84*	0.34	0.38	0.40	0.49†	0.28	0.37	0.35
Level of job responsibility	0.48*	0.06	0.43*	0.06	0.26†	0.05	0.28*	0.05
Hours worked/week	–*	0.26	0.29*	0.08	–*	0.21	0.20*	0.07
Years with present employer	0.16*	0.11	-0.01*	0.11	0.21*	0.09	-0.01*	0.10
Age	0.07	0.05	0.09*	0.05	0.02	0.04	0.09*	0.04
Organisation size	-0.03	0.05	-0.03*	0.04	-0.001*	0.04	-0.03*	0.03
Organisation type (1 = public sector)	-0.14	0.12	0.05*	0.10	-0.03	0.10	0.04	0.09
Relations with boss	0.19	0.06	0.13	0.06	0.18	0.05	0.08*	0.05
Trade union membership (yes = 1)	-0.17	0.12	-0.06†	-0.11	0.10	0.09	0.10	0.05
Equation characteristics								
R^2	0.26		0.22		0.18		0.15	
Adjusted R^2	0.24		0.20		0.17		0.13	
F	14.48***		10.73***		9.30***		6.80***	

Notes: †$p < 0.10$; *$p < 0.05$; **$p < 0.01$; ***$p < 0.001$.

and reveal that associations between level of responsibility and relations with one's boss are positive and significant at all levels for both sexes. The effect of the latter variable is greatest for job control and declines as the focus moves away from this immediate point.

An important characteristic of the sample was the proportion of women (41 per cent) who worked part-time. This group was less likely to report high levels of personal control at all levels, as indicated by the positive regression coefficients for hours worked shown in Table 7.6. This probably indicates their recognition of the lower-defined skill and quality of part-time work. Too few men worked part-time to allow a confident comparison that controlled for other factors. One-way ANOVA tests comparing males' and females' mean perceived control scores only for those working more than 30 hours per week found no persistant differences, affording an important elaboration of the gender comparisons above. Other variables that were important for perceived levels of control were organisation size, particularly for women on whom it exerted a negative influence; and longer tenure, which, for men, increased perceived control in the department and organisation as a whole.

Thus, to summarize, while gender has some explanatory significance with respect to satisfaction and management relations, it is not a powerful independent variable in its own right for drawing conclusions about employee commitment. Rather, gender effects may be a reflection of other variables – most obviously, job level, hours worked and perceptions of personal control within the workplace. Perceptions of control in particular are influenced by job level and relations with one's boss, for both men and women.

Communication, Consultation and Representation

The incidence of participation mechanisms in UK organisations (that is, downward and upward communication, financial involvement and representative participation) has been well documented (see, for example, Daniel 1987; Marchington *et al.* 1992; Millward *et al.* 1992; McNabb and Whitfield 1999) and overall reveals wide variation in practice and fairly low levels of consultation and involvement by British management. In the DTI survey, public-sector organisations tended to inform employees significantly more often about health and safety issues, the organisation's overall plans, and career opportunities. Private-sector employers communicated more on the organisation's overall efficiency and the performance of individual departments, although this amounted to only 40 per cent of private-sector organisations in both cases. Moreover, 20 per cent and 18 per cent of private- and public-sector employers, respectively, were reported as using no methods of communication at all.

We saw earlier that, on average, women reported slightly better relations with their immediate bosses than did men. Despite this, women seemed less likely to say they had received information about these aspects of their work from management than were men. This difference largely vanished, however, after controlling for the predominance of females among those working less than 30 hours per week (those few males in this category also reporting lower levels of information).

The DTI survey also asked employees to rate the effectiveness of different types of communication. These ratings are shown in Table 7.7 for men and women in both unionised and non-unionised organisations. The primary means of communication for learning about events in the workplace or making employee views known were circulars/internal memoranda (downward communication only), meetings between groups of employees and managers or supervisors, staff appraisals and, most prominently, informal conversations with managers/supervisors or colleagues. These were rated very or fairly effective for both purposes by the majority, as evidenced by the ratings of around 3 in Table 7.7 for unionised and non-unionised organisations. For most of these mechanisms, there were no significant differences by gender: women were more favourable only for suggestion schemes and informal conversations with managers. In non-unionised organisations, there was a significant interaction effect between gender and job level for ratings of conversations with managers; women managers and supervisors were more favourable towards informal conversations with superiors or colleagues than either their male managerial counterparts or female non-managerial employees (F = 3.91, $p < 0.05$ for conversations with superiors and F = 4.67, $p < 0.01$ for conversations with colleagues).

Thus informality was more highly rated by women as a vehicle for participation in non-unionised organisations, particularly if they were supervisors or managers. The effect of the union appeared to be the same for both men and women, with no major gender differences in perceptions of effectiveness. Where trade unions or staff associations negotiated with management on pay, formal methods of communication were also more likely, in keeping with an expected institutionalisation of employee relations. Informal mechanisms remained the most common means of communication in all organisations, however.

Of the overall sample, 14 per cent claimed no consultation prior to new initiatives being undertaken, these being chiefly new staffing levels (in 48 per cent of cases), the introduction of new working methods or conditions (44 per cent), quality control measures (36 per cent), and changes in equipment (31 per cent). Those who acknowledged any consultation reported mainly the notification of all employees (40 per cent), but also direct discussions with employees (34 per cent) or employee representatives (24 per cent).

Among those individuals reporting that changes had taken place, 6–7 per cent fewer women than men said they were aware of relevant consultation,

Table 7.7 Mean ratings of sources of information or methods of participation in unionised and non-unionised organisations: men and women

Information source/method of participation	Unionised organisation						Non-unionised organisation					
	Men			Women			Men			Women		
	n	M	SD	n	M	SD	n	M	SD	n	M	SD
Company												
Company report	136	2.88	0.88	95	2.96	0.89	67	3.16	0.79	64	2.98	0.86
Company videos	**105**	**2.91**	**0.87**	**75**	**3.27**	**0.81**	33	2.91	0.95	35	3.20	0.87
Company newspapers	188	2.83	0.84	154	2.86	0.92	74	2.80	0.91	82	2.84	0.88
Circulars/memos/notices	277	3.12	0.80	251	3.18	0.77	165	3.11	0.79	192	3.15	0.79
Management												
Management–employee meetings	188	3.21	0.79	176	3.22	0.69	118	3.34	0.79	131	3.39	0.74
Management/representative meetings (e.g. JCCs)	132	3.08	0.75	114	3.01	0.74	**37**	**3.08**	**0.96**	**67**	**3.36**	**0.67**
Staff appraisals	126	3.03	0.89	119	2.69	0.92	75	3.09	0.81	86	3.23	0.93
Employee attitude surveys	69	2.63	0.87	63	2.85	0.78	29	2.86	0.79	28	2.82	0.98
Letters/memos	81	2.68	0.89	75	2.65	0.85	45	2.96	0.67	45	2.93	0.86
Suggestion schemes	140	2.69	0188	1.07	2.86	0.85	57	2.86	0.83	61	2.97	0.88
Trade unions/staff associations												
Meetings with employees	161	3.11	0.78	114	3.06	0.92						
Through staff representatives	186	2.96	0.78	136	2.83	0.77						
Informal conversations												
With managers/supervisors	213	3.23	0.81	190	3.26	0.75	**189**	**3.27**	**0.83**	**217**	**3.42**	**0.72**
With other colleagues	205	3.11	0.84	175	3.19	0.85	165	3.10	0.89	187	3.18	0.84

Note: Only the one-way ANOVA tests for those shown in bold type are significant: company videos in unionised organisations ($p < 0.001$); management–representative meetings in non-unionised firms ($p < 0.10$); and informal conversations with managers/supervisors in non-unionised firms ($p < 0.05$).

132

whether through general notification, directly from management, or through representatives, but none of these differences was statistically significant. However, two groups where women were prevalent – among part-time employees and in feminised occupational categories – reported lower levels of consultation. For example, in personal and protective services over 75 per cent reported no discussion prior to changes, compared to an average of 63 per cent in other occupations.

These observations were confirmed in three stepwise regressions predicting the likelihood of consultation (i) between managers and employees; (ii) between managers and employee representatives; and (iii) through notification to all employees. The predictors were gender, job level, age, occupation, years with the organisation, trade union membership, organisational size, organisational sector (private or public) and interactions of each of these with gender. Job level emerged as a significant predictor of (i) and (iii); that is, the greater the level of responsibility, the more likely employees were to report direct employee/management consultation ($\beta = 0.43$, $p < 0.001$) and general notification ($\beta = 0.27$, $p < 0.01$). The two other variables to emerge were, first, tenure, which was significant for awareness of management/employee representative consultation ($\beta = 0.16$, $p < 0.01$) and general notification ($\beta = 0.17$, $p < 0.01$), and, second, size of organisation, where the larger the organisation, the more consultation of all types was reported (β values of 0.19, 0.18 and 0.13, all $p < 0.01$ for each regression, respectively). Belonging to a trade union seemed to provide no advantage in terms of increased awareness of consultation. Even in unionised firms, at least half the sample perceived that there had been no discussion or prior notification before changes were made.

In short, in the reported evaluations of communication or consultation channels, gender differences were rare. This challenges the expectations of opposing established views on gender differences. Other findings here, however, have suggested that, on average, women find themselves to be less well consulted or informed than men, suggesting that there may be structural differences in experience related to gender. We therefore consider the implications of gendered organisation theory for interpretation of some of the findings in the next section of the chapter.

Gendered Organisation?

We begin with the notion that organisations are dominated by masculine cultures that innately oppress women, and devalue female individuals and feminine characteristics (Calas and Smircich 1990; Savage and Witz 1992; Collinson and Hearn 1996; Kerfoot and Knights 1998). Acker (1992) argues that four sets of gendered processes can be identified in organisations: production of gender divisions (jobs, pay, power); creation of symbols and

images that justify divisions; gendered interactions embodying domi-
nance/subordination; and the internal construction by individuals of their
understanding of appropriate role behaviour. Although this model embod-
ies disadvantaging decision-making by managers, it recasts it as part and
parcel of this wider, more pervasive, gendered construction of organisational rules, criteria and *modus operandi*.

In this vein, Wilson (1995) reports research showing that women's leadership styles are still generally less valued than those of males, and that the
control of women managers is often compromised by aggressive male
subordinates. Critical studies of organisational cultures and structures have
argued that they tend to embody masculine values – although the precise
version of masculinity may shift over time – for example, from paternalism
to strategic rationalism and individualistic competitiveness (Kerfoot and
Knights 1998). Bureaucracy, too, is seen as a target for feminists to attack,
and in radical terms rather than within its own suffocating discourse
(Ferguson 1984). It is apparent that, if we are concerned with influence,
forms and experience of decision-making, and 'involvement', then a
gendered organisation perspective has profound implications.

At the same time, the notion that there are innately 'feminine' ways of
managing, and that women are disadvantaged unless (and probably even if)
they adopt 'male' styles is both appealing and problematical. The appeal is
the strength it lends to a gendered model of power and democracy, with the
additional promise of greater equality leading to a more democratic
management style for women, and arguably for men too. One problem is the
essentialist nature of parts of the argument, as well as its exclusive privileg-
ing of gender. Wajcman's (1996) research casts doubt on the more radical
claims that female managers adopt intrinsically different managerial styles,
for example.

If masculine bias is built into the relational fabric of the organisation, for
example, shaping mental work and identity as well as concrete practices,
then assessing attitudes at face value will be of only limited utility. The
tendency of women to see relations with their boss in better terms than do
men takes on a very different possible meaning within this framework,
rather than offering any means of testing it, to give just one example. But
there is no way to judge in this survey whether, for example, male and
female managers provoked differing assessments from male and female
employees.

While this limitation of the evidence is accepted, there are some observations that may guide other, more interpretative, research. Looking back over
findings, there is a discrepancy between women reporting on average better
relations with their boss while also reporting lower personal control and less
frequent consultation on changes at work. These differences were particularly bound up with the predominance of women among those working less
than 30 hours per week, as confirmed by the regressions predicting personal

control. This is at least suggestive of some patterns in a gendered organisational analysis of participation.

Exploring further, we recall first the findings on personal control reported earlier, wherein female managers appeared to be more disadvantaged than other female employees relative to their male counterparts in terms of perceived control. While a higher level of responsibility seemed to lead to increased commitment to the work unit only for men, it did not emerge as a significant determinant of perceived control. Wajcman (1996) implied that gender influences may be strongest towards the top of the organisation, but there was no significant interaction between gender and job level in the regressions for perceived consultation.

Our second stage of exploration modifies this observation to explore potential structural determinants of perceived personal control at non-managerial levels for full-time employees. The analysis examined environments in which gendered relations might operate differently, by dividing respondents into two groups: those in female-dominated occupations and those in male-dominated ones. The mean ratings of personal control for men and women within each sub-group are presented in Table 7.8 alongside those for managers and supervisors. Personal control is consistently lower for women than men within both types of occupations, and, as is particularly noticeable, lower for females in male-dominated occupations.

Acknowledging the relatively small number of women in the latter occupations and hence the need for caution in inferring a gender effect for this data, we carried out a two-factor ANOVA using gender and occupational category, including demographic and organisational variables as covariates. There was no significant interaction between gender and occupational category for any of the perceived control measures shown in Table 7.8, suggesting that women were not necessarily more disadvantaged in a male-dominated environment than in a female-dominated one. Similarly, gender did not emerge as a significant main effect, although the small sample of women in 'male' occupations may have limited the reliability of this comparison. However, in all cases, there was a significant main effect for occupational category, which, as the means suggest, implies that those in so-called 'male' occupations were likely to have much lower levels of personal control. In addition, tenure was a significant covariate in all cases, with personal control increasing with longer service in the organisation. Organisational size, meanwhile, contributed to significantly lower perceived personal control overall, despite its association with greater provision of formal channels for consultation and communication.

Interpreting these findings any more strongly would involve a disingenuous pretence that they have clear and unambiguous implications. None the less, the patterns observed are suggestive enough to indicate the need for a differentiated exploration of gendered organisational environments by other means.

Table 7.8 Effects of occupational type and gender on perceived personal control: men and women

Perceived personal control	Managers & supervisors				Non-managerial occupations								Two-factor ANOVA main effects and interaction (gender (G) and occupation type (O)) [a]		
					'Male' dominated				'Female' dominated						
	Men (n=328)		Women (n=203)		Men (n=186)		Women (n=29)		Men (n=87)		Women (n=182)				
	M	SD	M	SD	M	SD	M	SD	M	SD	M	SD	G	O	G×O
Job	3.29	0.78	3.24	0.79^{ns}	2.41	0.99	2.21	1.21^{ns}	2.82	0.93	2.67	0.97^{ns}	3.05^{ns}	9.15^{**}	0.01^{ns}
Working conditions	2.75	0.91	2.71	0.93^{ns}	2.14	0.97	1.86	0.92^{ns}	2.24	1.01	2.16	0.94^{ns}	3.12^{ns}	3.18^{ns}	0.76^{ns}
Dept/branch	2.82	0.97	2.83	0.91^{ns}	1.74	0.85	1.55	0.91^{ns}	2.01	1.01	1.91	0.94^{ns}	1.75^{ns}	10.36^{**}	0.04^{ns}
Organisation	2.24	0.94	2.20	0.93^{ns}	1.53	0.74	1.48	0.79^{ns}	0.79	0.79	1.57	0.78^{ns}	0.81^{ns}	1.43^{ns}	0.17^{ns}

Notes: Variables were measured on a 4-point Likert scale where 1 = 'none at all'; 4 = 'a great deal'. 'Male'-dominated occupations were: craft and related, and plant and machine operatives; 'female'-dominated occupations were: clerical/secretarial, personal and protective, and sales.
[a] Non-managerial occupations only. Main effects and interactions allowed for the effects of covariates tenure, age, organisation size and organisation sector (public or private). Tenure was a significant covariate for all measures of perceived control ($F_{(1,7)} = 7.94$, $p < 0.01$; $F_{(1,7)} = 6.52$, $p < 0.05$; $F_{(1,7)} = 14.66$, $p < 0.001$; $F_{(1,7)}$, $p < 0.01$, respectively) and organization size for perceived control overall in the organization ($F_{(1,7)} = 7.73$, $p < 0.01$).
$^{**}p < 0.01$; ns = not significant.

Trade Unions and Gender

The impact of employee organisations relate particularly to some aspects of the worker patriarchy argument. The fear that unions will replicate and rein-force the disadvantages imposed on women by management practice and other factors would lead to an expectation that unions might be associated with no improvement in women's experience of personal control or repre-sentative participation relative to men – and that they may even be worse off than non-unionised women, while men gain.

Sinclair (1995, 1996) offers evidence from a large-scale survey which shows that differences in propensity to unionise between men and women, and also in levels of activism, were best explained by pay levels and by how favourable attitudes to unions were. Attitudes to trade unions did not differ substantially between full- and part-time workers, nor with differences in attachment to work. Indeed, women were no less supportive of the principle of trade unionism, though they were seemingly rather less happy with their experience of unions. Sinclair speculates that domestic commitments, not measured in the DTI survey, were also likely to account for differences between the sexes, and between full- and part-timers. These findings are consistent primarily with the worker patriarchy and material constraints factors posited earlier.

The DTI data, however, appear to point to other and more complex conclusions. First, it is notable that, for men, union membership is generally associated with a marked reduction in perceived control at all decision levels compared to male non-unionists; in contrast, women union members reported slightly higher control than female non-unionists at all decision levels. Because of this contrary pattern, despite the overall gender inequality in perceived control discussed earlier, gender differences among union members all but vanish. Women appear to gain most from union member-ship in increasing personal control over, at least, organisational level deci-sions.

Second, it is possible that these differences are accounted for, in part at least, by the different patterns of union membership between men and women. Moreover, union membership had little effect on perceived control or ratings of communication or consultation for either men or women.

Overall, then, the DTI data lend highly qualified support, but support none the less, to a claim that being in a union has some positive rather than negative effects on control for women members relative to men. This does not refute claims that unions are often male-dominated and sexist in their policies and practices, but it nevertheless invites some reappraisal of any argument that being in a union is beneficial for men but not for women.

Part-time Workers and Feminist 'Fallacies'

This final section scrutinises more closely the differences between full-time and part-time working women, and its implications for gender differences on participation. As noted earlier, this issue has been brought to prominence by the analysis of Hakim (1991, 1995, 1996) which is presented as a critique of feminist 'fallacies'. Hakim argues that work commitment is lower among women as a group than among men, and that this is reflected in the proportion of women who either choose not to work outside the home or, increasingly importantly, elect to work part-time. In arguing that these are preferences, not choices forced by labour market discrimination and unequal opportunities, Hakim breaks with modern feminist orthodoxies. She also argues that part-time jobs are not typically poor or marginalised jobs, made thus by employer whim and prejudice, but in fact meet the needs of the women who take them. Confronting the 'part-time paradox', whereby women working shorter hours consistently report higher levels of job satisfaction than full-timers (male or female) despite on average having lower-paid and less skilled jobs (see Curtice 1993), she argues that this can be explained by these women having chosen the jobs to suit their lower work commitment – hence their satisfaction with the situation.

Hakim is correct, it seems, to assert a need to examine critically any *presumption* (a) that women have similar attitudes to those of men; or (b) that women can safely be treated as a homogeneous group. However, it does not follow that the present conclusions as to the pattern of attitudes concur with hers. First, we share Hakim's cautious view regarding relying solely on quantitative analysis of what may be insubstantial data in some ways; but we would argue that, if surveys have some value, then the independent or interactive effects of variables should be explored. Doing so here has already led to considerable qualification of findings, which might be misread from simple percentage comparisons such as those employed by Hakim. Second, an alternative viewpoint remains that women work part-time because circumstances require them to do so, because of a lack of childcare and other support in what are seen as inescapable responsibilities. One study on which Hakim relies, by Watson and Fothergill (1993), in fact reports that it is material constraints rather than normative reasons that account for most decisions to work part-time. The higher levels of satisfaction are accounted for by arguing that these women form lower expectations of jobs as a result of their experiences, and so come to appreciate the relative worth of conditions of which full-timers tend to be more critical.[3] Hakim herself does admit that: 'When male and female employees are matched closely on the jobs they do, organisational environment, and full-time hours, sex differentials fade and disappear' (1991: 109), but since she sees the overall lack of match as a matter of women's own choice, this is seen as reinforcing her argument rather than confirming that of her opponents. Sinclair (1995), however, finds no difference, in a large-scale sample, in work commitment between men, full-time women and part-time women.

Our concern with this debate, meanwhile, arises from competing implications of the different positions for gendered attitudes to participation. Hakim's findings would tend to promote the view that some women, at least, will be more acquiescent to management and more positive about their work, and would imply that part-time women will also be likely to have less interest in participation; her opponents would see any lower interest in participation by women, and part-timers in particular, as being driven primarily by poorer jobs, low self-esteem, weak influence, and possibly exclusion from the union, reinforced by the practical constraints that limit active participation as well as the opportunity to work longer hours. Thus, Hakim's position would logically entail simply accepting that things are as they are; while others would seek changes in management and union policies, and the provision of support facilities, to allow part-timers to participate more fully.

Some of the findings in the DTI study are consistent with those that have led to these competing interpretations. It was reported earlier that part-timers were much more likely to choose convenience of working hours as their key reason for taking a job, for example. Levels of commitment, to department or organisation, were also found to be quite similar, though a little higher for full-timers. Age, along with measures of perceived personal control in the workplace, was the predominant predictor of commitment to organisational success for women. Hours worked was, in turn, a strong predictor of perceived personal control at all levels; thus, while working part-time does not necessarily have a direct impact on commitment, it does have negative implications for perceived personal control in different aspects of work.

The consistent perception of lower control suggests that part-timers were aware of the limited participation afforded by their jobs. Though there were few part-time men in the survey, those responding reported a similar relative control deficit to part-time women. The nature of the DTI survey questions prevents us from being able to discern whether this lack of control is reflected in any way in wider measures of satisfaction.

However, the DTI data does allow the exploration of some of Hakim's assertions in a different way. In effect, she partitions the female workforce into full- and part-timers, treating the latter group as a bloc and as distinct from the former in their orientations. Our findings on personal control for different groups of women part-timers exhibited a clear and significant upward gradient as the number of hours worked per week increased, but hours worked was not a significant variable in the prediction of commitment. The danger of Hakim's assumptions appear in these findings: it is evident that the 16–29 hours group are more like the 30 hours and over group in their outlook than those working 15 hours or less, especially with respect to commitment. This casts severe doubt on Hakim's partitioning, and so on the proportion of women who might be seen as 'different', even before the caveats above are considered.

The tentative reading of the overall findings here is that they suggest that part-time jobs are experienced realistically by their holders as being inferior to full-time jobs. If this is a state of affairs to which expectations have been adjusted, there is no reason for such a finding not to be linked to higher recorded satisfaction levels. The lower levels of commitment of part-timers are not helpful *per se* in resolving the debate between Hakim and her opponents, since they may be seen as either being consistent with a lower normative attachment to work itself, or as a reaction to inferior job content and to exterior practical demands.

Moreover, the differences are not all that great in any of these findings (nor are they in Hakim's work), suggesting that many part-timers are not as different from full-timers as Hakim suggests. She may well have been right to emphasise the need to avoid blanket generalisations about women's views, but she then appears to have resorted to more complex yet almost equally parlous generalisations. Our analysis of the differences between those working different numbers of part-time hours illustrates the need for a more textured and less absolute approach.

Conclusions

This chapter has made the case for avoiding homogenisation of employees in discussions of organisational participation, and has specifically explored the gender differentiation in outlook and experience of the employment relationship. The findings reported above challenge both the view that women can be assumed to be the same as men, and the various stereotypes of female employees that are prevalent in much management thinking and practice. Factors such as age, occupational position, hours worked, relations with one's manager and union membership have all emerged as significant variables explaining differences in responses at various points in the analysis. In the process, the evidence has shown the danger of oversimplified generalisation within, as well as between, genders.

To summarise the main findings, women do appear to display more emphasis on convenient working hours (that is, to deal with commitments outside their job), and on good work relations with management, and show higher levels of overall satisfaction. This confirms previous evidence. Exploring further why this pattern exists, however, revealed that women were just as likely as men to find interesting work important – job level, sector and job type were more important predictors here than gender.

No differences in overall commitment were found between men and women, and generally we found the same correlations between attitude variables for both sexes, which indicates a danger in gender-stereotyping work orientations or attitudes. In any case, age, relations with boss and perceptions of control proved to be more important factors than gender in explaining differences in response. Certain interesting differences in the gendered pattern of experience also emerged between public- and private-sector organisations, with the public sector affording women better job relations and more control over job and department, though we did not deviate from our main purpose to explore these issues further. Job level proved to be a strong predictor of commitment, but only for men. Women managers emerged as more disadvantaged than their female counterparts in non-managerial jobs, but on other measures (for example, perceived consultation) and when controlling for hours worked, job level was not a major interactive factor.

Explanations of gender disadvantage based on a fundamental difference of outlook (basically the 'own worst enemies' and essentialist disadvantage models) do not appear to be well supported by the evidence. Limitations imposed on women by domestic circumstances, or by management patriarchal policies and practices, gain some support from this analysis. Moreover, there were some indications that male advantages over women in terms of perceived control, and some of the differences in patterns of experience across organisations, could lend support to a masculine cultures argument, though such claims remain weak without more appropriate qualitative evidence to support them. There were some indications, none the less, of structural conditioning of gender differences in experience, as well as of employee perceptions more generally. The importance of organisational size, and the public/private sector contrasts for women, are examples of this. The 'structural' examination of gendered environments was restricted by the small number of females in 'male' occupations; none the less, we can say that females were disadvantaged in terms of perceived control in both predominantly male and predominantly female occupational categories relative to men. It is also noteworthy that the 'male' occupations generally showed lower perceived control levels for employees than the 'female' ones.

Finally, considering the worker patriarchy argument, the analysis here does not support the view that unions make things worse, rather than better, for women. Union membership seems to improve ratings of personal control and of commitment for women, but not men. Union membership, though, has no effect on perceptions of being consulted.

It appears, then, that there are indeed important organisational participation issues that are gendered. Yet the problem is not at heart one of attitudes, but rather one of material constraints, structures and traditions. The next issue concerns the identification of paths of least resistance to change, and the consideration of whether reform has anything feasible to offer for a more democratic organisational future.

Notes

1 The sample was drawn from the electoral registers, seeking representativeness through a complex formula taking respondents from a range of constituency types, and adding a sample of non-electors aged over 15.
2 The DTI questionnaire did not allow examination of desired levels of control. This would have allowed the testing of debates regarding whether women express less desire for participation (Wall and Lischerson 1977; Allen *et al*. 1991; Drago and Wooden 1991).
3 Curtice (1993) argues this, as do Rose (1994) and Horrell *et al*. (1994), the latter two both analysing the data from the Social Change and Economic Life Initiative (SCELI) data. See also the reply to Hakim by Ginn *et al*. (1996).

References

Acker, J. (1992) 'Gendering Organizational Theory', in A. J. Mills and P. Tancred (eds) *Gendering Organizational Analysis* (London: Sage), 248–60.
Acker, J. and van Houten, D. R. (1974) 'Differential Recruitment and Control: The Sex Structuring of Organizations', *Administrative Science Quarterly*, 19:2, 152–63.
Allen, C., Cunningham, I. and McArdle, L. (1991) *Employee Participation and Involvement into the Nineties: Company Practice, Innovation and the Trade Union Role* (Stockton, UK: Jim Conway Foundation).
Angle, H. L. and Perry, J. L. (1986) 'Dual Commitment and Labor–Management Relationships Climates', *Academy of Management Journal*, 29:1, 31–50.
Baldwin, F. and Walpole, S. (1986) *Women, Affirmative Action and Industrial Democracy* (Canberra: AGPS).
Barker, D. L. and Allen, S. (eds) (1976) *Dependence and Exploitation in Work and Marriage* (London: Longman).
Beynon, H. and Blackburn, R. (1972) *Perceptions of Work: Variations Within a Factory* (Cambridge University Press).
Brown, R., Curran, M. and Cousins, J. (1983) 'Changing Attitudes to Employment?', Department of Employment, Research Paper No. 40 (London: HMSO).
de Bruijn, J. and Cyba, E. (eds) (1994) *Gender and Organizations – Changing Perspectives* (Amsterdam: VU University Press).
Calas, M. B. and Smirchich, L. (1990) 'Rewriting Gender into Organizational Theorizing: Directions from Feminist Perspectives', in M. Reed and M. Hughes (eds), *Rethinking Organization: New Directions in Organization Theory and Analysis* (London: Sage), 227–53.
Cavendish, R. (1982) *Women On The Line* (London: Routledge).
Clark, A. E. (1997) 'Job Satisfaction and Gender: Why Are Women So Happy at Work?', *Labour Economics*, 4 , 341–72.
Cockburn, C. (1983) *Brothers: Male Dominance and Technological Change* (London: Pluto).
Cohen, A. and Lowenberg, G. (1990) 'A Re-examination of the Side-bet Theory as Applied to Organizational Commitment: A Meta-analysis', *Human Relations*, 43, 1015–50.
Collinson, D. L. and Hearn, J. (eds) (1996) *Men as Managers, Managers as Men: Critical Perspectives on Men, Masculinities and Managements* (London: Sage).
Curtice, J. (1993) 'Satisfying Work – If You Can Get It', in R. Jowell, L. Brook and L. Dowds (eds), *International Social Attitudes: The 10th BSA Report* (Aldershot: Dartmouth) 103–22.

Daniel, W. W. (1987) *Workplace Industrial Relations and Technical Change* (London: Frances Pinter).

Dex, S. (1988) *Women's Attitudes Towards Work* (London: Macmillan).

Drago, R. and Wooden, M. (1991) 'The Determinants of Participatory Management', *British Journal of Industrial Relations* 29:2, 177–204.

Feldberg, R. and Glenn, G. N. (1979) 'Male and Female: Job versus Gender Models in the Sociology of Work', *Social Problems*, 26:5, 524–38.

Ferguson, K. E. (1984) *'The Feminist Case Against Bureaucracy'* (Philadelphia: Temple University Press).

Findlay, P. (1988) 'Fighting Plant Closure: Women in the Plessey Occupation', in D. Elson, and R. Pearson (eds), *Women's Employment and Multinationals in Europe* (London: Macmillan),183–206.

Gallie, D. and White, M. (1993) *Employee Commitment and the Skills Revolution* (London: PSI).

Ginn, J., Brannen, J., Dex, S., Moss, P., Roberts, C., Archer, S., Dale, A., Elias, P., Pahl, J. and Rubery, J. (1996) 'Feminist Fallacies: a Reply to Hakim on Women's Employment', *British Journal of Sociology*, 47:1, 167–74.

Guest, D. E. and Dewe, P. (1991) 'Company or Trade Union – Which Wins Workers' Allegiance? A Study of Commitment in the UK Electronics Industry', *British Journal of Industrial Relations*, 29:1, 75–96.

Hakim, C. (1991) 'Grateful Slaves and Self-made Women: Fact and Fantasy in Women's Work Orientations', *European Sociological Review*, 7:1, 101–21.

Hakim, C. (1995) 'Five Feminist Myths about Women's Employment', *British Journal of Sociology*, 46:3, 429–55.

Hakim, C. (1996) *Key Issues in Women's Work: Female Heterogeneity and the Polarisation of Women's Employment* (London: Athlone).

Horrell, S., Rubery, J. and Burchell, B. (1994) 'Gender and Skills', in R. Penn, M. Rose, and J. Rubery (eds), *Skill and Occupational Change* (Oxford University Press), 189–222.

Kaul, H. and Lie, M. (1982) 'When Paths Are Vicious Circles – How Women's Working Conditions Limit Influence', *Economic and Industrial Democracy*, 3:4, 465–81.

Kerfoot, D. and Knights, D. (1998) 'Management, Manipulation and Masculinity: A "Man"agerial Project', *Organization*, 5:1, 7–26.

Maddock, S. (1994) 'Women – a Democratic Force Within Organizations', in J. G. M. Bruijn and E. Cyba (eds), *Women in Organizations* (Amsterdam: VU University Press), 105–24.

Marchington, M., Goodman, J., Wilkinson, A. and Ackers, P. (1992) *New Developments in Employee Involvement*, Employment Department Research Paper No. 2 (London: Department of Employment).

Marsden, P. V., Kalleberg, A. L. and Cook, C. R. (1993) 'Gender Differences in Organizational Commitment', *Work and Occupations*, 20:3, 368–90.

Mathieu, J. E. and Zajac, D. (1990) 'A Review and Meta-Analysis of the Antecedents, Correlates, and Consequences of Organizational Commitment', *Psychological Bulletin*, 108, 171–94.

McNabb, R. and Whitfield, K. (1999) 'The Distribution of Employee Participation Schemes at the Workplace', *International Journal of Human Resource Management*, 10:1, 122–36.

Meyer, J. P. and Allen, N. J. (1997) *Commitment in the Workplace. Theory, Research and Application* (Thousand Oaks, Calif.: Sage).

Mills, A. J. and Tancred, P. (eds) (1992) *Gendering Organizational Analysis* (London: Sage).

Millward, N., Stevens, M., Smart, D. and Hawes, W. (1992) *Workplace Industrial Relations in Transition* (Aldershot: Dartmouth).

Mincer, J. (1966) 'Labor Force Participation of Married Women: A Review of Recent Evidence', in R. A. and M. Gordon (eds) *Prosperity and Unemployment* (New York: Wiley).

Pateman, C. (1970) *Participation and Democratic Theory* (Cambridge University Press).

Pateman, C. (1983) 'Some reflections on *Participation and Democratic Theory'*, in C. Crouch and F. Heller (eds), *International Yearbook of Organisational Democracy, Vol 1: Organisational Democracy and Political Processes* (Chichester: Wiley) 107–20.

Penn, R., Rose, M. and Rubery, J. (eds) (1994) *Skill and Occupational Change* Oxford University Press).

Phillips, A. (1991) *Engendering Democracy* (Cambridge: Polity Press).

Polachek, S. (1981) 'Occupational Self-selection: A Human Capital Approach to Sex Differences in Social Structure', *Review of Economics and Statistics*, February, 60–9.

Pollert, A. (1981) *Girls, Wives, Factory Lives* (London: Macmillan).

Pollert, A. (1996) 'Gender and Class Revisited; or the Poverty of Patriarchy', *Sociology*, 30:4, 639–69.

Ramsay, H. (1976) 'Participation: The Shop Floor View', *British Journal of Industrial Relations*, 14:2, 128–41.

Ramsay, H. (1996) 'Engendering Participation', Occasional Paper No. 8, Department of Human Resource Management, University of Strathclyde.

Ramsay, H. and Scholarios, D. (1996) 'Organizations, Democracy and Gender Analysis: Questions of Theory and Method', Paper presented at ISA Research Committee 10 Conference on Theoretical Approaches Towards Democracy in Organizations, Copenhagen, 11–14 June.

Ramsay, H., Panteli, N. and Beirne, M. (1997) 'Empowerment and Disempowerment: Active Agency, Structural Constraint and Women Computer Users', in R. Lander and A. Adam (eds), *Women In Computing* (Exeter: Intellect), 84–93.

Rose, M. (1994) 'Job Satisfaction, Job Skills and Personal Skills', in R. Penn, M. Rose and J. Rubery (eds), *Skill and Occupational Change* (Oxford University Press) 244–80.

Rose, M. (2000) 'How Far Can I Trust It? Job Satisfaction Data in the WERS98 Employee Survey', Working Paper No. 6: ESRC Future of Work Programme (Swindon: ESRC).

Savage, M. and Witz, A. (eds) (1992) *Gender and Bureaucracy* (Oxford: Basil Blackwell).

Sinclair, D. M. (1995) 'The Importance of Sex for the Propensity to Unionize', *British Journal of Industrial Relations*, 33:2, 173–90.

Sinclair, D. M. (1996) 'The Importance of Gender for Participation and Attitudes to Trade Unionism', *Industrial Relations Journal*, 27:3, 239–52.

Siltanen, J. (1994) *Locating Gender: Occupational Segregation, Wages and Domestic Responsibilities* (London: UCL Press).

Sloane, P. J. and Williams, H. (2000) 'Job Satisfaction, Comparison Earnings, and Gender', *Labour*, 14, 473–502.

Tillsley, C. (1994) 'Employee Involvement: Employees' Views', *Employment Gazette*, 102:6, June, 211–16.

Wajcman, J. (1993) *Women in Control: Dilemmas of a Workers' Co-operative* (Milton Keynes: Open University Press).

Wajcman, J. (1996) 'Desperately Seeking Differences: Is Management Style Gendered?', *British Journal of Industrial Relations*, 34:3, September, 333–49.

Wall, T. D. and Lischerson, J. A. (1977) *Worker Participation: A Critique of the Literature and Some New Evidence* (London: McGraw-Hill).

Walton, R. E. (1985) 'From Commitment to Control in the Workplace', *Harvard Business Review*, 63, March–April, 76–84.

Watson, G. and Fothergill, B. (1993) 'Part-Time Employment and Attitudes to Part-Time Work', *Employment Gazette*, May, 213–20.

Whirlpool Foundation (1995) *Women: The New Providers* (US survey) (New York: Whirlpool Foundation).

Whirlpool Foundation (1996) *Women: Setting New Priorities* (European survey) (London: Whirlpool Foundation).

Wilson, F. (1995) *Organizational Behaviour and Gender* (Maidenhead: McGraw-Hill).

Witt, L., Nye, A. and Lendell, G. (1992) 'Gender and the Relationship between Perceived Fairness of Pay or Promotion and Job Satisfaction', *Journal of Applied Psychology*, 77:6, 910–17.

8

Promoting Workplace Development: Lessons for UK Policy from Nordic Approaches to Job Redesign and the Quality of Working Life

Jonathan Payne and Ewart Keep

Introduction

Like most of its international competitors, the British government wants to transform the UK into a 'knowledge-driven economy' (DTI 1998). Unlike some of them, however, it has the additional problem of grappling with a long-standing and well documented low-skills equilibrium (PIU 2001; HM Treasury 2002). Since the 1980s, the dominant approach among policy-makers has been to rely on a succession of measures aimed almost exclusively at increasing the supply of skills and qualifications (Keep and Mayhew 1999). The election of a New Labour government in 1997 has not fundamentally altered the overall trajectory of policy (see Keep 1999). At the same time, several commentators have argued that this approach neglects deeply embedded structural weaknesses within the British economy that serve to depress employers' *demand* for, and *usage* of, skills (see Finegold and Soskice 1988; Keep and Mayhew 1999; Brown and Lauder 2001; Lloyd and Payne 2002a, 2002b). In particular, it is claimed that many UK organisations remain locked into neo-Fordist, cost-based competitive strategies, centred on relatively standardised goods and services, and associated Tayloristic forms of work organisation that make only limited demands on many employees' skills and capabilities (Keep and Mayhew 1998; Ackroyd and Procter 1998). Consequently, these commentators argue that UK skills policy needs to embrace a much broader range of 'demand-side' interventions, capable of changing the ways that firms compete, design jobs and manage their employees, if substantive progress is to be achieved.

With the exception of the somewhat isolated example of the Cabinet

146

Office's Performance and Innovation Unit's project on workforce development (see PIU 2001), such arguments have tended to make little impression on policy-makers.

Since the project's publication two years ago, UK policy-makers have struggled to come to terms with its possible implications. A brief glance at the 'new' Skills Strategy for England (see DfES 2003) suggests that the temptation to revert to supply-side measures has, once again, proved irresistible (for some of the reasons for this, see Keep 2002). Were policy-makers to become serious, however, about the need for effective interventions, measures would have to be directed at improving work organisation and generating far higher levels of participation in workplace innovation by employees. This chapter argues that a useful starting point may be to consider the experience of the Nordic countries, generally regarded as world leaders in the field of job redesign and workplace development (see Ennals and Gustavsen 1999).

A note on job redesign and workplace development

Before we move to substantive issues, paying some attention to definitions may be useful. Work organisation or job design 'concerns the ways jobs are defined or configured within the overall organization of production', whether employees work individually or in teams, and the extent to which they enjoy autonomy or discretion in their work (see Bélanger *et al.* 2002: 17). However, to grasp the full meaning of such terms requires them to be placed in their wider historical context. In the 1960s and 1970s, *job redesign* came to be associated with what was variously labelled work humanisation, job enrichment or quality of working life (QWL) initiatives. These experiments took place against the background of severe labour shortages and trade union militancy, and were an attempt to deal with problems of worker alienation, rising absenteeism and high labour turnover, often linked to Fordist/Taylorist production systems. Specifically, the aim of workplace reformers was to reconfigure *job content* with a view to improving employees' job satisfaction and motivation by giving them greater control over their labour and enhanced opportunities for self-actualisation through their work. Such experiments were initiated mainly by management and intellectuals, but in some countries governments and trade unions were also active in launching programmes (Durand 1998).

With labour surpluses and declining union power in the 1980s, management interest in such initiatives went into rapid decline. Instead, the restructuring of work became part of a new managerial agenda emphasising the need to improve quality, productivity, organisational flexibility and responsiveness to customers in an environment characterised by intensifying competitive pressures (see Buchanen 1994). Nevertheless, the impact of new forms of work organisation on employees remains deeply controversial (see

Appelbaum 2002). Whereas, for some commentators, this has meant a renewed opportunity to develop more empowering and participative forms of labour, others see a familiar managerial ploy to intensify work. A further analytical shift has occurred with the growing Anglo-US literature on 'high performance work organisations' (see Harley, Chapter 3 in this volume). These theories stress the complementarities existing between 'bundles' or 'clusters' of work organisation and human resource practices, and see more participatory work systems being introduced as part of a much broader process of organisational change. How far such practices have spread, and the extent to which they in fact increase worker control, autonomy or job satisfaction is a subject of some considerable debate (see Appelbaum 2002; Geary 2003).

At the time of writing, publicly-supported *workplace development* or *innovation* programmes reflect this temporal shift, having a much broader focus on improving competitiveness and productivity, albeit alongside more traditional QWL and industrial relations goals (see Brödner and Latniak 2002; Ennals and Gustavsen 1999). In this sense, 'workplace innovation' has come to mean a broader process of organisational renewal consistent with 'high quality, high skill, high trust' business approaches. An important question is the extent to which publicly-supported programmes aimed at supporting and resourcing this kind of development are able to achieve success and, critically, whether they deliver 'better jobs' for employees that, in line with original ambitions of workplace reformers, expand their opportunities to exercise skill, discretion and autonomy at work. This is a key question that we shall return to later in our discussion of contemporary workplace innovation programmes in Norway and Finland.

Workplace Development in the UK: A Case of Sorry Neglect

Even in the 1960s and 1970s, UK experiments with 'job enrichment' tended to fall a long way behind those attempted elsewhere in Northern Europe (see Elliot 1978; Lupton *et al.* 1979). At company level, certain job redesign experiments did take place, notably at Esso's Fawley oil refinery in 1960 and ICI's British Nylon Spinners in 1968, but these were confined to a small handful of organisations. In terms of the scope or depth of such experiments, there was certainly very little to compare with the introduction of 'semi-autonomous work groups' at Volvo's celebrated Kalmar car plant in Sweden[2]. Indeed, whereas in Norway, Sweden and Germany, the whole debate came to be coloured by notions of worker involvement and industrial democracy, in the UK the emphasis was much more on easing industrial relations problems and boosting efficiency (see Elliot 1978; Geary 1994).

Why, then, was it that initiatives aimed at improving job design and the quality of working life put down such shallow and fragile roots in the UK?

Part of the explanation is that, historically, such issues have tended to lack resonance with employers, trade unions or the state. British employers have long resisted any formal negotiation with trade unions over 'production issues' which were felt to infringe upon their hallowed 'right to manage' (see Hyman 1995), and have been fiercely hostile to any form of industrial democracy (see Bullock 1977; Coates 1980: 131–42). The hostility of UK private capital towards worker or union participation at the political level of the enterprise is indicative of a deeply-felt belief that managerial power and prerogative must be defended if economic efficiency and shareholder interests are to be preserved.

Historically, British trade unions have also shown relatively little interest in initiating experiments in work reorganisation and job redesign, preferring to concentrate their energies on more 'traditional' forms of collective bargaining over wages and conditions (Elliot 1978; Brannen 1983). Even at the time of the Bullock Report on industrial democracy, many British trade unionists remained wary of being co-opted into areas of managerial decision-making that threatened to compromise their status as a 'permanent and independent opposition'. Powerful unions with strong shop-floor organisation were able at certain times, however, to exert a degree of defensive control over job content, the pace of work and the introduction of new technology. But, as Terry (1994: 229, 228) reminds us, this was largely an 'opportunistic' response, premised on a 'managerially-derived division of labour' that rarely involved a strategic challenge to Taylorist forms of work organisation. If one leaves aside the odd exceptional case such as the Lucas Aerospace joint shop stewards' committee (see Elliot 1978: 79–80), British unions at this time more or less accepted that it was for management to run the enterprise, organise production and design work systems, while they got on with the business of collective bargaining.

Work organisation disappears as a policy issue

Since the 1980s, issues of work organisation and job redesign have all but vanished from UK public policy debates. The overriding assumption has been that global competitive pressures, rapid technological change and more sophisticated patterns of consumer demand would propel firms increasingly to adopt high-value-added, high-skill production approaches, linked to theories of Human Resource Management (HRM) and the 'high performance work organisation' (HPWO), and that this would eventually culminate in a shift towards flatter, less hierarchical organisations populated by empowered 'knowledge workers'. Within such workplaces, work would be reconfigured to allow employees greater scope for autonomy and creativity, and to maximise job satisfaction and employee commitment. Provided employers could be guaranteed enough of the right kind of skills, the design of work systems was assumed to be relatively unproblematic. Despite such high skills rhetoric, however, successive Conservative governments in the 1980s and 1990s pursued a policy of a flexible, deregulated labour market designed to attract inward investment and achieve a competitive advantage on the basis of relatively low labour costs (Brown and Lauder 2001). This reliance on a low waged and increasingly casualised workforce undermined investment in human capital and encouraged 'low road' approaches to competitiveness and productivity based on cost-cutting and work intensification (see Coates 2000). The present Labour government led by Tony Blair has continued much of this legacy, relying mainly on supply-side interventions, insistent that 'flexible' labour markets must be pursued in an era of 'globalisation' (Blair 1998), and wary of any strategy that threatens to encroach on areas of managerial prerogative (Lloyd and Payne 2002b).

Despite such political and ideological obstacles, there are good grounds for thinking that the UK needs to develop a role for public policy in promoting work and work organisation development that extends beyond exhortation and the diffusion of 'best practice' (see DTI 1998). The bulk of research, from both case studies (West and Patterson 1997; Ackroyd and Procter 1998; Dench *et al*. 1998; Guest 2000), and from surveys such as the DTI/ESRC's 1998 Workplace Employee Relations Survey (WERS) (Cully *et al*. 1998), indicates that low-skill, highly routinized jobs, offering limited opportunities for trust, creativity and discretion, remain relatively commonplace in the UK economy. The most recent Skills Survey available at the time of writing (Felstead *et al*. 2002: 11) highlights a 'marked decline in task discretion', with the proportion of respondents reporting a great deal of choice over the way they do their work falling from 52 per cent in 1986 to 39 per cent in 2001 (Felstead *et al*. 2002: 13). On this evidence, the opportunities for displaying initiative and creativity at work appear to be contracting rather than expanding, with a more qualified workforce able to use their skills and knowledge in ever more tightly circumscribed ways.

Other studies confirm that leaving work organisation and job design solely in the hands of individual employers may not be sufficient to bring about the shift in patterns of work design and skills usage that UK policymakers would clearly like to see. Guest *et al*.'s (2001) study of the limited take-up of progressive people-management practices in the UK, based on interviews with forty-eight senior executives in a range of organisations, shows that job redesign continues to be viewed with extreme suspicion in many UK boardrooms. Furthermore, 'a number of interviewees were baffled by what job design and job redesign meant, and confused it with involving employees in initiatives to improve workplace productivity' (Guest *et al*. 2001: 48). One CEO even questioned whether employees always wanted more interesting and varied work, saying: 'Certain people want to have eight hours for work, eight hours for rest and relaxation, and eight hours in bed. And it wouldn't matter what you made their job, however interesting it was, that is the way they want to live' (Guest *et al*. 2001: 48). There is also mounting evidence to suggest that the reliance on a flexible, deregulated labour market is actively encouraging alternative strategies to 'up-skilling' – including work intensification (Warhurst and Thompson 1998; Green 2001) and long working hours (see TUC 2001).

Supporting workplace innovation in the UK: playing catch up

Unfortunately, the UK finds itself trailing some distance behind a number of other European countries when it comes to putting in place a supportive infrastructure and policy framework for workplace development (Totterdill 1999; Ennals *et al*. 2001; Brodner and Latniak 2002). At the time of writing, the UK lacks either a national institute or major government-sponsored programme concerned explicitly with the modernisation of work organisation.

The government's only foray into this area comes in the shape of the Department of Trade and Industry's (DTI) Partnership Fund designed to 'improve employer–employee relationships, workplace productivity and job satisfaction' (DTI 2002). The scope of funding is clearly very limited, however. By early 2002, the Fund had awarded grants to 160, mainly small-scale, projects at a total cost of just £5 million. The projects address a galactic range of issues, including new ways of working, health and safety issues, training, equal opportunities, service quality, bullying, sexual harassment and work–life balance. Even allowing for some positive outcomes, there remain major doubts as to whether this constitutes a serious strategic attempt to modernise work organisation in Britain. It is striking that the Fund's own promotional material makes hardly any reference to work reorganisation or the quality of working life, with the overriding emphasis being placed on developing a new consensual-type psychological contract between employer and employees (significantly, the DTI appears indifferent as to whether 'partnership' should involve trade unions).

The chronic neglect of work organisation development within the UK public policy framework has meant that the baton has had to be carried instead by a small group of interested academics to be found mainly among the UK Work Organisation Network (UK WON). Started in 1997, UK WON is a 'loose coalition of universities, business support organisations, employers and trade unions with a commitment to developing and disseminating new forms of work organisation' (Totterdill 1999). Despite managing to pick up some funding from the European Social Fund and the DTI, its organisers concede that it remains hamstrung by the lack of core public funding (Ennals *et al*. 2001: 269). To sum up, then, the measures available in the UK at the time of writing to promote the development of better forms of work organisation appear to be weak and fragile compared with the scale of the problem they confront. In the next section, we turn to the experience of two Scandinavian countries, namely Norway and Finland, in a bid to see how far

they are able to provide convincing answers as to what a more robust institutional and policy framework for supporting workplace development
might look like.

Workplace Development in Scandinavia

Since the 1960s and 1970s, the Scandinavian countries, particularly Sweden
and Norway, have carved out something of an international reputation as
'world leaders' in the field of publicly-supported programmes aimed at
workplace and work organisation development (see Heller 1998; Ennals and
Gustavsen 1999). In the mid-1990s, Finland also entered the scene, launching
a National Workplace Development Programme that has begun to attract
international interest (see Ashton et al. 2003). Given the experience these
countries have presumably accumulated in this area, it seems sensible to ask
what lessons they might hold for the UK.

Norway

Norway has a forty-year history of programmes aimed at improving work
organisation, job design and work–life democracy (see Gustavsen et al. 2001;
Qvale 2002). Underpinning such efforts is a long-established tradition of co-
operation and social dialogue between the main employers' organisation
(NHO) and the leading trade union confederation (LO) that dates back to the
original Basic Agreement signed by the parties in 1935. Historically, the
social partners have played an important role in programmes aimed at
workplace development in Norway. These can be traced to the famous
Industrial Democracy Programme of the early 1960s and 1970s, when the
social partners were first approached by a social scientist, Einar Thorsrud,
with a view to initiating a series of 'socio-technical' experiments in selected
industrial plants aimed at developing autonomous work groups (see Emery
and Thorsrud 1976). Looking back, Dolvik and Stokland (1992: 154) suggest
that 'the direct effects of the project on work organisation and industrial
democracy seem to have been limited partly because it was initiated from
"above" without sufficient motivation at the workplace'. Another key problem to emerge was the failure of the experiments to spread to other firms
even within the same industrial sector (see Heller 1998; Qvale 2002). By the
end of the 1970s, the results of these 'first wave' experiments, in both
Norway and elsewhere, had collapsed amid 'an atmosphere characterised
by lack of conclusions' and little agreement as to what an alternative to
Taylorism might consist of (see Ennals and Gustavsen 1999: 19).

In the early 1980s, collaboration between social partners in the area of
workplace development deepened in Norway. An 'Agreement on
Development' (HF-B) was included as an appendix to the general agreement

that is negotiated every four years by NHO and LO. The HF-B agreement sets out how the parties will co-operate on enterprise development and adds considerable legitimacy to such efforts. HF-B has its own board, which funds local development efforts. In 1988, a six-year national enterprise development programme was started, linked to the National Work Life Centre (Senter for Bedre Arbeidsliv – SBA), designed explicitly to aid Norway's international competitiveness (see Qvale 2002). Once again, there are indications that the SBA programme met with some success, but that diffusion remained limited, with key firms failing to sign up (Davie *et al*. 1993; Heller 1998: 183).

When SBA ended in 1994, the social partners decided to approach the newly-formed Research Council of Norway (RCN), with a view to launching a new seven-year programme under the title 'Enterprise Development 2000' (ED2000). The primary aim of the new programme was to enable Norwegian enterprises to generate added value and be more competitive in the international marketplace (see RCN 1996), by putting in place 'an infrastructure for social innovations in and between enterprises' (Mikkelsen 1997: 72). At the same time, the programme was expected to develop 'the Norwegian model' of employee participation and labour/management co-operation (Gustavsen *et al*. 2001: 14). Significantly, ED2000 was the first time the social partners had initiated, as opposed to being simply participants in, such a programme. In addition to sharing funding with the Research Council, NHO and LO played an active co-ordinating and managerial role, receiving seats on both the national management board and the secretariat.

A core feature of the programme was the emphasis placed on social science 'action research' in supporting organisational innovation processes (see Levin 2002a). To assist this, and to create a mechanism for the exchange of knowledge and experience between firms, enterprises were linked to one of seven research centres as part of a 'module' (see Gustavsen *et al*. 2001: 114–228). Some modules focused on supporting innovation at the level of the individual enterprise, while others took as their point of departure the need to nurture interorganisational networks. Emphasis was placed on the 'broad participation' of employees in the developmental process, using devices such as work conferences, project groups and workplace meetings, and based on principles of 'democratic dialogue' (see Gustavsen *et al*. 2001). In total, around 100 enterprises and the same number of researchers came to be involved in the programme (Gustavsen *et al*. 2001: 14).

There are indications that ED2000 met with a good deal of success. An evaluation carried out as part of the benchmarking process found that the vast majority of enterprises (86 per cent) wanted to take part in future efforts, given the same level of financial and research support (Gustavsen *et al*. 2001: 55). Positive improvements were reported across a range of areas, including labour/management co-operation (around 80 per cent of participating enterprises), productivity (80 per cent), product quality (70 per cent), product development (45 per cent) and marketing (25 per cent) (see Gustavsen *et al.* 2001: 15, 39–70). However, as Gustavsen *et al.* (2001: 16) note, 'in assessing the impacts of the program, the benchmarking group as well as the social partners relied primarily on impressions gained through open interviews with management, union representatives and employees in the participating enterprises ... On this basis ... the program was given a highly positive evaluation.'

In several cases, many of the researchers openly concede that 'we did not achieve ... significant structural and innovative changes' (Claussen and Kvadsheim 2002: 109). Two themes emerge particularly strongly in all these accounts. The first is that successful development work requires a high level of trust and commitment on the part of both management and employees; and the second is that change often takes considerable time and energy. As Falkum (2002) neatly puts it, 'development coalitions demand trust, legitimacy, lots of time, and open dialogues between the parties involved'. While the module reports offer a collection of interesting vignettes concerning some of the challenges that researchers faced, it is much less clear what these programmes have in fact delivered in relation to the specific questions of work reorganisation and job redesign. Not only is little actual evidence advanced in support of claims, but the statements are often so vague as to be unhelpful in determining what has really happened to the organisation of work and who has benefited. Indeed, in many cases, the question 'what did the programme really deliver?' still seems to be unanswered.

The latest initiative in the area of enterprise development in Norway is 'Value Creation 2010' (VC2010). The main impetus for this came from the social partners, who approached the government with the view to setting up a new programme. Launched in 2000, VC2010 started with a ten-year life expectancy, a financial base three times that of its predecessor, and the participation of ten research centres (see Qvale 2002). The programme takes as its starting point the need to forge '*regional* development coalitions' (see Ennals and Gustavsen 1999). The intention is that research centres will now work in much closer partnership with employer organisations and the labour market associations at a regional, sectoral and national level (Qvale 2002: 49). Casting a backward glance over Norwegian efforts since the 1960s to promote workplace development, Qvale (2002) acknowledges that progress has occurred, albeit very slowly. He suggests that the most positive result has been the creation of a new culture of co-operation around development activity that includes researchers and enterprises, as well as social partners and other public agencies. Indeed, what the Norwegians came to realise from the 1980s onwards was that workplace development could not be confined to single enterprises but required the building up of relations between firms and other actors through networks, coalitions and supply chains, particularly at regional level.

Finland

In comparison with Norway, Finland can be considered a 'late starter' when it comes to programmatic, research-assisted workplace development, having moved into this area only relatively recently (see Alasoini 1997). Launched in 1996, the Finnish Workplace Development Programme (FWDP) is a joint initiative between the government and its social partners. A key strategic goal has been to locate workplace development as an integral part of Finland's 'national innovation system' rather than seeing economic growth simply in terms of investments in new technology and workforce skills (see Alasoini 1997, 2003). The main aim of the programme is to 'boost productivity and the quality of working life by furthering full use and development of staff know-how and innovative power at Finnish workplaces' (Alasoini 1997: 62). To this end, the programme funds the use of external experts, such as researchers and consultants, in various workplace development projects. The role of lead actor is taken by the Ministry of Labour, which finances and co-ordinates the programme, while managing it on a joint basis with the main labour market organisations. Around 1,300 workplaces and 120,000 employees have participated to date, in some 550 projects (Alasoini 2003).

The programme design is informed by several key principles. All development projects have to be 'workplace-initiated' and are expected to promote a balanced development between productivity and the quality of working life. The idea is not to solve specific problems for organisations but rather to put in place permanent structures that will allow them to meet their own developmental needs in the future. FWDP aims to promote projects that strive to achieve a comprehensive and holistic change in a company's mode of operation, including technologies, management, work organisation, staff skills, working conditions and occupational health (see Alasoini 1997). As such, it shares certain common theoretical underpinnings with the Anglo-American literature on 'high performance work systems' as well as Scandinavian notions of 'concept-driven development' (see Gustavsen *et al.* 1996). Successful workplace development is said to require the 'broad participation' of employees in the formulation and implementation of developmental goals. A further aim is to create 'learning networks' that allow researchers and practitioners to share ideas and experiment with new practices, thereby helping to build a 'critical mass' for workplace development (see Alasoini 2003). FWDP is engaged in three main types of activity. First, the programme funds expert support for projects in both the private and public sectors, based on applications submitted. The second main area of activity is the dissemination of knowledge about workplace development by means of various research publications, seminars, workshops, focus groups and an internet home page. Finally, the programme attempts to strengthen the workplace development infrastructure in Finland by supporting networking between workplaces and enabling researchers and practitioners to meet through seminars. In this way, the programme operates as a forum for dialogue and co-operation between key stakeholders, such as workplaces, R&D institutes, funding bodies, labour market organisations and policy-makers.

As with ED2000, FWDP has received some extremely positive evaluations, based mainly on feedback from management and staff at workplaces as well as researchers and consultants involved in the projects. The approach relies heavily on self-assessment questionnaires completed by a representative or representatives of each of three main parties at the completion of a project. Drawing on 502 such questionnaires covering 186 development projects completed by July 2000, Ramstad (2001) found that 84 per cent of respondents considered their project to have been fairly successful or highly successful. At the same time, positive improvements were recorded across a range of areas, including productivity (66 per cent of respondents), product or service quality (76 per cent), quality of operations (73 per cent) and responsiveness to client needs (70 per cent). Positive effects were also found in the area of work organisation. An improvement in team working was recorded by 89 per cent of respondents, 78 per cent said that co-operation between management and employees had got better, 67 per cent felt that there had been an improvement in social interaction in the workplace, and 74 per cent thought there were improved opportunities to use and develop professional skills. Interestingly, fewer gains were recorded in relation to the quality of working life. Nevertheless, 58 per cent still felt that there had been improvements in mental well-being at work, while 35 per cent reported better working conditions.

This picture of generally positive gains has been confirmed by a subsequent evaluation carried out on 108 development projects two and a half years after they had reached completion (see Rissanen and Arnkil 2003). While both these evaluations paint an extremely positive picture, such findings need to be handled with caution, given that they are based on the subjective views of respondents who have a stake in the continuation of the programme and the public funding that goes with it. Moreover, it is not clear what such evaluations can tell us about the specific impact these projects have had on work organisation. They suggest clearly that some projects may have helped with the introduction or further development of various forms of team or cell-based working, for example. However, the literature on team working has shown that this can have both positive and negative effects on employees' experience of work, depending upon the particular context in which it is introduced and the manner of its implementation. There is ample evidence from case studies to indicate that team working can, for example, be associated with increased peer surveillance and work intensification (see Delbridge and Turnbull 1992; Marchington and Grugulis 2000; Proctor and Mueller 2000).

If we allow for certain problems with the evaluation methodology, there seems little doubt, however, that Finnish policy-makers have made a determined effort to embed a publicly-supported programme that seeks to improve aspects of work organisation. The backing of both the government and its social partners means that FWDP enjoys considerable political legitimacy. However, as Alasoini (2003) notes, there are still many mountains left to climb. Finland is said to lack a strongly supportive infrastructure for workplace development at regional level, while the links between technology and workplace innovation policy remain underdeveloped.

There are also indications that 'broad workforce participation' may not be as deep or as extensive as many of the programmes' designers might have hoped. Using material drawn from development projects in fifty-four Finnish workplaces funded between 1996 and 2000, Alasoini (2001: 20) notes that 'there were only a few companies and public bodies which were successful in workforce mobilisation and achieving critical mass in support of development work', suggesting that 'a genuinely participatory approach . . . based on actual personnel participation, may still be fairly superficial at many Finnish workplaces'. In some cases, the problem was found to be 'a deeply rooted general atmosphere of distrust in the workplace or general uncertainty about how the project would benefit the employees' (Alasoini 2001: 14).

Other commentators have found that, apart from a minority of more innovative firms, many organisations remain wedded to bureaucratic, hierarchical management approaches and Taylorist forms of work organisation that make limited use of employees' skills (see Ylöstalo 1999). One might conclude, therefore, that even in a relatively high-wage country, with a well-regulated labour market, strong trade unions and legally-embedded co-determination arrangements (see Lilja 1998), the micro-foundations for successful development activity – in particular the critical ingredient of 'high trust' relations – are often found wanting.

All the indications are that workplace development in Finland confronts many difficult and complex challenges. At the same time, however, the future of FWDP looks reasonably bright and secure. Workplace innovation is accepted as a legitimate area of public policy concern and enjoys the continued support of the social partners. In January 2003, a joint memo from the Ministry of Labour and the central labour market organisations recommended that the new government in Finland should continue the programme, with increased financial support (see Alasoini 2003).

Evaluation of the Norwegian and Finnish programmes

Despite their many similarities, it is important to highlight some key differences between the Norwegian and Finnish workplace development programmes. The most recent Norwegian programmes – ED2000 and

VC2010 – are aimed primarily at supporting innovation in and *between* private companies at the front line of international competition, with an emphasis on nurturing *regional* development coalitions or networks. By contrast, FWDP can be said, perhaps, to pay more specific attention to work organisation at the level of the workplace, spans the private/public boundary, and aims explicitly to improve both productivity and the quality of working life across a broader range of organisations. A further distinction is that whereas in Norway it is the social partners that have been at the forefront of these initiatives, in Finland the main impetus has come from the Ministry of Labour, working in close association with the labour market organisations.

The question is, how are we to assess and evaluate the impact of these programmes in terms of their ability to improve the organisation and design of work? Two main points are worth emphasising. First, there is the issue of the way the programmes have been evaluated. In what are normally regarded as high-trust societies, this has taken the form of 'soft' measures such as surveys, questionnaires and interviews, with a strong element of self-evaluation. Second, if we are to evaluate these programmes critically, more attention will need to be given to what constitutes 'success'. A key aim of these programmes is to promote organisational or business innovation, where innovation is understood as a social process (Levin 2002b). In part, this reflects the wider shift that has taken place in workplace development programmes over time, away from the explicit concern with job redesign of the 1970s and towards supporting organisational change and innovation, conceived more broadly, and where there is a much stronger emphasis on achieving improvements in competitiveness, quality and responsiveness to customers (Alasoini 1997). At the same time, 'innovation' is a very vague and diffuse concept that can mean almost anything.

At one level, there seems to be considerable merit in adopting such a 'holistic' approach. Employee relations systems, work organisation and job design, much like skills, are often second- or third-order issues, dependent on broader organisational aims and objectives. Attempts to change what happens in the workplace are likely to be significantly more successful, therefore, where shifts in work organisation are linked to efforts to upgrade product market strategies, and product and service specification. The problem is, however, that if 'change' and 'innovation' are now the criteria for success, then in most cases it becomes relatively straightforward to demonstrate that some success has been achieved. This is indeed the story of the ED2000 programme. What we do not have is a very clear picture of how effective this new generation of programmes have been in terms of helping to design new approaches to work organisation that expand employees' opportunities for the exercise of skill, discretion and autonomy.

Despite a supposedly favourable institutional environment for programmatic workplace development, those closely involved with the programmes indicate that many problems and challenges remain, and that their generalisation across whole sectors remains an elusive goal. There are strong indications that broad workforce participation in such activities remains more the exception than the rule, and that without a culture of trust and commitment on all sides the development process soon runs into difficulties. A final point, common to both countries, appears to revolve around the need for major long-term capacity building to support workplace innovation. Progress seems to demand a range of actors external to the firm whose help and intervention may be necessary to act as catalysts for change and to support the development process. This pool of expertise is plainly finite in both Norway and Finland, and, as the Norwegian example demonstrates, the development of experts and organisations capable of fulfilling this role is certainly a lengthy and demanding one. How best to go about this developmental, capacity-building task, however, remains unclear.

Where Does the UK Go From Here?

If the experience of Norway and Finland can be said to illustrate anything, it is that workplace development is an extremely lengthy and challenging process. In comparison with the UK, both these countries accept that there is a legitimate role for public policy in this area, alongside more traditional measures aimed at diffusing new technology and increasing investment in workforce skills. The challenge facing UK policy-makers, were they to try to emulate such efforts, is compounded by the position from which they would have to start out. Having spent the years since the 1980s hammering away on the 'supply-side' of the skills problem, the UK currently finds itself without an infrastructure for promoting workplace and work organisation development that is in any way comparable to what exists in either Finland or Norway. This much alone suggests that *if* UK policy-makers were to become serious (and this is a very big 'if') about trying to close the gap with the Scandinavians in the area of programmatic workplace development, then they would face a major challenge. Assuming that UK policy-makers were to contemplate such a project, how might they feasibly go about this? One possible avenue of progress might be to provide core funding to UK WON and to see what progress it can make in terms of forging active 'coalitions' or 'networks' for development. At the same time, the DTI could take a stronger leadership role by launching a Finnish-style productivity/quality of working life programme. In doing so, it is vital that policy-makers take a long-term perspective and are realistic about what such a programme can be expected to achieve within a relatively short time-scale. A key strategic goal must be to build up the research expertise needed to support workplace development activity while developing the necessary confidence among both the policy-makers and the business community to enable the project to take hold and expand into the future.

Elsewhere we outline what kind of programme policy-makers might usefully consider in stimulating employer demand for skills (Payne and Keep 2003). This would include product market measures such as new forms of business support and advice aimed at helping firms to shift their strategies towards higher-value-added goods and services, and labour market reforms – in particular, higher national minimum wages to encourage firms to move away from low-cost competitive strategies. Most importantly for the themes of this book, a strong emphasis should be put on legislation and other forms of encouragement to create a more supportive environment for social partnership, employee involvement, and consultation and information.

By UK standards this would certainly constitute a fairly radical agenda, though it would not be recognised as such in Northern Europe. Persuading UK policy-makers to develop such a strategy will be far from easy, however. Were they to change their mind, they would certainly meet resistance from UK employers, many of whom remain wedded to low-value-added, low-skill production strategies. The opposition mounted by UK employer organisations to recent European Union directives on information, consultation and working time, as well as the Labour government's extremely modest proposal to give statutory recognition to union learning representatives (union members given paid time off work to engage in training-related activities), is a case in point. It is perhaps more through political conviction than any loss of nerve, however, that New Labour has acted to weaken and dilute such measures (see Hutton 2002).

Conclusion

Even if policy-makers could be persuaded to pursue the agenda outlined above, many other obstacles remain. A major problem is the decline in collective bargaining in the UK since the late 1970s. At the start of the 2000s, only around one in three British employees belongs to a trade union. Moreover, the fact that unions are virtually absent from private-sector services, while at least a third of British workplaces are without any formal structure at all for representing employee interests (see Cully *et al.* 1998: 43), is a further sobering reminder of the problems involved in developing 'partnership-based' approaches to workplace development in the UK. If involving employees and their representatives in planning and implementing change is the hallmark of successful workplace innovation, then all the indications are that the UK hardly offers the best environment in which to try to develop such projects. Furthermore, in a business environment characterised by severely weakened trade unions, where companies are under intense pressure to maximise short-term shareholder profits (Hutton 1995) and can easily resort to effort-intensive and cost-cutting strategies for raising productivity, persuading more than a few firms to take the high-quality, high-skill, high-trust 'road' is likely to be extremely difficult (see Keep 1999; Bach and Sisson 2000; Geary 2003). Faced with such pressures, many firms simply lack the capacity to initiate and sustain comprehensive and holistic programmes of organisational change where the pay-back period is long and the rewards uncertain.

Yet the experience of concerted, state-sponsored attempts at promoting workplace change in the Nordic countries examined in this chapter suggests that development activity is still an extremely lengthy, complex and challenging process. At the same time, there are serious questions to be asked about what these programmes have really delivered in terms of improvements in job design and the quality of working life that are only likely to be fully answered through further case-study-type research.

Unfortunately, the UK lacks many of the structural and political conditions that appear to be prerequisites for success, such as a high level of trust and commitment among the social partners. Even if policy-makers could be persuaded to launch a Finnish-style workplace development programme, there is still the possibility, therefore, that, faced with major institutional constraints, the project would backfire, leading policy-makers to conclude, 'we've tried that and it doesn't work'. As we have argued, much depends on how such a programme is framed, what the expectations are, and how success is measured (and over what time-scale). If such a programme could only demonstrate the potential that exists for enriching people's experience of work by allowing them to use and develop their talents in better-quality jobs, then that, in itself, would be no mean achievement. Moreover, only by becoming engaged in such efforts are policy-makers likely to shift their perceptions of *what else* needs to be done to address the underlying causes of Britain's skills problem (see Lloyd and Payne 2002a, 2002b). In brief, there is an urgent need to involve policy-makers in a different and better learning curve. A publicly-supported workplace development/quality of working life programme in the UK may be a small step in the right direction, and a long overdue one at that.

Note

The authors would like to thank Dr Caroline Lloyd of the ESRC's Centre for Skills, Knowledge and Organisational Performance (SKOPE) for providing comments on a first draft of this chapter. Thanks also to the editors, in particular Paul Thompson, for their help with editing the final version of this chapter prior to publication. All errors, of course, remain the authors' own.

References

Ackroyd, S. and Procter, S. (1998) 'British Manufacturing Organisation and Workplace Relations – Some Attributes of the New Flexible Firm', *British Journal of Industrial Relations*, 36:2, 163–83.

Alasoini, T. (1997) 'The Finnish National Workplace Development Programme: Background, Starting Premises and Initial Experiences', in T. Alasoini, M. Kyllönen and A. Kasvio (eds), *Workplace Innovations – A Way of Promoting Competitiveness, Welfare and Employment* (Helsinki: Ministry of Labour), 53–71.

Alasoini, T. (2001) 'A Concept-driven Model for Workplace Change – Evidence from 54 Finnish Case Studies', Paper presented at the 6th European IIRA Congress, Oslo, 25–29 June. Accessed on: http://mol.fi/tyke/new/english/articles4.htm.

Alasoini, T. (2003) 'Promotion of Workplace Innovation: Reflections on the Finnish Workplace Development Programme', Paper presented to the SKOPE Skills, Innovation and Performance Conference, Cumberland Lodge, UK, 31 March–1 April.

Appelbaum, E. (2002) 'The Impact of New Forms of Work Organisation on Workers', in G. Murray, J. Bélanger, A. Giles and P.-A. Lapointe (eds), *Work and Employment Relations in the High Performance Workplace* (London: Continuum), 120–49.

Ashton, D., Sung, J. and Raddon, A. (2003) *Raising Employer Demand for Skills: Lessons Form Abroad*, Report prepared for the DTI (London: DTI).

Bach, S. and Sisson, K. (20000) Personnel Management in Perspective, in S. Bach and K. Sisson (eds), *Personnel Management*, 3rd edn (Oxford: Basil Blackwell), 3–42.

Bélanger, J., Giles, A. and Murray, G. (2002) 'Towards a New Production Model: Potentialities, Tensions and Contradictions', in G. Murray, A. Giles and J. Bélanger (eds), *Work and Employment Relations in the High Performance Workplace* (London: Continuum), 15–71.

Blair, T. (1998) 'Foreword' in DTI White Paper, *Fairness at Work* (London: HMSO).

Brannen, P. (1983) *Authority and Participation in Industry* (London: Batsford).

Brodner, P. and Latniak, E. (2002) *Sources of Innovation and Competitiveness: National Programmes Supporting the Development of Work Organisation* (Brussels: European Commission).

Brown, P. and Lauder, H. (2001) *Capitalism and Social Progress* (Basingstoke: Palgrave).

Buchanen, D. A. (1994) 'Principles and Practice of Work Design', in K. Sisson (ed.), *Personnel Management: A Comprehensive Guide to Theory and Practice in Britain* (Oxford: Basil Blackwell), 85–116.

Lord Bullock (1977) *Report of the Committee of Inquiry on Industrial Democracy* (London: HMSO).

Claussen, T. and Kvadsheim, H. (2002) 'Networking Industrial Development', in M. Levin (ed.), *Researching Enterprise Development: Action Research on the Cooperation between Management and Labour in Norway* (Publishing Company: Amsterdam: John Benjamins), 93–111.

Coates, D. (1980) *Labour in Power? A Study of the Labour Government 1974–79* (London: Longman).

Coates, D. (2000) *Models of Capitalism: Growth and Stagnation in the Modern Era* (London: Polity Press).

Cully, M., O'Reilly, A., Millward, N., Forth, J., Woodward, S., Dix, A. and Bryson, A. (1998) *The 1998 Workplace Employee Relations Survey: First Findings* (London: ESRC/ACAS/PSI).

Davies, A., Naschold, F., Pritchard, W. and Reve, T. (1993) *Evaluation Report Commissioned by the Board of the SBA Programme* (Oslo: Work Research Institute).

Delbridge, R. and Turnbull, P. (1992) 'Human Resource Maximization: The Management of Labour Under Just-in-time Manufacturing Systems', in P. Blyton and P. Turnbull (eds), *Reassessing Human Resource Management* (London: Sage).

Dench, S., Perryman, S. and Giles, L. (1998) *Employers' Perceptions of Key Skills*, IES Report No. 349 (Brighton: Institute of Employment Studies).

DfES (Department for Education and Skills) (2003) *21st Century Skills: Realising Our Potential* (London: HMSO).

Dolvik, J. E. and Stokland, D. (1992) 'Norway: The "Norwegian model" in Transition', in A. Ferner and R. Hyman (eds), *Industrial Relations in the New Europe* (Oxford: Basil Blackwell), 143–67.

DTI (Department of Trade and Industry) (1998) *Our Competitive Future: Building the Knowledge-Driven Economy* (London: HMSO).

DTI (Department of Trade and Industry) The Partnership at Work Fund (2002) Accessed at: http://www.dti.gov.uk/partnershipfund/index.html.

Durand, J. P. (1998) 'Is the "Better Job" Still Possible Today?', *Economic and Industrial Democracy*, 19:1, 185–98.

Elliott, J. (1978) *Cooperation or Conflict: The Growth of Industrial Democracy* (London: Kogan Page).

Emery, F. E. and Thorsrud, E. (1976) *Democracy at Work* (Leiden: Niijhoff).

Ennals, R. and Gustavsen, B. (1999) *Work Organization and Europe as a Development Coalition* (Amsterdam: John Benjamins).

Ennals, R., Totterdill, P. and Ford, C. (2001) 'The Work Research Foundation: A National Coalition for Working Life and Organizational Competence', *Concepts and Transformation*, 6:3, 259–73.

Falkum, E. (2002) 'Fragile Coalitions', in M. Levin (ed.), *Researching Enterprise Development: Action Research in Cooperation between Management and Labour in Norway* (Amsterdam: John Benjamins), 77–92.

Felstead, A., Gaillie, M. and Green, F. (2002) *Work Skills in Britain 1986–2001* (Nottingham: DfES).

Finegold, D. and Soskice, D. (1988) 'The Failure of Training in Britain: Analysis and Prescription', *Oxford Review of Economic Policy*, 4:3, 21–53.

Geary, J. (1994) 'Task Participation: Employers' Participation Enabled or Constrained', in K. Sisson (ed.), *Personnel Management: A Comprehensive Guide to Theory and Practice in Britain* (Oxford: Basil Blackwell), 634–61.

Geary, J. (2003) 'New Forms of Work Organization: Still Limited, Still Controlled, but Still Welcome?', in P. Edwards (ed.), *Industrial Relations*, 2nd edn (Oxford: Basil Blackwell), 338–67.

Green, F. (2001) ' "It's Been a Hard Day's Night": The Concentration and Intensification of Work in Late Twentieth-century Britain', *British Journal of Industrial Relations*, 39:1, 53–80.

Guest, D. (2000) 'Piece by Piece', *People Management*, 6:15, 26–30.

Guest, D., King, Z., Cinway, N., Michie, J. and Sheehan-Quinn, M. (2001) *Voices from the Boardroom* (London: CIPD).

Gustavsen, B., Finnie, H. and Oscarrson, B. (2001) *Creating Connectedness: The Role of Social Research in Innovation Policy* (Amsterdam: John Benjamins).

Gustavsen, B., Hofmaier, B., Ekman-Phillips, M. and Wikman, A. (1996) *Concept-driven Development and the Organization of the Process of Change: An Evaluation of the Swedish Working Life Fund* (Amsterdam: John Benjamins).

Heller, F. (1998) 'Playing Devil's Advocate: Limits to Influence Sharing in Theory and Practice', in F. Heller, E. Pusic, G. Strauss and B. Wilpert (eds), *Organizational Participation: Myth and Reality* (Oxford University Press), 144–89.

HM Treasury (2002) *Developing Workforce Skills: Piloting a New Approach* (London: HM Treasury).

Hutton, W. (1995) *The State We're In* (London: Jonathan Cape).

Hutton, W. (2002) *The World We're In* (London: Little, Brown).

Hyman, R. (1995) 'The Historical Evolution of British Industrial Relations', in P. Edwards (ed.), *Industrial Relations: Theory and Practice in Britain* (Oxford: Basil Blackwell), 27–49.

Keep, E. (1999) 'UK's VET Policy and the "Third Way": Following a High Skills Trajectory or Running Up a Dead End Street?', *Journal of Education and Work*, 12:3, 323–46.

Keep, E. (2002) 'The English Vocational Education and Training Policy Debate – Fragile "Technologies" or Opening the "Black Box": Two Competing Visions of Where to Go Next, *Journal of Education and Work*, 15:4, 457–79.

Keep, E. and Mayhew, K. (1998) 'Was Ratner Right? Product Market and Competitive Strategies and Their Links With Skills and Knowledge', *EPI Economic Report*, 12:3, 1–14.

Keep, E. and Mayhew, K. (1999) 'The Assessment: Knowledge, Skills and Competitiveness', *Oxford Review of Economic Policy*, 15:1, 1–15.

Keep, E. and Mayhew, K. (2003) 'Skills in Their Workplace Context: Where Are We Going and Will This Take Us To Where We Want To Be?' Paper presented to the SKOPE Skills, Innovation and Performance Conference, Cumberland Lodge, Windsor Great Park, UK, 31 March–1 April.

Levin, M. (ed.) (2002a) *Researching Enterprise Development: Action Research on the Cooperation of Management and Labor* (Amsterdam: John Benjamins).

Levin, M. (2002b) 'Enhancing Innovations: A Core Issue of ED2000', in M. Levin (ed.), *Researching Enterprise Development: Action Research on the Cooperation between Management and Labour in Norway* (Amsterdam: John Benjamins), 207–22.

Lilja, K. (1998) 'Finland: Continuity and Modest Moves Towards Company-level Corporatism', in A. Ferner and R. Hyman (eds), *Changing Industrial Relations in Europe* (Oxford: Basil Blackwell), 171–89.

Lloyd, C. and Payne, J. (2000a) 'Developing a Political Economy of Skill', *Journal of Education and Work*, 15:4, 365–90.

Lloyd, C. and Payne, J. (2002b) 'On "the Political Economy of Skill": Assessing the Possibilities For a Viable High Skills Project in the UK', *New Political Economy*, 7:3, 367–95.

Lupton, T., Tanner, I. and Schnell, T. (1979) 'Manufacturing System Design in Europe', in C. Cooper and E. Mumford (eds), *The Quality of Working Life in Western and Eastern Europe* (London: Associated Business Press).

Marchington, M. and Grugulis, I. (2000) ' "Best Practice" Human Resource Management: Perfect Opportunity or Dangerous Illusion?', *International Journal of Human Resource Management*, 11:6, 1104–24.

Mikkelsen, L. N. (1997) 'The Norwegian R&D programme: Enterprise Development 2000: Building an Infrastructure for Improvement', in T. Alasoini, M. Kyllönen and A. Kasvio (eds), *Workplace Innovations: A Way of Promoting Competitiveness, Welfare and Employment* (Helsinki: Ministry of Labour), 72–90.

Payne, J. and Keep, E. (2003) 'Revisiting the Nordic Approaches to Work Reorganisation and Job Redesign: Lessons for UK Skills Policy', *Policy Studies*, 24:4, 205–25.

PIU (Performance and Innovation Unit) (2001) *In Demand: Adult Skills for the 21st Century* (London: Cabinet Office).

Proctor, S. and Mueller, F. (eds) (2000) *Teamworking* (London: Macmillan).

Qvale, T. U. (2002) 'A Case of Slow Learning? Recent Trends in Social Partnership in Norway with Particular Emphasis on Workplace Democracy', *Concepts and Transformation*, 7:1, 31–55.

Ramstad, E. (2001) *Kehittämisprojektien itsearviointi* (*Self-Assessment of Development Projects*) (Helsinki: Finnish Workplace Development Programme, Finnish Ministry of Labour).

RCN (Research Council of Norway) (1996) *Enterprise Development 2000: Conceptually Managed Productivity Development and Organizational Renewal in Working Life*, Programme Memorandum (Oslo: RCN).

Rissanen, P. and Arnkil, R. (2003) *Just in Time: Main Findings of the Effects of the Finnish Workplace Development Programme* (Helsinki: Finnish Workplace Development Programme, Finnish Ministry of Labour).

Terry, M. (1994) 'Workplace Unionism: Redefining Structures and Objectives', in R. Hyman and A. Ferner, *New Frontiers in European Industrial Relations* (Oxford: Basil Blackwell), 223–49.

Totterdill, P. (1999) *Britain's Advantage? Work Organization, Innovation and Employment*, (Mimeo, The UK Work Organization Network).

TUC (Trades Union Congress) (2001) 'They Call It Red Tape – Burnout Britain (London: TUC). Accessed to: http://www.tuc.org.uk/work_life/tuc-28260-f0.cfm?theme=redtape.

Warhurst, C. and Thompson, P. (1998) 'Hands, Hearts and Minds: Changing Work and Workers at the End of the Century', in P. Thompson and C. Warhurst (eds), *Workplaces of the Future* (London: Macmillan), 1–24.

West, M. and Patterson, M. (1997) *The Impact of People Management Practices on Business Performance* (London: Institute of Personnel Development).

Ylöstalo, P. (1999) 'Preconditions for Successful Workplace Development', in T. Alasoini and P. Halme (eds), Learning *Organizations, Learning Society* (Helsinki: Finnish Ministry of Labour), 140–51.

9
New Union Strategies and Forms of Work Organisation in UK Manufacturing

Andy Danford

Introduction

Since the end of the 1970s, trade union influence at work has declined significantly as a result of a range of political, economic and cultural factors. In the case of the UK, the industrial and political organisation of trade unions came under particularly severe attack from employers and politicians alike in the neo-liberal, Thatcherite period of 1979–97. In what Smith and Morton (1993) referred to as a process of 'decollectivization of industrial relations', unions suffered marginalisation in the face of the Conservative government's anti-union laws, state-sponsored attacks on militant worker organisation, and employer hostility through combinations of 'macho-management' and more subtle human resource management techniques. Many analysts have subsequently focused on the implications for union power of the loss of membership in this period, down from thirteen million in 1979 to just under seven million in 2003. Much of this work assesses the prospects for recruitment and retention in unionised sectors, in new firms and in new job territories, and therefore engages with certain quantitative dimensions of union power, such as levels of membership, its density and spread (see, for example, Heery *et al.* 2003; Waddington and Kerr 1999).

However, important as this work is, there is another dimension to the current problematical nature of union power that addresses directly the political economy of workplace relations. This more qualitative dimension relates to the extent to which labour organisation, and in particular workplace union organisation, is able to shape and influence events at the point of production. During the second half of the twentieth century the gradual development of a shop steward system of union regulation in many workplaces helped to establish local labour standards that set parameters for the nature of work organization and for the pace, content and quantity of work. For the workers themselves, these standards provided, and indeed can still provide, significant collective constraints against the arbitrary decisions of

166

supervisors and managers. They have a direct bearing on the quality of working life on the shop-floor and they continue to form the terrain of a frontier of control between workers' rights and managerial prerogatives.

The concept of local labour standards is associated most strongly with industrial relations in the USA's manufacturing sector. Here, work rules defining job content and the division of labour were often introduced by management to create a sense of fairness and to build employees' loyalty and commitment to the firm. During the post-Second World War economic boom, American unions in such sectors as autos and steel were able to mobilise their members in a series of militant campaigns that succeeded in converting management's 'work rules' into new sets of workers' rights. These included mutually-agreed seniority rights governing who could be selected for lay-off, promotion and job transfer, and the institutionalisation of trade union bargaining rights over such questions as job specifications, staffing levels and the speed of work (Tolliday and Zeitlin 1986; Lichtenstein 1988; Parker and Slaughter 1988). In the UK, a more informal regulatory system developed, characterised by the collective defence of 'custom and practice' rather than a set of specific shop-floor rules. The system required a more proactive shop steward organisation involved in continuous day-to-day negotiations with supervisors and line managers. The effect was similar to the American experience in that workers came to expect a sense of dignity, autonomy and fair treatment at work, based on the maintenance of labour standards and underpinned by trade union participation in work organisation.

In this chapter, trade union participation is analysed critically by operationalising union power as an index of workers' ability to mobilise collective resources to secure an acceptable degree of control and autonomy at work. In taking this approach we effectively transcend what has become a false dualism between industrial relations and the labour process. This requires the analysis of trade union behaviour at work within the terms of structural antagonisms in the capitalist employment relationship and the indeterminacy of labour, and it involves an examination of the connections between forms of work organisation, worker interests and trade union strategy.

In many respects, such an analytical approach becomes more compelling in the context of the post-1997 politico-economic conditions in the UK. Since the first New Labour government came to power in 1997 there has been a shift away from state hostility to collective union organisation *per se* towards encouraging a form of trade unionism that adopts co-operative relationships with employers. This has become known as New Labour's 'industrial relations settlement' (Undy 1999). It comprises modest legislative support for union recognition, new sets of individual workers' rights, such as the national minimum wage, and the promotion of workplace partnerships involving more extensive information and consultation rights for both unions and their members. At the same time, public policy debates on the competitiveness of British firms and the economy have been emphasising positive links between the development of high performance work organisation and the adoption of partnership practices (DTI 2002; TUC 2002). As a result, managerial demands for higher labour productivity through the new management techniques of the high-performance workplace are increasingly likely to be accompanied by attempts at injecting a new 'social cohesion' into the employment relationship, and to reverse the traditions of opposition in bargaining relations with trade unions.

This chapter will argue that these shifts in state and employer policies have profound implications for the maintenance of labour standards and autonomous job control at work, and for independent, oppositional forms of workplace unionism. By the use of case study evidence in high-performance manufacturing settings it will also contend, however, that innovations in independent union activity, rather than partnership strategies, contain the greater potential for a renewal of union organisation and influence at work. The chapter first considers both the meaning and growth of labour standards and job controls in post-war British manufacturing industry and the politico-economic factors that placed new limits on this during the 1980s and 1990s. It then analyses critically the role of workplace unions in the restructured high-performance workplace and assesses current debates on workplace partnership. This is followed by multiple case study evidence of union strategies and high-performance work practices in the aerospace sector.

The Traditions of Job Control

The organisational strength of workplace unionism in British manufacturing derives primarily from the development of the shop steward system. Although this has a long history in British industrial relations it only became the prime means of local representation of worker interests, and of mediation between worker and supervisor, two decades after the Second World War. During the 1960s and 1970s in particular, the limited achievements of national union bargainers, embodied in national agreements that served only to set a basis of minimum standards of pay and conditions, meant that pressures were placed on union representatives at the workplace level to negotiate improved local terms and conditions. These pressures became particularly acute in the wider environmental conditions of economic stability, full employment, and growth in product markets, which in turn fuelled a new worker confidence and demands for more advantageous settlements. In addition, many manufacturing employers came to see plant-level bargaining as the appropriate method for gaining acceptance of new working methods, job evaluation and new technology (Terry 1995). This view was given further institutional support by the findings of the Labour Government's Donovan Commission in 1968.

Partly as a result of these processes, the system of shop steward representation spread throughout manufacturing industry. By 1980, 85 per cent of private manufacturing firms and virtually 100 per cent of larger firms with recognised unions had on-site union representatives (Millward *et al.* 2000). Economic growth, a decentralisation of industrial relations and new local management agendas had combined to ensure that, as Terry put it, 'shop stewards had become in many ways the pivotal figures of British trade unionism' (1995: 206). The salience of rank-and-file unionism can also be attributed to the imperatives of post-war mass production. New consumer demands and the rationalisation of management (involving production techniques that aimed to increase managerial control and intensify the exploitation of labour) materialised as a series of challenges to the quality of life on the production line. Prominent here were increasing workloads, speeding up the line, pressures on staffing levels, and new managerial prerogatives over task flexibility and working time. In this context, the new shop stewards were not merely additional agents or mediators in a more fragmented and localised system of collective bargaining. Instead, in those workplaces where union organisation was sufficiently strong, shop stewards became the leading agents of local solidarities aimed at countering managerial control and asserting autonomous worker control (Hyman 1975). One classic study of this autonomous control is provided by Beynon's (1984) analysis of rank-and-file unionism at Ford's Halewood auto plant. Beynon's study reminds us that while everyday struggles over the minutiae of job timings, staffing ratios, work allocation and overtime might, to some observers, appear mundane and inconsequential, for the workers and shop stewards who are subject to these processes they constitute focal points of a major struggle for a degree of job control. When workers won these struggles they established 'the basis for a say in the way their lives were to be regulated while they were in the plant' (Beynon 1984: 141).

The extent to which workplace unions secured a significant degree of autonomous control prior to the new conditions of the 1980s is a matter of debate. In well-organised workplaces, many shop stewards succeeded in maintaining a good deal of influence, if not control, over decisions affecting local pay systems, skill demarcations, informal seniority rights, job timings, overtime and shift allocation. But in the weakest of the organised plants, as Hyman (1975: 153) has noted, none of this occurred. Moreover, in some of the core sites of union struggle, such as autos, the penetration of union job control was partly contingent on the magnitude of employer hostility (Tolliday and Zeitlin 1986). Nevertheless, the overall pattern was one of organised constraint against the excesses of management control and the development of labour standards, often informal and local, that set parameters for the conditions in which workers laboured on the production lines of private capitalist firms (Stewart *et al.* 2004).

Many writers have emphasised the limits, and indeed the work-based inequalities, caused by the inherent 'sectionalism' of this shop steward system. A custom of informal accountability between a shop steward and his/her local work group, where the prime concern is to defend the interests of the immediate worker constituency, meant that class solidarity could often be undermined by rivalries and demarcations that were a corollary of a capitalist division of labour (Lane 1974; Tolliday and Zeitlin 1986). Moreover, it has been argued that this sectionalism contributed to a 'narrowness of vision', a 'lack of strategic vision' and a union approach to work organization and control that was largely reactive, defensive and unfocused (Thompson and Wallace 1994: 58; Terry 1995: 208). These arguments contain many truths. However, with the benefit of hindsight and in the contemporary context of relative union weakness, a lack of independent 'employee voice' at work, and increasingly unconstrained managerial prerogatives, the profoundly democratic nature of the shop steward form of union organization retains much appeal. The proximity of the steward to the membership, the ensuing mutual bonds of trust, and the possibility that workers could have their views presented to management without distortion are all important facets of this. Together they still provide the potential for a more powerful challenge from below compared to the current prospects offered by workplace partnership.

The means by which workplace unions and their members were able to assert autonomous control came under sustained attack during the 1970s, and more intensively so in the last two decades of the twentieth century. For many British manufacturing firms this was the era of the ideologies and management practice of the new workplace flexibility: 'Japanisation', 'flexible specialisation' and 'total quality management'. What united these changes was not the attraction of 'worker empowerment', because for most workforces this proved elusive. Instead, this period was marked by a return to the central capitalist problematic of labour control and the closer management of time (Tomaney 1990: 51). For many employers, the development of rank-and-file unionism, autonomous control and protective labour standards constituted key constraints against their attempts to overcome a growing productivity crisis. As Tomaney argues, the source of this crisis lay not in the limits of Fordist–Taylorist forms of work organisation but rather in the ability of workplace unions to exploit the management-defined demarcations and fragmented work processes of the mass production assembly line. In order to raise the rate of capital utilisation, employers were determined to reintegrate work tasks through new task flexibility measures, and these same measures would raise rates of labour exploitation through an inevitable intensification of work. As a result, the 1980s and 1990s saw sustained employer attacks on the local labour standards that had developed in many traditional manufacturing sectors, such as aerospace, autos and shipbuilding. These attacks were fully supported and partly facilitated by the interventions of neo-liberal Thatcherite governments. Eventually, this assault on workers' rights and protective custom and practice crystallised in the more coherent form of the lean production factory regime (Stewart *et al.* 2004). It is to union influence on work organisation under this regime, and its latest derivative, the high-performance workplace, that we now turn.

The High-performance Workplace and Partnership: Union Marginalisation?

In the context of British industry's labour productivity performance, much academic and public policy discourse is currently promoting the use of high-performance work systems (HPWS) as the 'high road' option to competitive advantage (DTI 2002; Michie and Sheehan 2002). At the conceptual core of HPWS is the notion of a more systematic mobilisation of tacit knowledge and worker discretion through managerial practices that permit workers to participate in decisions that affect their organisational routines. In the interests of organisational flexibility and efficiency, workers are assumed to experience more autonomy over job tasks and working methods, and to enjoy a greater input into managerial decision-making processes through extensive systems of organisational communications. Examples of HPWS practices that are considered to provide such employee involvement are self-managed teams, different types of problem-solving groups, two-way communications, and stronger representation and consultation rights. Although these techniques are not new, advocates of HPWS argue that, when used together in coherent 'clusters' or 'bundles', they enhance organisational performance as well as providing a new emphasis on 'mutuality' and 'social cohesion' in the employment relationship (Appelbaum *et al.* 2000; J. Bélanger *et al.* 2002). It is this new emphasis that is intended to mark them out from the more tightly controlled Japanese-style lean production systems. That is, in return for the prospect of a better quality of working life and greater job security, workers and their unions may be expected to become more committed and more loyal to their employers; in essence, forming a workplace partnership.

The role for trade unions in the high-performance workplace is somewhat ambiguous. There is a burgeoning amount of explicitly managerialist literature from North America which argues that trade unions have much to gain – and little to lose – from co-operative engagement with the new management agendas. For example, the idea of trade union involvement with the design of HPWS and wider participation in a firm's strategic planning has been advanced in facile terms as a route to bridging opposing sets of interests between employers and their workers and unions. Leaving aside the complication of management resistance, it is assumed here that if unions take a lead in ensuring that new participative forms of work organisation are sustained, then this approach is more likely to lead to outcomes that meet the requirements of both the employers and their workforces (Kochan and Osterman 1994; Appelbaum *et al.* 2000; Frost 2001).

The implications of this approach are spelt out more candidly by P. R. Bélanger *et al.* (2002). These authors argue that trade unions in the high-performance workplace have little option but to adopt a position that involves 'exchanging' employee involvement for the acquisition of new partnership rights (P. R. Bélanger *et al.* 2002: 161). To put this more bluntly, in return for greater input into managerial decision-making, the union is expected to support line management prerogatives and to abandon its opposition to direct employee communications and employee involvement. This position is embodied in an emerging model of union participation in management:

1. a significant weakening of those work rules that constrain managerial prerogatives and provide some protection for workers.
2. the organization of work and the economic and financial management of the firm become the principal goals of co-operative workplace bargaining.
3. labour–management relations shift towards co-operation and continuous problem-solving around integrative issues.
4. union participation in joint committees and the substitution of a strict division of roles and responsibilities by power-sharing means that unions become concerned with a firm's economic performance and both workers and unions come to perform duties that used to belong exclusively to management. (P. R. Bélanger *et al.* 2002: 162)

Such a model of partnership has stark implications for the British shop steward system and trade union attempts to maintain a degree of autonomous worker control. Perhaps the key question for those at the point of production becomes: does partnership present new spaces for worker resistance, or does it instead move the 'frontier of control' much closer to management? Terry's (2002) updated account of the state of shop steward activism in the UK postulates the latter. The current hegemonic control of management in manufacturing characterised by its ability to transfer and relocate production rapidly and to impose unilateral control over work organisation has removed the base upon which independent workplace unionism prospered. For many shop stewards who organise workers on the assembly lines of the new high-performance work regimes, acts of opposition are likely to be met by the withdrawal of management support for union organisation itself. At the same time, the pragmatic pressures for co-operation with managerial initiatives can seem overwhelming (Terry 2002: 270).

Terry is not alone in offering a pessimistic prognosis for the traditions of independent workplace unionism. For example, Bacon *et al.*'s (1996) account of trade union strategy in the British steel industry argues that conventional shop-floor union organisation is an increasingly ineffective model of worker influence. In the context of privatisation, steel plant closures and local work restructuring, the practice of national-level union participation has disappeared, while workplace-based trade unionism has become characterised by relative weakness, fragmentation and accommodation to management demands. For these authors, the corollary of this is that if the frontier of control has moved so decisively towards management, then trade unions need to adopt new partnership strategies based on the promotion of individual worker rights and co-operative union participation in work redesign. Similarly, Bacon and Storey (1996) have argued that a combination of individualistic management practices (for example, non-standard employment contracts, individualised pay, and direct communications) and new forms of collectivism (for example, teamworking and group-based employee involvement schemes) together threaten to undermine the collective basis of workplace unionism. New trade union strategies seeking employees' dual commitment to the company and the union, and based on a social relationship of co-operation with management constitute the only realistic option in these contexts.

There is a developing body of work in the UK that seeks to provide a theoretical underpinning to such partnership strategies. This neo-pluralist literature advances a combination of material and ethical concerns to explicate the idea of union co-operation. For example, Ackers (2002) contends that a new ethical foundation for the normative institutions and practices of social partnership will strengthen trade union participation at work, in civil society and the state. Rejecting Marxist concepts of exploitative class relations and struggle, we are presented with an alternative of potential social cohesion through trade union participation in management agendas. Or, we could put this another way, the traditions of autonomous control on the shop-floor would be replaced by a new ethic of worker accommodation.

These advocates for trade union participation in HPWS and partnership practices highlight important shifts in the material basis of rank-and-file workplace unionism and they certainly reflect much of the current 'Third Way' public policy discourse on work relations. However, the problem with the 'mutual gain' argument is that its assessment of progressive management practice is excessively speculative and it offers very little concrete analysis of the real politics of production. As a result, high-performance work systems, and those who labour under them, are effectively abstracted from the labour process itself. If, instead, we locate trade union attempts to defend worker interests in the context of contemporary capital accumulation strategies we may find a dwindling number of issues upon which unions and managers can co-operate, and an expanding number about which they differ. And these differences may be fundamental. For although nobody is denying that workers and their union representatives may often display both a commitment to organizational success and a desire to participate in work decisions (for some evidence of this, see Martínez Lucio and Stuart 2002) these co-operative attitudes may well be negated by the underlying exploitative conditions of the high-performance workplace.

To assess the implications of this for trade union strategy at work it is better to consider exactly what employers really expect of their workers and their workplace representatives in the new conditions. In one of the most widely-quoted papers of the partnership debate, Taylor and Ramsay (1998) argued that the new management discourse, whether categorised as 'soft' HRM or partnership, may seek to capture employee commitment and to marginalize union influence while maintaining a semblance of normal bargaining relations. It may also seek a shift in rank-and-file activity in that union representatives may be manoeuvred into 'policing management-led changes rather than protecting members from them' (Taylor and Ramsay 1998: 127). Writing in a similar vein, and adopting a Critical Social Relations framework, Stewart et al.'s (2004) international studies of quality of working life under lean production in the auto industry also reject assumptions of worker and union empowerment. Instead, they offer a framework that views lean production as a systemic attempt to weaken independent trade unionism and to secure a new cultural control in the workplace. Cultural control is defined as 'the creation of a workplace which is framed around management's own corporate agenda of productivity and quality whereby collective rights are seen as subordinate to those of the corporation' (Stewart et al. 2004: 263). For many workers, the outcome of this process has been an intensification of work, an extension of working hours and the loss of collective counter-controls over managerial actions. Looked at in this way, lean production (and its HPWS derivative) constitutes a continuation and refinement of the 1970–1980s employer offensives against rank-and-file trade unionism and associated protective labour standards. The key strategic issue for trade unions is that if they respond to this challenge by seeking some influence, perhaps damage limitation, through engagement with partnership, then they may find themselves cut adrift from the collective foundation of their *raison d'être*. In other words, shop stewards may become isolated and distanced from their rank-and-file base, they may be deprived of the job control mechanisms that protect shop-floor worker interests, and their partnership agreements may in reality grant management a new latitude to determine changes in work practices and organisation (Taylor and Ramsay 1998; Whitston et al. 1999; Danford et al. 2002).

All this does not mean to say that the appropriate alternative union strategy is always to adopt a traditional form of opposition. The more fragmentary collective base of the new forms of work organisation and the normative power of 'soft' human resource management have shifted the material and ideological terrain of workplace industrial relations a little too much for outright opposition to be effective in all cases. Moreover, in the current politico-economic conditions, where class struggle from above continues to be more prominent than class struggle from below, the more rudimentary forms of union resistance rarely enjoy impunity from the employer. In these circumstances, trade union activists may be forced to participate in the new management agendas, but to do so from an independent position. This independence would require broadening the scope of free collective bargaining. It would also warrant an awareness of the insidious process of incorporation through the institutional practices of partnership. Therefore, such a strategy would not mean that shop stewards had to submit to change, or embrace change, but instead, as one senior trade union official has argued, stewards must critically engage with HRM and such HPWS practices as teamworking and continuous improvement (Fisher 1997).

There is a growing number of case studies of workplace union behaviour that provide evidence to counter the pessimism of inevitable union weakness under HPWS and partnership: or indeed, of the necessity of an ethics of accommodation. These studies suggest that a new, creative form of opposition can be developed. For example, Stewart and Wass's (1998) analysis of workplace union responses to the implementation of high-performance management techniques at Rover and Vauxhall auto plants revealed how union activists can often contest and redirect management objectives by reinterpreting the partnership postures of their national unions. By eschewing 'embrace and change' and, instead, engaging critically with the management techniques, new sets of member concerns were brought within the scope of the shop-floor unions' collective bargaining agendas. The Rover and Vauxhall shop stewards were able to broaden their influence over such issues as absence control, labour mobility and the role of the teamleader. In the case of the Vauxhall plant, this influence extended to monitoring and controlling any aspect of the labour process addressed by management's direct communications strategies. Therefore, while in both companies management succeeded in introducing technical reconfigurations to the labour process (in terms of the reorganisation of machinery and labour) they were prevented from securing their new labour control agendas. A further example of this is provided by Martínez Lucio *et al.*'s (2000) study of the introduction of teamworking and TQM at Royal Mail. A similar pattern of dissonance between nation union policy and shop steward concerns is presented. Despite the acquiescence of the national Communication Workers Union (CWU) to management change programmes during the 1990s, the local representatives of Royal Mail workers were able to mobilise opposition to work restructuring. This opposition was not a question of knee-jerk rejection of the 'ethics' of partnership but instead something more significant than this, a reflection of the negative impact of HPWS practices on the material interests of shop-floor workers. As Martínez Lucio *et al.* (2000: 275) argue, it is quite invalid to abstract team work and similar practices from the organisational and political context. In the case of Royal Mail, team working threatened to fragment worker representation and solidarity; it reduced the range of skills of teamworkers; it had detrimental effects on work rates and health and safety; it raised the prospects of redundancies; it threatened the traditions of worker deployment by seniority; and it sought to develop new competitive market relations between workers. In these conditions, and the wider political context of deep distrust of management motives, CWU activists were able to mount considerable opposition to team working, and to construct different forms of shop steward autonomy by establishing new networks and forums of rank-and-file activity.

These case studies (for further examples of similar processes, see Newsome 2000; Danford *et al.* 2003) emphasise that sophisticated forms of trade union opposition to HPWS and partnership cannot only be successful but can also raise the prospects for trade union renewal, a grass roots renewal, around the issue of new work organisation. It is to this issue that we now turn.

New Work Organisation and the Prospects for Trade Union Renewal

The term 'trade union renewal' encompasses changes in both the role and interrelations of the state, union officials, lay representatives and union members (Gall 2003: 3). As a thesis of potential union revitalization in the public sector it is most closely associated with the work of Fairbrother (1996; 2000). Essentially, the argument is that structural changes in public-sector management and work organisation may in turn catalyse structural and ideological shifts in the public-sector unions. A combination of centralised decision-making (involving the setting of new financial controls and targets) and devolved management at the local workplace level is bringing about a de-standardisation of employment conditions and a potential degradation of employees' quality of working life. If union activists can exploit these changes they may provide the conditions for the emergence of a new form of participative unionism. By this is meant a process of rank-and-file democratisation that strengthens the active involvement of members in union organising, collective bargaining and union policy formation. It also weakens the traditions of bureaucratic control and centralised bargaining by professional union officers. Some writers have objected to this argument on the basis that an excessive emphasis on local rank-and-file participation may lead to problems of sectionalism and organisational fragmentation. These objections are not quite sustainable, however, since Fairbrother's thesis does not demand the outright substitution of 'bottom-up' for 'top-down' but instead the establishment of a more dynamic two-way democratic process (2000: 29). Nevertheless, his conceptualization of union renewal is at times problematic in its excessive focus on the public sector, its virtual exclusion of trade unions in the manufacturing sector, and the latter on the basis of an assumption that the manufacturing unions are locked into strategies of reactivity and survival rather than proactivity and organisational renewal (Fairbrother 2000: 315, 327).

An alternative approach that adapts the union renewal thesis to structural changes in the management of work across industrial sectors is provided by Danford *et al.* (2003). This research analysed workplace union responses to the restructuring of work and work relations in aerospace, manufacturing, insurance, private utilities and the public sector. It uncovered contrasting patterns of union renewal in some contexts and severe organisational weakness in others, irrespective of sector. Danford *et al.* (2003) adopted the precepts of Kelly's (1998) mobilisation theory in an attempt to identify the material workplace conditions that engendered new patterns of worker discontent, and the factors that contributed to successful – or unsuccessful – union attempts to collectivise these discontents. While their research did not operationalise directly worker consciousness, or any of the many processes that shape the formation of worker interests, it did provide evidence of a significant relationship between work restructuring, the depth of worker discontent and union influence. In contrast to those who have argued that employers adopt new management techniques to counteract the spread of unionism (see Gallie *et al.* 1998), Danford *et al.* (2003) showed the opposite relationship. That is, where the mass of HPWS and HRM techniques is greater in workplaces then there is a likelihood that worker grievances will increase and a tendency for the scope of union bargaining (and influence) to expand accordingly. In other words, the new management techniques can provide conditions for union renewal rather than decline.

Danford *et al.* (2003) found that in the aerospace and manufacturing sectors especially, workplace unions had not been inactive in the face of significant work reorganisation. Neither had they turned away from the rising incidence of worker discontent to embrace partnership. Instead, a good number of unions had maintained their influence by consciously *adapting* their traditional forms of independent union organisation to the new conditions of the high-performance workplace. Three short case studies of this *process* of organisational renewal in a traditional but dynamic manufacturing sector will now be presented.

Case Studies of Work Restructuring and Union Response in the Aerospace Sector

The three case studies are of design and assembly plants owned by UK-based multinational firms. AircraftCo manufactures airframe assemblies; EngineCo manufactures jet engines; and AvionicsCo manufactures flight control systems and instrumentation. The analysis presented here is of the shop-floor union organising activity of primarily AEEU (now AMICUS-AEEU) and TGWU shop stewards. Each case study factory employed large numbers of production workers and technical staff, the average size being 3,700 employees. Trade union membership densities for the two unions were close to 100 per cent. Interviews were carried out with shop stewards, senior stewards and personnel managers at each factory during 1999–2000.

The British aerospace industry has been subject to immense restructuring since the late 1980s as a result of state deregulation, changes in civil and defence markets, and an intensification of global competition. The impact of this restructuring on work organisation and its regulation has taken the form of widespread labour rationalisation, a decentralisation of management into business units, the introduction of such HPWS techniques as teamworking and *kaizen*, and attempts to adopt workplace partnership relationships. The three case study plants were affected by these changes to varying degrees. All three had seen significant reductions to their shop-floor workforces over this period; two plants were divided into a complex of smaller business units; team working was introduced at all three plants; and a partnership agreement was reached at one plant (AircraftCo), while the management at the remaining two plants made recurrent overtures to their shop-floor unions to adopt partnership practices.

The first notable feature of each workplace union was the extent of organisational recovery following steward victimisation during a peak redundancy period between 1990 and 1995. In all three plants, the shop-floor workforce was reduced by 50 per cent over this period, whereby 75 per cent of EngineCo shop stewards, 90 per cent of AvionicsCo stewards and all the AircraftCo stewards lost their jobs. And yet, by the end of the 1990s, sufficient numbers of new shop stewards had been recruited to bring member-representative ratios up to the same level as the pre-redundancy period (around 35:1). The process by which this recovery was achieved consisted of a combination of tapping the shoulders of individuals with potential leadership skills and depending on volunteers to emerge. But the reason why individuals plucked up the courage to come forward lay in the resilience of a strong collective consciousness on the shop-floor. This consciousness was of a type that frequently is ignored by those who argue that the employment relationship has become irrevocably fragmented and individualised by the new employment conditions. One manager at EngineCo reflected somewhat ruefully on this:

> You also have to remember that it's a collective out there, the shopfloor is a collective unit, they think in the same way and they believe that if the company won't treat them as real individuals then they would prefer to remain as a collective. They know they have tremendous power against the company, as a collective the company can't do anything without their consent.

An example of how rank-and-file activism drew on this collective consciousness and the bonds of respect that often exist between workers and their elected shop stewards was provided by AvionicsCo. At this plant, a series of redundancies had reduced the number of recognized stewards from thirty-eight to just three. When the management then decided to take advantage of a further redundancy by sacking the plant's long-standing AEEU union convenor the two remaining shop stewards responded to this victimisation by ignoring the threat to their own positions and organising unofficial overtime bans, go-slows and non-cooperation. These actions proved successful in the context of the vulnerability of lean, HPWS work organisation. The management was forced to back down and reappoint the dismissed convenor, whose description of this incident is instructive:

> I was the first works convenor in this country to get reinstated. It was because that workforce wanted me back. That was the happiest day of my life. I walked in that canteen and they clapped me in. That's what you call respect. That's what I've always said to this company, you'll never be able to touch me because this workforce won't let you. It was brilliant, it really was. £56,000 they offered me to go and I wouldn't go on principle. I'd sooner have got put out by them because I was no good.

The second feature of union activity was a refusal to remain static in the face of work restructuring and new production techniques. The fragmentation of both a cohesive factory organisation into a plethora of business units (at AircraftCo and EngineCo) and of manufacturing functions into matrices and production cells (at all three plants) constituted the main threat to the traditions of autonomous job control on the shop-floor. The creation of multiple profit centres at AircraftCo and EngineCo was aimed at establishing a more flexible, market-responsive factory organisation with ostensibly more autonomous unit managers made more accountable for cost control and unit performance. The implications for industrial relations were that previously site-wide employment conditions could be dismantled in favour of divergent unit-based conditions. For the shop-floor unions, this violated the guiding principle of equal employment rights and conditions for all workers irrespective of their location in the factory. The introduction of team working involved further organisational fragmentation. In all three plants, the conversion of function-based manufacturing areas into a series of smaller, multi-functional cells responsible for specific product families and sub-assemblies threatened the organisational base of the shop-floor unions. The use of cellular team working to introduce new multi-tasking practices and the devolvement of some managerial responsibilities to teamleaders could undermine shop steward control over such issues as staffing levels, skill deployment and the fair allocation of overtime and shift work. Thus, the decentralisation and fragmentation of the management of work organisation threatened not just shop steward influence but also the unifying and egalitarian ethos that underpinned the maintenance of site-wide labour standards.

The response of the workplace unions to these new challenges could be characterised as critical engagement by 'exploiting partnership' at AircraftCo, and critical engagement by 'strategic opposition' at EngineCo and AvionicsCo. The shop stewards at AircraftCo had signed a partnership agreement with management in 1996. This agreement sanctioned shop steward membership of new project management teams and steering groups empowered to implement work reforms such as cellular working, just-in-time and workflow. The stewards' approach to this activity was first to educate themselves on the possibilities and dangers of the new management techniques, and then to use their influence and organisation to frustrate those initiatives that were deemed to be harmful to their members' interests. One senior steward described this:

> We went on one of the first AEEU workplace change courses at Esher college. They were chatting to us about Japanisation, globalisation, all this sort of stuff. They gave us a lot of good information, but what we found is that we've done most of it. Team Leaders, TQM, Quality Circles, Brainstorming, Action Planning Teams. You name it, AircraftCo must read the DTI/CBI casebook and hang the lot out here. We were well prepared for all of it. Instead of approaching it with outright opposition we would set up things like pilot schemes, see how they went. Put our own terms of reference around them. If it didn't work we would stop them more or less. But most of the time because we were well involved with it we said 'Look; we don't want to stand in the way of change, but it should be controlled change.'

The AircraftCo senior stewards maintained control over these changes by strengthening the lines of accountability between shop stewards and the plant's Joint Shop Stewards' Committee (JSSC), and by placing new union controls over the management's direct communications policies. All stewards who attended the project management teams had to report proposed changes to the JSSC to highlight any issues that should be subject to collective bargaining. The threat to union influence by way of teamleaders' prerogatives and direct communications was curtailed in three ways. First, by removing the teamleaders' disciplinary powers. Second, by gaining recognition rights for teamleaders and thus ensuring that their role became subject to union regulation. And third, by securing an agreement that allowed shop steward influence over management communications by giving the stewards rights to attendance at all communications meetings between managers and teamleaders, and at all team briefings. The stewards also secured the right to monitor the content of communications cascades. In achieving this, the stewards succeeded in appropriating management's own partnership discourse to ensure that the shop-floor unions did not become marginalised by the changes. The frontier of control had been extended to the battle for the hearts and minds of factory workers, and on management's communications terrain. The senior steward commented:

> We were worried about the employee communications, we saw the shop stewards as a key communicator. We were using jargon back to the company at the time that we saw stewards as key communicators and you needed that relationship between the team leader, manager and steward. By circumventing the steward you were going to damage that relationship and become reactive. If the steward was part of the team it would be more proactive.

The strategy adopted by the unions at EngineCo and AvionicsCo was far more oppositional to partnership, though this did not mean that the union activists relied totally on traditional forms of rank and file organisation. Unlike their counterparts at AircraftCo, the stewards felt that the risk of incorporation through partnership was too great to warrant experimental engagement with management teams. It was believed that partnership relationships inevitably induced a distancing of the steward from the membership. A senior steward at EngineCo put it like this:

> I think the result of partnership would be that people would fail to come to you and worst of all, would see the union as a sop to the management. And that would have an effect on recruitment, retention of membership and the aspirations of the membership . . . That's the biggest danger of all, to my mind. Becoming isolated from the membership and being seen as an unpaid manager and part of the management team rather than representing the membership and the views of the membership. I think it's important that we divide the two.

In this quite different relational context, the shop stewards at both plants accepted the inevitability of the use of such HPWS practices as cellular working – they did not have the power to do otherwise – but they did succeed in placing significant constraints on the imposition of managerial prerogatives. They also succeeded in maintaining site-wide regulation of employment conditions and labour standards. As with the workplace union at AircraftCo, this strategy involved adapting the conventional lines of steward accountability to the new conditions of decentralised management. The traditional work-group-based model of steward representation was altered so that steward accountability to a site union executive took precedence over steward accountability to the local work group. This meant that the freedom of action of line managers and cell leaders was restricted by placing new limits on local steward autonomy, and imposing much stricter lines of accountability between the local stewards and the site union executive of senior stewards. A senior steward at AvionicsCo described the outcome of this:

> So yes, we've maintained accountability between the manager, the shop steward and the site executive of the union. We still control it 100 per cent. They can't do anything, they can't move labour without our permission, they can't work extra overtime without our permission. We're in charge. It's a good job here.

Therefore, although the local shop steward's autonomy was reduced, the tradition of autonomous job control was maintained, and in many ways enhanced, by the new lines of accountability. Moreover, at all three plants, local labour standards were also protected by regular use of unofficial actions. For example, although rarely reported by media commentators or by strike data, the use of the unofficial overtime ban, variously referred to as 'morris dancing', 'going shopping' and 'going fishing', was a common response to the arbitrary decisions of teamleaders and line managers. Overall, a combination of union innovation, adaptation and traditional forms of opposition had ensured union resilience and, indeed, renewal in these restructured, 'high-performance' manufacturing plants.

Conclusions

The new management agendas in manufacturing industry seek to increase labour productivity through the use of high-performance work practices and the adoption of co-operative partnership relationships with trade unions. These agendas have called into question the traditions of autonomous job control, the maintenance of local labour standards at work and the future of independent forms of workplace unionism. A key question posed earlier in this chapter was whether the practices of HPWS and partnership open up new spaces and issues for worker mobilisation and collective resistance, or whether these changes inevitably move the frontier of control ever closer to management. The dominant view in the media, in political circles, and increasingly in academia, is that trade unions have little choice but to adopt more co-operative relationships with employers in order to secure at least some limited influence and regulation over new forms of work organisation and the employment relationship. This is the soft, New Labour variant of the Thatcherite 'there is no alternative'. However, this chapter has argued that there *is* an alternative to the 'ethic of worker accommodation'. Much case study research has exposed the reality of lean production and the high-performance workplace in terms of an intensification of labour, a deterioration in the quality of working life and an attempt to substitute managerial cultural control for an autonomous worker control. In this context, if trade unions adopt a partnership strategy in order to retain a vestige of influence then their activists may well become distanced from the rank and file, and disempowered by the loss of traditional job control practices. Both a qualitative and quantitative decline in union power may result, through loss of workplace control and loss of membership. The new 'partnership trade union' may indeed become a hollow shell. The alternative for trade unions is one of organizational renewal based on critical engagement with the new partnership agendas. The case studies presented in this chapter have shown how this is possible when local union activists exploit the new spaces created by management's partnership agendas to carve out independent, and where necessary, oppositional, stances. They also show how existing forms of rank and file democracy can be adapted to meet the challenges of the decentralised workplace.

Finally, it is interesting to note that, in the context of the critiques of the inherent plant-based sectionalism of this form of independent workplace unionism, a good number of the shop stewards in the three aerospace case studies were highly critical of the national AEEU's decision to dismantle district committees and branches during the 1990s. These forums were regarded as essential means of spreading rank-and-file union innovations to new workplaces. As one shop steward put it, 'we were able to cross-fertilise ideas, we were up to date on everything that was happening in the area. But the AEEU has abolished all of that'. In 2002, Derek Simpson was elected as the new General Secretary of AMICUS-AEEU. He was elected on a platform of handing control of the union back to the rank and file. At a local meeting with the shop stewards of the companies discussed in these case studies at the end of 2002, Derek Simpson's first pledge was to reintroduce district committees and new activists' networks once the gradually changing balance of power at the union's executive level allowed this (fieldwork notes). One year later, left-wing candidates came within a couple of seats of becoming the majority group on a traditionally right-wing executive. This example is one of many of the currently shifting sands of union politics. It should serve to remind us that prescriptive models of workplace union behaviour and national union identity often obscure as much as they explain, not least the potential for radical change in the politics of union relations. New union strategies at the workplace level and political changes at the national level suggest that there is an alternative to the blind alley of accommodation to the employers' work organisational agendas.

References

Ackers, P. (2002) 'Reframing Employment Relations: The Case for Neo-pluralism', *Industrial Relations Journal*, 33:1, 2–19.

Appelbaum, E., Bailey, T., Berg, P. and Kalleberg, A. L. (2000) *Manufacturing Advantage: Why High Performance Work Systems Pay Off* (Ithaca, NY: Cornell University Press).

Bacon, N. and Storey, J. (1996) 'Individualism and Collectivism and the Changing Role of Trade Unions', in P. Ackers, C. Smith and P. Smith (eds), *The New Workplace and Trade Unionism* (London: Routledge).

Bacon, N., Blyton, P. and Morris, J. (1996) 'Among the Ashes: Trade Union Strategies in the UK and German Steel Industries', *British Journal of Industrial Relations*, 34:1, 25–50.

Bélanger, J., Giles, A. and Murray, G. (2002) 'Towards a New Production Model: Potentialities, Tensions and Contradictions', in G. Murray, J. Belanger, A. Giles and P. A. Lapointe (eds), *Work and Employment Relations in the High-Performance Workplace* (London/New York: Continuum).

Bélanger, P. R., Lapointe, P. A. and Lévesque, B. (2002) 'Workplace Innovation and the Role of Institutions', in G. Murray, J. Belanger, A. Giles and P. A. Lapointe (eds), *Work and Employment Relations in the High-Performance Workplace*, (London/New York: Continuum).

Beynon, H. (1984) *Working for Ford*, 2nd edn (Harmondsworth: Penguin).

Danford, A., Richardson, M. and Upchurch, M. (2002) ' "New Unionism", Organising and Partnership: A Comparative Analysis of Union Renewal Strategies in the Public Sector', *Capital and Class*, 76, 1–27.

Danford, A., Richardson, M. and Upchurch, M. (2003) *New Unions, New Workplaces. A Study of Union Resilience in the Restructured Workplace* (London: Routledge).

DTI (Department of Trade and Industry) (2002) *High Performance Workplaces. The Role of Employee Involvement in a Modern Economy*, Discussion paper, July.

Fairbrother, P. (1996) 'Workplace Trade Unionism in the State Sector', in P. Ackers, C. Smith, and P. Smith (eds), *The New Workplace and Trade Unionism* (London: Routledge).

Fairbrother, P. (2000) *Trade Unions at the Crossroads* (London: Mansell).

Fisher, J. (1997) 'The Challenge of Change: The Positive Agenda of the TGWU', *The International Journal of Human Resource Management*, 8:6, 797–806.

Frost, A. C. (2001) 'Reconceptualising Local Union Responses to Workplace Restructuring in North America', *British Journal of Industrial Relations*, 39:4, 539–64.

Gall, G. (2003) 'Introduction' in G. Gall (ed.), *Union Organising. Campaigning for Trade Union Recognition* (London: Routledge).

Gallie, D., White, M., Cheng, Y. and Tomlinson, M. (1998) *Restructuring the Employment Relationship* (Oxford University Press).

Heery, E., Simms, M., Delbridge, R., Salmon, J. and Simpson, D. (2003) 'Trade Union Recruitment Policy in Britain. Form and Effects', in G. Gall (ed.), *Union Organising. Campaigning for Trade Union Recognition* (London: Routledge).

Hyman, R. (1975) *Industrial Relations: A Marxist Introduction* (London: Macmillan).

Kelly, J. (1998) *Rethinking Industrial Relations* (London: Routledge).

Kochan, T. and Osterman, P. (1994) *The Mutual Gains Enterprise* (Boston, Mass.: Harvard Business School Press).

Lane, T. (1974) *The Union Makes Us Strong* (London: Arrow).

Lichtenstein, N. (1988) 'The Union's Early Days: Shop Stewards and Seniority Rights', in M. Parker and J. Slaughter (eds), *Choosing Sides: Unions and the Team Concept*, A Labor Notes Book (Boston, Mass.: South End Press).

Martínez Lucio, M. and Stuart, M. (2002) 'Assessing the Principles of Partnership. Workplace Trade Union Representatives' Attitudes and Experiences', *Employee Relations*, 24:3, 305–20.

Martínez Lucio, M., Jenkins, J. and Noon, M. (2000) 'Management Strategy, Union Identity and Oppositionalism: Teamwork in the Royal Mail', in S. Procter and F. Mueller (eds), *Teamworking* (London: Macmillan).

Michie, J. and Sheehan, M. (2002) 'Labour "Flexibility" – Securing Management's Right to Manage Badly?', in B. Burchell, S. Deakin, J. Michie and J. Rubery (eds), *Systems of Production. Markets, Organization and Performance* (London: Routledge).

Millward, N., Bryson, A. and Forth, J. (2000) *All Change at Work? British Employment Relations 1980–98, as Portrayed by the Workplace Industrial Relations Survey Series* (London/New York: Routledge).

Newsome, K. (2000) 'Exploring Changes in the Organization of Work in the Graphical Industry. Threats to Union Organization', *Employee Relations*, 22:5, 503–22.

Parker, M. and Slaughter, J. (1988) 'Work Rules and Classifications: The Balance of Power', in M. Parker and J. Slaughter (eds) *Choosing Sides: Unions and the Team Concept*, A Labor Notes Book (Boston, Mass.: South End Press).

Smith, P. and Morton, G. (1993) 'Union Exclusion and the Decollectivization of Industrial Relations in Britain', *British Journal of Industrial Relations*, 31:1, 97–114.

Stewart, P. and Wass, V. (1998) 'From "Embrace and Change" to "Engage and Change": Trade Union Renewal and the New Management Strategies in the UK Automotive Industry?', *New Technology, Work and Employment*, 13:2, 77–93.

Stewart, P., Lewchuk, W., Yates, C., Saruta, M. and Danford, A. (2004) 'Patterns of Labour Control and the Erosion of Labour Standards. Towards an International Study of the Quality of Working Life in the Automobile Industry (Canada, Japan and the UK)', in E. Charron and P. Stewart (eds), *Work and Employment Relations in the Automobile Industry* (Basingstoke: Palgrave Macmillan).

Taylor, P. and Ramsay, H. (1998) 'Unions, Partnership and HRM: Sleeping with the Enemy?', *International Journal of Employment Studies*, 6:2, 115–43.

Terry, M. (1995) 'Trade Unions: Shop Stewards and the Workplace', in P. Edwards (ed.), *Industrial Relations: Theory and Practice* (Oxford: Basil Blackwell).

Terry, M. (2002) 'Employee Representation: Shop Stewards and the New Legal Framework', in P. Edwards (ed.), *Industrial Relations: Theory and Practice*, 2nd edn (Oxford: Basil Blackwell).

Thompson, P. and Wallace, T. (1994) 'Trade Unions and Organizational Innovation', *Employee Relations*, 16:2, 55–64.

Tolliday, S. and Zeitlin, J. (1986) 'Shop-Floor Bargaining, Contract Unionism and Job Control: An Anglo-American Comparison', in S. Tolliday and J. Zeitlin (eds), *The Automobile Industry and its Workers* (Oxford: Polity Press).

Tomaney, J. (1990) 'The Reality of Workplace Flexibility', *Capital and Class*, 40, 31–55.

TUC (Trades Union Congress) (2002) *High Performance Workplaces*, TUC Submission on the Government's discussion document, November.

Undy, R. (1999) 'New Labour's "Industrial relations Settlement": The Third Way?', *British Journal of Industrial Relations*, 37:2, 315–36.

Waddington, J. and Kerr, A. (1999) 'Trying to Stem the Flow: Union Membership Turnover in the Public Sector' *Industrial Relations Journal*, 30:3, 184–96.

Whitston, C., Roe, A. and Jefferys, S. (1999) 'Job Regulation and the Managerial Challenge to Trade Unions: Evidence from Two Membership Surveys', *Industrial Relations Journal*, 30:5, 482–98.

10
'You've Got to Admit It's Getting Better . . .': Organised Labour and Internationalisation

Nigel Haworth

Introduction

Harvie Ramsay contributed to many debates, scholarly and activist alike, but none was more important than his involvement from the late 1970s with the thorny issue of organised labour's apparent weakness when faced with the power and scope of international capital. Like the footballer, Martin Peters, Ramsay was 'ten years ahead of his time' when he became involved with this issue.[1] At that stage, few academics and trade unionists had a coherent analysis of the issue, and many of the academics who had addressed the issue were quite comfortable with the view that internationalisation was both inevitable and beneficial, and that labour's stake in the process was best reflected within national labour relations systems. Ramsay's most significant contributions were to offer analyses of, first, the capacity of workers within multinational corporations (MNCs) to challenge global decision-making; second, to provide a coherent intellectual framework, which explained why organised labour found effective strategies to deal with global decision-making hard to identify; third, to assess the potential of structural contradictions within MNC management decision-making to provide organised labour with *points d'appui* capable of empowering labour's representatives; fourth, to begin the assessment of regional integration's impact on labour's capacity to influence the global economic order, particularly in the context of the European Union. Many of these contributions derived from Ramsay's seminal contribution to the industrial democracy and worker participation debates (see, for example, Haworth and Ramsay 1988).

This chapter begins with an exposition of the impact of the thinking about labour and internationalisation that began in the 1970s and crept into the early 1980s.[2] Levinson's contribution (Levinson 1972) is central because, in the critiques offered of his work, ideas were raised that continue at the heart of contemporary debate. This exposition is not simply an account of 'dead' history. Rather, it helps us to understand the dramatic shifts in the circum-stances surrounding internationalisation over the intervening three decades. It shows how much of the earlier debate became locked in a narrow coun-terposition of the MNC to the organising capacity of labour, a debate that resulted predictably in a pessimistic assessment of labour's opportunities to match MNC power. Predictably, because the range of challenges to interna-tionalisation that exist at the start of the twenty-first century was unimagin-able in the 1970s.[3] Thereafter, the chapter moves to the current, more optimistic, assessments of labour's future *vis-à-vis* internationalisation. The chapter concludes with some rudimentary explanations of the environment giving rise to a renewed optimism.

Reflecting on Recent History

The 1970s was an important decade for any understanding of the relation-ship between trade unions and internationalisation. Two intellectual tradi-tions emerged and combined in that decade, just as a politics of trade union response to internationalisation also began a slow gestation. The two intel-lectual traditions were, first, the growth of a mainstream analytical literature on the MNC and foreign direct investment (FDI). The second was a commensurate, if tentative, analysis of the basis for a trade union response to economic internationalisation. The mainstream literature on the MNC and FDI proceeds from the middle 1960s (Vernon's (1966) product cycle model) through Dunning's eclectic paradigm (Dunning 1976, 1995) and on to Buckley and Casson's theory of international operations (Buckley and Casson 1979). These approaches constituted a new strand in international trade theory and may be seen loosely as theories of market failure. They explained MNC and FDI activity in terms quite different from existing economic orthodoxy, which emphasised country-specific resource endow-ments. Instead, the new trade theories emphasised three factors, conceived in terms of the OLI relationship. These factors were the exclusive possession of certain assets (ownership advantages – O); the internalisation of income generating assets (as a response to market failure – I); the location-specific advantages of enterprises (L). Clearly, the new approaches to the MNC and FDI emphasised particularly the organisation and behaviour of the interna-tional firm; that is, the management structures and beliefs that underpinned internationalisation. This mainstream literature emerged as an analytical response to a pressing empirical circumstance – the post-Second World War movement of (primarily US) FDI into international manufacturing and the consequent emergence of new layers of MNC activity, complementing the longer-established international firms in primary sectors.

The OLI model has explicit HRM dimensions. Ownership advantages may include 'possession' of key managers and core workers. Internalisation may lead to active internal labour markets as companies try to hold on to important staff. Location specific HRM advantages may vary from access to high-skill, high-value-adding employees to access to large volumes of low-skill, low-paid manufacturing employees. The impact of MNCs and FDI on labour markets became a significant area of study as, on the one hand, the human resource needs of MNCs were examined, and, on the other, the impacts of MNC behaviour on local, regional and national labour markets were studied.

However, we are less concerned here with the substance of these debates than their emergence in the literature. By the end of the 1970s, sophisticated mainstream analyses of MNCs and FDI existed. They tended to take for granted the internationalisation phenomenon. They were less interested in the limits to internationalisation (if such limits exist) or its extended impacts, preferring to emphasise the firm and its decision-making as an aspect of an evolutionary development towards a global economy. Existing at the boundaries of economics and a variety of management disciplines, these theories melded, albeit not without controversy, with the emerging emphasis on strategies for company and national competitiveness,[4] and became an invaluable intellectual resource for companies and governments pursuing further internationalisation.

Inevitably, a radical alternative emerged to confront this new orthodoxy on MNCs and FDI. It drew on a number of traditions, including classical political economy from Hobson to Lenin and Bukharin, and on an anti-imperialist literature that grew in the 1960s. This was echoed by the United Nations Economic Commission for Latin America's (ECLA) structuralism and the Dependency School. In turn, the Development Studies tradition took up the baton. A significant labour-related literature was a feature of this radical tradition. However, despite some common roots, the orthodox and radical literatures rarely engaged as institutional and disciplinary boundaries, methodologies, emphases and client groups separated them.

The second relevant intellectual tradition that emerged in the 1970s related to trade union responses to MNCs and FDI. As might be expected, it has both mainstream and radical components, both of which focused initially on the potential for international collective bargaining. The orthodox tradition mirrored the new orthodoxy surrounding MNCs and FDI and generally came to the conclusion that international bargaining was difficult to put in place.[5] As Press (1984) summarised at the time, seven major obstacles to international collective bargaining were identified:

• Management hostility to an extension of collective bargaining into the international arena, reflecting a broader concern about the internationalisation of demands for industrial democracy;
• National trade unions fear(ed) loss of sovereignty;
• Lack of membership support;

- Differences between national IR systems;
- Lack of an international regulatory framework;
- International actions lack(ed) political legitimacy; and
- Political fragmentation of trade unions.

More extreme orthodox views went so far as to argue that international collective bargaining was undesirable (for example, Northrup 1978).

The counterview to this negative response to international collective bargaining was the seminal work of Levinson (1972), which in turn gave rise to a significant debate among radical theorists about the future of international trade unionism in a period of economic internationalisation.

Charles Levinson and International Trade Unionism

The importance of Levinson's work is not widely recognised in a world that has accepted globalisation into common parlance. However, in the 1970s, Levinson broke new ground with his analysis of MNCs and their implications for collective bargaining. His argument was straightforward. Capital was internationalising and, consequently, the power of management was increasing. The trade union response had to match the scope and level of MNC power. This required direct negotiation with MNCs, achieved by stages – company-wide union support for national action in one country against one MNC subsidiary, followed by multiple negotiations with a company in several or many countries, followed in turn by integrated, comprehensive international bargaining. In Levinson's view, the first stage was in place. Further development through the stages was possible, given the appropriate conditions.

We can judge the significance of Levinson's work by the response it generated.[6] Four reactions stand out particularly. The first is the initial wave of support for Levinson's arguments (for example, Litvak and Maule 1972; Ulman 1975). The second is the sometimes intemperate attempt by Northrup and Rowan (1979) to debunk Levinson from an orthodox management perspective. The third is the wave of empirical work undertaken to assess types and levels of international union action (for example, Blake 1973; Hershfield 1975; Weinburg 1978). Most studies in this tradition offered some support for Levinson's assertion that his first stage had been reached.

However, the fourth reaction took the debate forward into more analytical territory. In Olle and Schoeller's seminal piece in 1977, the idea that the internationalisation of capital would result logically or automatically in an equal and parallel growth of an international trade union opposition was challenged (Olle and Schoeller 1977). Rather, they argued, the differential national effects of FDI established competitive international economic relations that were not susceptible to the equalisation of wages and conditions, or the institutional integration of national union bodies into an effective international presence. They also rejected the economism implicit in Levinson's direct association of international unionism with the rise of the MNC. Finally, notions of global governance, seen by some to be an important context for international trade unionism, would emerge only through politico-military action, which would not provide the political conditions for effective international trade union activity. Olle and Schoeller argued for working-class political action as the only effective response to the internationalisation of capital.

Olle and Schoeller's critique of Levinson is in many ways as dismissive as that of Northrup and Rowan. Thus the Levinson thesis was assailed from left and right, the only (partial) support emerging in studies suggesting that some levels of international union activity had occurred.

The 1970s debate was at its most downbeat in the work of Haworth and Ramsay (1984, 1988). They based their analysis on two strands of thought – the one drawn from practical involvement in attempts to resist plant closures in Scotland in the late 1970s;[7] and the other found in extending the line of thinking begun by Olle and Schoeller. The central issue addressed by Haworth and Ramsay was an asymmetry between labour and capital in an internationalising world. The asymmetry was presented in terms of value theory and a more 'sociological' argument. The value analysis suggested that international capital seeks to increase value appropriation on a global scale. Hence the MNC is potentially less concerned about any particular labour group (that is, less concerned about the particular nature of concrete labour) and is probably more concerned about the general form of labour power as a value-creating commodity. In contrast, the worker experiences value creation in terms of concrete labour and the production of use values. Equally, the worker betrays no evidence of the production of abstract labour, embodied in the commodity and providing the means of value appropriation. The key issue here is the impact of the relationship between concrete and abstract labour. In the case of concrete labour, the consciousness of the worker is defined in part by his/her experience as a use value, engaged in the real world of the labour process. In contrast, management understands the role of concrete labour, but also understands labour in terms of abstract labour, value creating and, potentially, homogeneity. For management, internationalisation opens up the possibility of access to vast pools of labour, approximating the status of homogeneous inputs. In sum, value theory suggests a useful way of understanding an asymmetry between labour and capital in an internationalised world – labour experiencing the world primarily in its capacity as concrete labour, as a use value, engaged in specific labour processes in defined physical locations (plants, communities). Capital sees labour in these terms too, but also, crucially, sees it as an increasingly homogeneous, substitutable, international opportunity for value creation and expropriation.

The sociological argument was commonplace, but still important. It posited an inverse relationship between identity and consciousness, on the one hand, and distance, on the other. It then suggested a growing divergence between the locations in which worker identity and consciousness are formed and the locations in which management decision-making takes place. In relation to identity and consciousness, workers create collaborative relationships in workplaces and communities, based on common interests, shared experiences, physical proximity and frequent interaction. As one moves away from the location in which identity and consciousness are formed and nurtured, identity and consciousness dissipate and become more inchoate. Simultaneously, management decision-making has shifted from that same location as a result of changing company structures. Eventually, with the growth of the MNC, decision-making may be geographically very distant from the location in which workers live and work.

The value theory and sociological approaches were suggesting the same conclusion. Internationalisation of capital has created a significant distance between the strongholds of labour and capital. This distance is both physical and conceptual. Managements increasingly operate in global mode, while workers organise best locally. Management is increasingly viewing labour as a homogeneous, substitutable quality (indeed, as abstract labour), but labour still experiences the world primarily in terms of its characteristics as concrete labour and the producer of use values. This is a fundamental asymmetry between labour and international capital and, argued Haworth and Ramsay, a potent explanation of labour's difficulties in creating an effective response to internationalisation. This explained why labour's capacity to influence capitalist decision-making is weak. Efforts to extend worker participation and industrial democracy on the international stage seemed likely to fail because labour had little or no leverage on international capital (Haworth and Ramsay 1988).

Tentative Political Responses from the International Labour Movement

The late 1960s and 1970s highlighted these difficulties. This was the period in which the scope of internationalisation was first recognised by national trade union movements. Peak organisations began training activities on MNCs. Representations to government on the economic and industrial relations impacts of FDI became common. The international organisations – the International Confederation of Free Trade Unions (ICFTU), World Federation of Trade Unions (WFTU) and World Council of Labour (WCL) – began to make regular pronouncements about MNCs and FDI. The International Labour Organisation (ILO) took up the issue, as did the United

Nations proper. On the margins, but playing an important role in fostering debate, numerous pro-labour NGOs became active on the relationship between Labour and MNCs (though their activities were not always met with gratitude by the official trade union movement). There were many incidents of international solidarity action, providing the raw material for Northrup and Rowan, Blake and others to study. These actions tended to be spontaneous, principled and short-term, and are illustrated by the global response to the 1973 Pinochet coup in Chile. They were rarely sustained beyond the important but limited context of information exchange.

The thrust of trade union argument centred on two key dimensions – first, state level control of FDI – that is, the imposition at nation-state level of regulation of MNC activities; second, the development of appropriate international bargaining institutions, such as the ICFTU's World Corporation Councils (WCCs).

The conjuncture was not propitious for these union initiatives. Pressure on governments to control MNCs grew at a time when most economies had entered a long phase of economic restructuring in which priority was given to economic efficiency and competitiveness. FDI was widely seen to be a vital component of that restructuring process and was generally courted with reduced, rather than increased, regulation. International trade integration was also promoted strongly in the General Agreement on Tariffs and Trade (GATT) and elsewhere. MNCs were seen to be key elements in greater trade integration. Trade regulation also raised the issue of international flows and an orthodox consensus began to grow, indicating that, just as trade should be encouraged, so should ever-freer international capital flows. The power of trade unions, both national and international, to confront this orthodoxy was limited.

Initiatives such as the WCCs suffered from exaggerated expectations. As Olle and Schoeller (1977) point out, they had a limited effect on MNCs and were remote from the rank and file. This remoteness gave rise to a debate that continues at the time of writing, about the 'organic' nature of international trade union institutions – that is, the extent to which transnational union agencies reflect the interests of, and involve, rank and filers. However, today, it is clear that a fundamental weakness of initiatives such as the WCCs lay in part in the absence of a supportive regulatory regime at either regional or global levels, but also in the lack of an appropriate internationalist politics.

Optimism Resurgent

Contemporary analysis of internationalisation and its impact on labour internationalism is striking because of its more positive assessment of labour's capacity to wield effective global influence. The analysis has three related elements. First, there is a rejection of 'left pessimist' analysis (to paraphrase Armbruster (1998) and Borgers (n.d.)) and the emergence of positive analyses of organised labour's capacity to respond effectively to internationalisation, which have pointed to potential organisational and political strategies open to labour. Second, visions of global governance inconceivable in the 1970s are now posing questions about popular representation on a global scale. When these elements are combined, grounds become apparent for a rekindled optimism about the influence of organised labour in an internationalised world.

The contemporary critique of left pessimism

Contemporary thinking about labour internationalism combines a rejection of the 'left pessimism' associated with, among others, Ramsay's earlier work, and counterposes both organisational and political responses as key elements of a more positive perspective. The contemporary debate has had to deal not only with the pessimism of the late 1970s and early 1980s, but also heavyweight analysis that might promote further pessimism. Castells, in his seminal work on the information society, highlights the 'divide and rule' approach adopted by international capital in the global economy (Castells 1996). Capital has used a variety of techniques in this approach including workforce downsizing, sub-contracting, the use of casualised labour in various forms, automation or relocation of high-cost jobs, and measures to gain the acquiescence of workers to inferior work conditions. In Castells' view, this approach effectively destroys the collective power of 'old' labour. Other leading analysts (for example, Tilly 1995; Touraine 1986) provide collateral support for the Castells argument.

Much of the critique of left pessimism begins from either a direct or indirect rejection of the determinism implicit in many contemporary perspectives on globalisation. Commentators reject the notion that globalisation is a homogeneous and inexorable unilinear process. In a variety of different formulations, globalisation is argued to have limits and contradictions that provide opportunities for international action by labour. Key to those opportunities is the capacity of labour to operate organisationally and politically around those limits and contradictions. The key elements of a successful new labour internationalism identified in the contemporary literature include:

- *A view that the structural barriers to effective cross-border trade union organisation are not insuperable and have limits* (Armbruster 1998). Given appropriate conditions, strategic cross-border union organisation is possible, but its success will be governed by contingent circumstances (Armbruster, 1998; Ramsay 1999). Contingent factors include the quality of strategic thinking available to labour, the effectiveness of labour organisation and the quality of information available (allowing labour to identify and take advantage of weaknesses in corporate strategy). The potential for sustained trade union membership involvement in international activities is now greater than was the case in the 1970s.

- *The existence of improved trade union strategy at both national and international levels.* Unions have improved strategic capacity increasingly in terms of international developments, in part because national trade union bodies have developed improved capacity, and in part because of the role played by the ICFTU (a role allowed the develop by the end of the Cold War splits within the international trade union movement). Moreover, Hodkinson (2001) suggests that international activities have been radicalised by the pressure imposed by globalisation, just as national union movements have had to consider a more activist role on international matters. At the heart of these radicalised roles is the notion of agency, wherein Herod's (1998) suggestion that globalisation has from its inception been shaped by the actions of workers is further developed. Improved trade union strategy has sought to identify the limits to globalisation and, in the political space created by those limits, has mobilised national and international union activities. Lambert and Webster (n.d.) discuss this mobilisation in terms of the creation (see Touraine 1986) of a 'future vision' for labour internationalism (Lambert and Webster n.d.).

- *New forms of labour networking.* Labour organisations and their memberships are now using modern technology not only in terms of simple information flow but also as the basis for a 'net internationalism'. Numerous analyses of this phenomenon exist (see, for example, Waterman 1993; Lee 1997; Hodkinson 2001). Perhaps the most established variation on this theme is that provided by Waterman (1993), in which he develops in a number of contributions the idea of a 'global solidarity culture' leading to 'organic solidarity' based on knowledge shared in a global system of labour communication.

- *The emergence of social movement unionism.* Munck (with Waterman 1993, and Moody 1997, among others) has suggested that the emergence of new social movements and what he describes as a 'politics of reconstruction' are key factors in the creation of opportunities for successful labour internationalism (see Munck 1999). As new social movements appear in response to the impacts of internationalisation, opportunities arise for new types of trade union organisation which move beyond traditional economistic trade union behaviour. Central to Munck's view is the rejection of a strong counterposition of 'old labour' and 'new social movements'. Rather, a politics of transformation provides opportunities for traditional trade union activity to become broader in its political perspectives. The transformation can be understood in the shifts denoted in following table (Lambert and Webster, n.d.).[8]

Table 10.1   Key elements of 'old' and 'new' labour international

Old Labour Internationalism	New Labour internationalism
Hierarchy	Network
Centralisation	Decentralisation
Command	Participation
Control	Empowerment
Restricted debate	Open debate
Slow decision-making	Quick decision-making
Large bureaucracy	De-layered
Formal	Flexible
Diplomatic orientation	Mobilisation orientation
Focus on workplace and trade unions only	Focus on coalition building with new social movements and NGOs
Predominantly North	Predominantly South

Source: Lambert and Webster (n.d.)

- *Consequences and agency*. A series of economic and financial crises in Latin America, Asia and Russia in the 1980s and 1990s, coupled with the international scope of market-driven policy frameworks, has highlighted the social and economic consequences of global economic integration (see, for example, Lee 1998). Previously unimaginably large numbers of people have faced changes in workplace and community that vary from the disruptive to the catastrophic. Disaffection with national policy-makers has been accompanied by dissatisfaction with the current global order (Kapstein 1996). In turn, dissatisfaction has turned into mobilisation at many levels – from violence during WTO ministerial meetings to the international emergence of sophisticated representative bodies within civil society. Labour organisations are among the most powerful and extensive of these bodies and, as we discuss below in terms of global governance, are a force in contemporary global discourse.
- *The production of developed theoretical perspectives*. Primarily as an effect of the previous five elements, the volume and quality of theoretical work on labour internationalism has improved markedly. This is as true for scholarly journals as it is for activist agencies such as the ICFTU and the International Trade Secretariats (ITSs). Strategic intervention into global corporates, or into regulatory issues such as the trade–labour standards debate has required an improved analytical quality and, inevitably, the devotion of greater resources.

Labour internationalisation and global governance

If optimism has grown about the organisational and political capacity of labour to organise internationally in terms of its internal capacities and external actions, the external environment has also changed in a positive fashion. Global regulation has developed in numerous contexts as a direct effect of global economic integration. This is true for trade, human rights, the use of the sea, intellectual property and many other issues. Emergent global regulation provides some of the important 'spaces' in which a new labour internationalism may prosper. For our purposes, four key aspects of this environment – the emergence of regime fusion, the internationalisation of social protection, the impacts of regional integration and, finally, what might be called the effects of production volatility – stand out.[9] In sum, these constitute important dimensions of an emergent global governance system (see, for example, Held 1995; Cox 1996; Murphy 2000; Wilkinson and Hughes 2002).

Regime fusion

Regime fusion refers to the fusion between international regimes. Regimes in this sense are international governance processes, consisting of governments, other actors and institutions in civil society, and the shared rules, values and norms that bind the participants to the regime. In particular, two international regimes – an international labour relations regime and the global trade regime – are at the time of writing grappling with fusion (Haworth and Hughes 2000, 2003; Haworth *et al.* 2003). The vehicle for that fusion is the trade–labour standards debate, and its institutional setting lies on the World Trade Organisation (WTO)–ILO axis.

The trade–labour standards debate, renewed once more in the Doha ministerial meeting of the WTO, was given life in the final stages of the Uruguay Round of the GATT. Under pressure from the USA and some European states in particular, the WTO has been forced to address the issue of the trade–labour standards relationship. The recent history of the trade –labour standards debate permits the plausible conclusion that the relationship between the international trade regime and labour standards (and, for that matter, other standards too) will be consolidated institutionally on a global scale. Its institutional basis will be a relationship between the ILO and the WTO or their successors – an institutional fusion reflecting the fusion of global regimes. The establishment of international regulation linking trade and labour standards will open up the potential for a more general internationalisation of industrial relations institutions and practices, in turn providing an important framework for international labour participation. This would also be one significant moment, among many, in the establishment of a wider popular international representation and participation.

Popular representation and social protection

A second process supporting the emergence of popular representation and participation in global institutions is the internationalisation of social protection. While this has been a key perspective of the ILO since its inception, the combination of economic internationalisation and significant regional crises has raised international social protection measures to new significance. This is particularly the case in the aftermath of the 1997 Asian crisis. At the time of writing, all significant international agencies (and particularly the international financial institutions – IFIs) are committed to social protection agendas. The need for internationally supported safety nets is not contested. The political and social stability of the international economic order is now seen to rest in part in effective global social protection measures. The debate is now about their configuration and the levels and mode of popular representation in that configuration. Most agencies now engage actively with non-governmental organisations (NGOs), but the extent to which that engagement shifts agency perspectives is an open question. Human resource development (HRD) is a key dimension of that social protection. Trade union agencies such as the ICFTU are key representatives of popular sectors in the configuration of a global social protection regime.

Regional integration

A third process to consider is regional integration. The emergence of international labour participation in the APEC process has been discussed above. Elsewhere, in NAFTA through the side agreement, and in the European Union (EU) through its social agendas, the voice of labour has been institutionalised to a greater or lesser extent. In the case of the EU, the institution of European Works Councils is the most significant of a series of measures in place. To this may be added the range of international trade secretariat initiatives with individual MNCs such as Danone and Accor. Supranational regional integration opens the door to regional labour representation in regional intergovernmental processes.

Production volatility

Finally, there is the issue of production volatility. Traditionally, the global organisation of production on the basis of a variety of contracting arrangements between core companies and sub-contractors has been interpreted as weakening the power of domestic and international labour organisations. The internationalisation of production regimes appears to take place at a level and in a form not susceptible to the traditional strategy and tactics of labour organisation, domestic or international. Yet, these production regimes are increasingly vulnerable to popular, particularly consumer, assessment. Companies such as Adidas-Salomon and Nike have established internationally vetted standards of engagement with contracting firms, based on ILO conventions. Independent audit agencies such as the Fair Labour Association have sprung up. The Clinton Administration used these initiatives to introduce a code of practice for international production by US firms in the apparel industry. The drive for these measures comes neither from labour nor from a moral conversion on the part of the companies. It comes from the joint effect of mobilised consumer pressure and government intervention. Internationalisation may have opened up tremendous opportunities for companies to take advantage of cheap labour and less demanding compliance arrangements, but it has also allowed an equivalent mobilisation of consumers and their representatives on the basis of intensified information flows. Care needs to be taken in interpreting the long-term impact of these developments. It would be easy to read too much into their present form. However, the active involvement of the ILO in this type of standard setting suggests a possible route for popular labour activity in the global governance of production.

Taken together, these four issues suggest a trend towards the regulation of the international economic order, associated with a trend towards global governance. The outcome of the trends is, obviously, not known. It is, however, realistic to argue that we are in the early stages of a global debate about the relationship between national and supranational governance, the international economic order and popular participation in both. International labour, and particularly the ICFTU, is a significant popular sector participant in that debate.

Understanding the Origins of the New Environment

Thus far, we have shown how, in the recent times, a rejection of 'left pessimism' can be justifiably based on new political and organisational opportunities open to labour on the international stage, on the one hand, and the effect of emerging global governance on the other. In the final substantive section of this chapter, a rudimentary explanation for the contemporary environment is offered. While sharing some themes with, for example, Tilly (1995), it goes somewhat further than Tilly in suggesting that popular representation in global governance is now a serious consideration, in which the role of labour internationalism will be an important building block. Moreover, in tune with Herod (1998), it emphasises the importance of political action by civil society in the creation of future global governance institutions.

How are we to explain this new environment? In the 1970s, as we have seen, critics from both left and right argued that Levinson's (1972) view of international collective bargaining was unrealisable. Effective trade union representation at the global level seemed to be impracticable. In 2001, views are more sanguine about trade union representation on the international stage, and we have presented four contexts giving rise to this change of heart. In searching for an explanation of this shift, we must try to understand what has changed in the configuration of global political economy over the last thirty years. For example, has there been a slow maturation of circumstances that has brought about a scenario presaged by Levinson, or are there other interpretations of the period that offer better accounts of change?

We can put to one side the argument for the maturation of the Levinson model. The types of development discussed above are far wider in scope than the move towards international collective bargaining envisaged by Levinson. There is little evidence of the aggregation of international bargaining through the stages suggested by Levinson, and despite its presence in some labour standards arguments, equally little evidence of an equalisation of wages and conditions. In sum, the arguments presented by Olle and Schoeller (1977) against Levinson are borne out by the passage of time. We must, therefore, look elsewhere for the origins of the shift in circumstances between the 1970s and the early 2000s.

One explanation, warranting further consideration, is found in the interrelationship between the economic and political processes that mark the modern capitalist era[10]. The contemporary emergence of new possibilities for global labour activity reflects the asymmetry between popular political representation at national and international levels. National level political representation emerged in the advanced capitalist economies not only as political representation, but also as a means of influencing the economic power of capital. By the late nineteenth and early twentieth centuries national level accommodations were either in place or being formed. However, the internationalisation of capital that developed from the late nineteenth century created a new asymmetry – emerging global economic power without a parallel political accommodation. Hence this tentative argument suggests that the current opportunities for labour movements on the global stage are the extension of the demand for national political representation into the global environment. In other words, emerging global governance is not only about global political representation, but also about the use of global political power to constrain the global reach of capital.

Asymmetry Constrained?

The early years of the twenty first century look to hold more promise for labour representation on the international stage than the limited world of the 1970s. The opportunities arising are, paradoxically perhaps, a consequence of internationalisation. The internationalisation agenda has for over 100 years been substantially set by international capital, in many ways beyond the constraint of nation states and their domestic political accommodations. However, as the level of internationalisation has become more profound, the twin challenges of popular representation and necessary regulation have emerged to provide labour with avenues unsuspected in the

1970s. And, of course, we should here repeat Herod's argument about the essential contribution of labour to the shaping of internationalisation throughout its phases (Herod 1998).

These avenues are by no means straightforward. As we noted above, the history of popular representation and trade union organisation has been marked by both success and failure, and by struggle and pain. Moreover, similar contradictions to those that mark domestic political accommodations exist on the global stage. One has only to look at the condemnation heaped by some commentators and NGOs upon the ICFTU for their engagement with regional bodies such as APEC, or the similar response by others to the labour standards model to see how these contradictions may be played out. However, at least in the 2000s, the global environment offers the option of general engagement, a far cry from the negativism of the 1970s.

Conclusion

Borgers (n.d.) notes that Ramsay wavered between left pessimism and measured optimism in his work on labour internationalism. This is a fair assessment. There was in his work a fundamental belief in the capacity of the labour movement nationally and internationally to seek out and support democratic challenges to an overweening international capitalist order. For Ramsay, the key to success lay in the cogency and effectiveness of political action across civil society. The thrust of his analysis was to recognise that opportunities for such action were expanding as the limits and contradictions within the dominant global order became ever more apparent. There was nothing easy or obvious about success. It was inevitably going to be a hard-fought clash between competing, and in many ways opposed, global perspectives. In these circumstances, measured optimism is an appropriate posture.

Notes

1   Referring to England manager Alf Ramsay's assessment of Martin Peters, the West Ham player, in the 1966 English World Cup squad.
2   This chapter draws extensively on a collaboration with Ramsay, begun in the 1970s, which was planning an 'auto-critique' of an earlier 'left pessimism'. The chapter is drawn in part from project notes held by Ramsay.
3   Perhaps one should qualify this. Peter Waterman, for example, always stood out as a more positive analyst, basing his views in part on a prescient understanding of how the communications revolution offered by IT might be used to labour's advantage. Dan Gallin would be another important exception, as would Rob Lambert and Eddie Webster.
4   Note, for example, the debates on Porter's Diamond – Porter 1990; Dunning 1992, 1993; Rugman and Verbeke 1993.

5 See, for example, Gunter (1972); Blake (1973); Tudyka (1973); Flanagan and Weber (1974); Roberts and May (1974); Ulman (1975); Banks and Steiber (1977); Morgan and Blainpain (1977); Northrup and Rowan (1979).
6 Press (1984) offers a helpful account of this debate.
7 See Baldry *et al.* (1983, 1984).
8 Lambert and Webster contrast the two modes but subscribe broadly to the 'transformation' view developed by Munck.
9 The ideas in this section are developed at some length in Haworth (2002a).
10 This argument has still to be fully developed and is offered here as a tentative framework for further consideration.

References

Armbruster, R. (1998) 'Cross-border Labor Organizing in the Garment and Automobile Industries: The Phillips Van-Heusen and Ford Cuautitlan Cases', *Journal of World-Systems Research*, 4:1, Winter, 20–51.

Baldry, C., Haworth, N., Henderson, S., Ramsay, H. (1983) 'Fighting Multinational Power: Possibilities, Limitations and Contradictions', *Capital and Class*, nos. 20 and 21, 157–67.

Baldry, *et al.*, (1984) 'Multinational Closure and the Boundaries of Resistance: Implications of the Massey Ferguson Case', *Industrial Relations Journal*, 15:4.

Banks, R. and Steiber, J. (1977) *Multinationals, Unions and Labor Relations in Industrialised Countries* (Ithaca, NY: Cornell University Press).

Blake, D. (1973) 'Cross-national Cooperative Strategies: Union Responses to the Multinational Corporation', in K. Tudyka, *Multinational Corporations and Labour Union* (Njimegen: University of Nijmegen Press).

Borgers, F. (n.d.) 'Networked Capitalism – Networked Unionism? Theorizing International Unionism'. Accessed at http://www.lmu.ac.uk/ies/im/people/swalker/labournetworking/Borgers-NetworkedCapitalism.pdf.

Buckley, P. J. and Casson, M. (1979) 'A Theory of International Operations', *European Research in International Business*, 10, 45–50.

Castells, M. (1996) *The Information Age: Economy, Society and Culture Vol. I, The Rise of the Network Society* (Oxford: Basil Blackwell).

Cox, R. (1996) 'Structural Issues of Global Governance: Issues for Europe', in R. Cox and T. Sinclair, *Approaches to World Order* (Cambridge University Press).

Dunning, J. H. (1976) 'Trade, Location of Economic Activity and the MNE: A Search for an Eclectic Approach', in B. Ohlin, P.-O. Hessleborn and P. M. Wijkman (eds), *The International Allocation of Economic Activity*, Proceedings of the 35th Nobel Symposium, Stockholm.

Dunning, J. H. (1992) *Multinational Enterprises and the Global Economy* (Reading, UK: Addison-Wesley).

Dunning, J. H. (1993) 'Internationalizing Porter's Diamond', *Management International Review*, 2, 7–15.

Dunning, J. H. (1995) 'Reappraising the Eclectic Paradigm in an Age of Alliance Capitalism', *Journal of International Business Studies*, 26:3, 461–91.

Flanagan, R. and Weber, A. (1974) *Bargaining without Boundaries* (Chicago: University of Chicago Press).

Gunter, H. (1972) *Transnational Industrial Relations* (London: Macmillan).

Haworth, N. (2002a) 'International Labour and Its Emerging Role in Global Governance: Regime Fusion, Social Protection, Regional Integration and Production Volatility', in R. Wilkinson and S. Hughes, *Global Governance: Critical Perspectives* (London: Routledge).

Haworth, N. (2002b) 'Labour and Internationalisation: How 30 Years Makes a Difference', Mimeo, Geography and Industrial Relations Conference, University of Sydney, November.

Haworth, N. and Hughes, S. (2000) 'Internationalisation, Industrial Relations Theory and International Relations', *Journal of Industrial Relations*, 42:2, 195–213.

Haworth, N. and Hughes, S. (2003) 'International Political Economy and Industrial Relations', *British Journal of Industrial Relations*, 41:4, 665–82.

Haworth, N. and Ramsay, H. (1984) 'Grasping the Nettle: Problems with the Theory of International Trade Union Solidarity', in P. Waterman (ed.), *For a New Labour Internationalism* (The Hague: ILERI).

Haworth, N. and Ramsay, H. (1988) 'Workers of the World, Untied: International Capital and Some Dilemmas in Industrial Democracy', in R. Southall (ed.), *Trade Unions and the New Industrialisation of the Third World* (London: Zed Press).

Haworth, N., Hughes, S. and Wilkinson, R. (2003) 'The International Labour Standards Regime: A Case Study in Global Governance', Paper delivered at the ESRC Global Governance Symposium, Oxford, November.

Held, D. (1995) *Democracy and the Global Order: From the Modern State to Cosmopolitan Governance* (Cambridge: Polity Press).

Herod, A. (ed.) (1998) *Organizing the Landscape: Geographical Perspectives on Labor Unionism* (Minneapolis/London: University of Minnesota Press).

Hershfield, D. (1975) *The Multinational Union Challenges the Multinational Company*, Conference Board Report No. 658.

Hodkinson, S. (2001) 'Problems@Labour: Towards a Net-internationalism?', Paper delivered at the 'International Labour (and Other) Networking' Panel, GSA Conference, Manchester, July.

Hymer, S. (1970) 'The Multinational Corporation and the Law of Uneven Development', in J. Bhagwati (ed.), *Economics and World Order* (New York: World Law Fund).

Kapstein, E. (1996) 'Workers in the World Economy', *Foreign Affairs*, 75:3, 16–38.

Lambert, R. and Webster, E. (n.d.) 'Social Emancipation and the New Labour Internationalism: A Southern Perspective'. Accessed at (http://www.ces.fe.uc.pt/emancipa/research/en/ft/internacionalismo.html)

Lee, E. (1997) *The Labour Movement and the Internet: The New Internationalism* (London: Pluto).

Lee, E. (1998) *The Asian Financial Crisis: The Challenge for Social Policy* (Geneva: ILO).

Levinson, C. (1972) *International Trade Unionism* (London: George Allen & Unwin).

Litvak, I. and Maule, C. (1972) 'The Union Response to International Corporations', *Industrial Relations*, 11, 62–71.

Moody, K. (1997) 'Towards an International Social-Movement Unionism', *New Left Review*, 225, 52–72.

Munck, R. (1999) 'Labour Dilemmas and Labour Futures', in P. Waterman and R. Munck (eds), *Labour Worldwide in the Era of Globalisation: Alternative Union Models in the New World Order* (New York: St Martin's Press).

Murphy, C. (2000) 'Global' Governance: Poorly Done and Poorly Understood', *International Affairs*, 76:4, 789–804.

Morgan, A. and Blainpain, R. (1977) 'Legal Barriers Restricting International Labour Action', in OECD, *The Industrial Relations Impact of MNEs* (Paris: OECD).

Northrup, H. (1978) 'Why Multinational Bargaining Neither Exists Nor Is Desirable', *Labor Law Journal*, 330, 330–42.

Northrup, H. and Rowan, R. (1979) *Multinational Collective Bargaining Attempts* (Pittsburgh: University of Pennsylvania).

Olle, W. and Schoeller, W. (1977) 'World Market Competition and Restrictions upon International Trade Union Policies', *Capital and Class*, 2, 56–75.

Porter, M. E. (1990) *Competitive Advantage of Nations* (New York: Free Press).

Prahalad, C. K. and Doz, Y. L. (1981) 'An Approach to Strategic Control in MNCs', *Sloan Management Review*, 22:4, 5–13.

Press, M. (1984) 'The Lost Vision: Trade Unions and Internationalism', in P. Waterman (ed.) *For a New Labour Internationalism* (The Hague: ILERI).

Ramsay, H. (1999) 'In Search of International Union Theory', in J. Waddington (ed.), *Globalization and Patterns of Labour Resistance* (New York: Mansell).

Roberts, B. and May, J. (1974) 'The Response of Multinational Enterprises to International Trade Union Pressures', *British Journal of Industrial Relations*, 12/4, 403–16.

Rugman, A. M. and Verbeke, A. (1993) 'Foreign Subsidiaries and Multinational Strategic Management: An Extension and Correction of Porter's Single Diamond Framework', *Management International Review*, Special Issue, 2, 71–84.

Tilly, C. (1995) 'Globalization Threatens Workers' Rights', *International Labour and Working Class History*, 47, 1–23.

Touraine, A. (1986) 'Unionism as a Social Movement', in S. M. Lipset (ed.), *Unions in Transition. Entering the Second Century* (San Francisco: ICS Press).

Tudyka, K. (1973) *Multinational Corporations and Labour Union* (Njimegen: University of Nijmegen Press).

Ulman, L. (1975) 'Multinational Unionism: Incentives, Barriers and Alternatives', *Industrial Relations*, 14, 1–31.

Vernon, R. (1966) 'International investment and international trade in the product cycle', *Quarterly Journal of Economics*, 80, 2, 190–207.

Waterman, P. (ed.) (1984) *For a New Labour Internationalism*, (The Hague: ILERI).

Waterman, P. (1993) 'Globalisation, Civil Society, Solidarity: The Politics and Ethics of the World Both Real and Universal', Working Paper No. 147 (The Hague: ISS).

Waterman, P. and Munck, R. (eds) (1999) *Labour Worldwide in the Era of Globalisation: Alternative Union Models in the New World Order* (New York: St Martin's Press).

Wilkinson, R. and Hughes, S. (2002) *Global Governance: Critical Perspectives* (Routledge: London).

Weinberg, P. (1978) *European Labour and Multinationals* (London: Praeger).

11
Trojan Horses or Paper Tigers? Assessing the Significance of European Works Councils

Mark Hall and Paul Marginson

The most significant institutional innovation in European-level company-based industrial relations has been the establishment of European Works Councils (EWCs) in well over 600 multinational companies (MNCs) as a result of the EU's 1994 EWCs Directive. Prior to the adoption of the Directive, there were widely divergent views of the likely impact of this new institution. These ranged from predictions that, because of their limited statutory remit and the lack of guaranteed trade union involvement, EWCs were doomed to become ineffective 'paper tigers', to, at the other end of the spectrum, concerns on the part of some employers that EWCs might prove to be a 'Trojan horse', opening the door to European company-level collective bargaining. The aim of this chapter is to review, almost a decade after the adoption of the Directive, the accumulating research evidence on the operation and impact of EWCs and offer a (necessarily still provisional) assessment of its significance.

Writing just after the Directive's commencement in September 1996, Harvie Ramsay (1997) reviewed the extensive literature on the theory and practice of the local- and national-level works councils that have long existed in many west European countries in order to reach a preliminary assessment of the potential of the new European-level employee information and consultation structures. He distilled three propositions which usefully frame such a venture. First, formal participation rights, as specified in the legislation or central agreements that establish works councils, often bear only an indirect relationship to actual practice and outcomes. Second, contingent factors, including the nature of the legislation, industrial relations institutions, employee attitudes and organisation, and management's approach will 'shape outcomes in different ways between and within countries' (Ramsay, 1997: 316). Third, evaluation of the impact of works councils 'should consider potential sources of strength and weakness, instead of vesting all in scrutinising precise form and statute. In the end, only an empirical investigation, sensitised to various possibilities, is adequate to the task of assessment' (ibid.).

These propositions form the basis for the review of the impact of EWCs that we present in this chapter. While placing EWCs in the context of the legislation that conceived them, and the agreements negotiated between group management and employee representatives that have established them, our main emphasis – following Ramsay's injunction – will be on assessing the growing evidence on EWC practice. The chapter begins by establishing the innovative nature of the regulation underpinning EWCs and their significance as transnational industrial relations structures. It briefly surveys their diffusion to around a third of the multinational companies potentially covered by the Directive, and then the provisions of the agreements negotiated between central management and employee representatives establishing EWCs. The assessment of EWC practice that follows draws attention to the substantial variation in their activity, effectiveness and impact, and reviews the contingent factors accounting for such variation.

The Significance of EWCs as an Institutional Innovation

Adopted under the Maastricht 'social chapter' from which the UK had opted out, the Directive originally applied to all EU member states apart from the UK, and was subsequently extended to cover the three other member states of the European Economic Area (EEA). In 1997, the UK became subject to the Directive following the end of the UK's social chapter opt-out (Carley and Hall 2000). The Directive will also apply to the ten accession countries following the EU enlargement in 2004, making a total of twenty-eight countries that fall within the territorial scope of the Directive.

The central objective of the Directive is to promote the establishment of European-level information and consultation arrangements in 'Community-scale' companies – that is, those with 1,000 or more employees in the EEA, and operations employing 150 or more in at least two EEA, states. Some 1,850 multinational companies (MNCs), including the EEA operations of companies headquartered in the USA, Japan and other non-EEA countries were estimated by the European Trade Union Institute to be covered prior to EU enlargement (Kerckhofs 2002). EU enlargement will have the effect of bringing more companies within the scope of the Directive as multinational companies' operations and employees in the ten new EU member states will count towards the Directive's employment thresholds.

The Directive placed a strong emphasis on the negotiation of arrangements tailored to the circumstances of the enterprise. Under Article 13, companies in which 'an agreement, covering the entire workforce, providing for the transnational information and consultation of employees' was in existence at the Directive's implementation date (22 September 1996) were exempt from the terms of the Directive for as long as the agreement continues to apply.

Since that date, the Directive's 'special negotiating body' (SNB) procedure has applied, under which negotiations about the arrangements for an EWC (or, alternatively, an information and consultation procedure) can be triggered unilaterally by either employee representatives or management. The constitution of the SNB – made up of employee representatives from each member state in which the enterprise has operations – is determined by law, and Article 6 of the Directive requires any resulting agreement to address certain points, but the parties still have the discretion to agree enterprise-specific arrangements.

Statutory EWCs, as set out by the Directive's 'subsidiary requirements', are applicable only where management refuses to open negotiations despite an employee request, where the negotiations via an SNB do not produce an agreement after three years or where management and the SNB agree to adopt the statutory model. The subsidiary requirements set out a basic constitution for an EWC, identify the transnational issues on which central management must inform and consult the EWC, and provide for annual meetings with the scope for additional meetings in 'exceptional circumstances' – essentially in the event of major restructuring. While there has been no known case in which a company has been required to establish a statutory EWC, as discussed below, the Directive's subsidiary requirements have had a strong influence on EWC arrangements introduced by agreement, providing a benchmark for negotiators on the main constitutional and operational issues.

The framing of the Directive was innovative, reflecting the principle of 'subsidiarity' in a range of different ways (Hall 1992). Among other things, this involved devolving to the member states considerable scope for determining important elements of the legal framework for the establishment of EWCs. Thus the provisions of the EEA member states' national transposition legislation have generally been 'customised' to reflect national industrial traditions and practices (Carley and Hall 2000: 110). Most notably, however, the Directive gave precedence to arrangements negotiated between management and employee representatives over the subsidiary requirements it specified, constituting a fall-back model of last resort. Similarly, Müller and Platzer (2003) argue that the novelty of the Directive lies in 'its combination of three principles: regulation (procedural rules and an enforceable set of statutory minimum provisions), subsidiarity (adaptability to national and corporate conditions), and the primacy of negotiations (which give the parties at national level considerable leeway in shaping their institution)' (p. 58).

The innovative nature of the EWCs Directive as a regulatory instrument has direct implications for the first two of Ramsay's propositions. On the first, formal participation rights of employee representatives in effect derive from regulation at three levels: the Directive itself, the national transposition legislation giving legal effect to the Directive in each member state; and the

provisions of the agreements between management and employee representatives that establish individual EWCs. The relationship of the Directive's
formal participation rights to actual practice is rendered even more indirect
by the insertion of the further two regulatory tiers. The scope for contingent
factors to play a substantial role – the second of Ramsay's propositions – is
therefore even wider.

Of probably greater significance is that the EWCs Directive established
for the first time transnational industrial relations structures within MNCs
operating within the EU. In so doing it sought to bridge the 'representation
gap' between increasingly transnational corporate decision-making and
employees' nationally-defined information and consultation rights in the
context of the creation of the single European market (Hall 1992). The widespread restructuring and rationalisation that accompanied the integration of
MNCs' operations on a European-scale footing (Ramsay 1995) has increasingly involved transnational management decisions which affect workforces
simultaneously in more than one country. Hitherto, workforces and their
representatives had not had any right of consultative access to transnational
management decision-making structures, as the high-profile controversy
over Hoover's 1993 decision to relocate production from a French to a
Scottish site, involving the closure of the former, graphically underlined
(EIRR 1993). As Ramsay (1997: 320) put it, EWCs are now 'the main current
channel for seeking to match the internationalisation of capital's decision-
making'.

Yet, as many observers alongside Ramsay have underlined, the information and consultation rights provided by the Directive, and the national
legislative measures implementing it, are limited in terms of formal participation. In particular, the Directive defines 'consultation' in general terms as
'the exchange of views and establishment of dialogue' between employee
representatives and management – a formulation that very few of the agreements subsequently establishing EWCs depart from. Only a handful provide
more specific consultation procedures, involving, for example, the right for
employee representatives to respond formally to management proposals
and to receive a considered response from management before it acts, or
even before negotiation (Carley and Marginson 2000). None the less, it
would be premature to conclude that as a result of such formal weakness
EWCs are 'paper tigers', doomed to be ineffective:

> the Directive's lack of rigorous regulatory specification does not mean
> that the EWC as a company-level forum for 'social dialogue' and an
> instrument of participation is necessarily weak. Rather its effectiveness is
> achieved [or not] by practical operation. (Müller and Platzer 2003: 68)

EWCs also have potential institutional significance for both trade unions
and employers. For unions, they provide a platform for the development of

cross-border networks among national- and local-level trade union-based and works council-based representative structures within MNCs, in which it becomes possible to exchange information on matters relevant to local negotiations and eventually to develop common positions and press for similar bargaining outcomes. Crucially, since – in line the Directive – virtually all agreements specify that management shall bear the expense of the EWC's basic functioning (including the costs of organising meetings, travel, administration and necessary translation and interpretation) the resource implications for unions of developing such networking are substantially lower than previously. For these reasons, since the proposals for the Directive were first tabled, employers have feared that EWCs might constitute a 'Trojan horse', opening the door to European-level collective bargaining. However, EWCs also potentially offer a forum through which management can secure an understanding of the rationale for its cross-border decisions that affect employees' interests, and even acceptance. They offer the prospect of key decisions gaining greater legitimacy among the wider workforce, precisely because they have been the subject of a transnational process of information disclosure and dialogue. Interaction between these two dynamics can be expected to shape the nature and influence of EWCs.

The Spread of EWCs

The primacy accorded to negotiated arrangements in implementing the requirements of the EWCs Directive has prompted European-level negotiations between management and employee representatives (frequently trade unions) on an unprecedented scale. By October 2002, an estimated 639 MNCs had negotiated agreements establishing a total of 739 EWCs – the difference being accounted for by the existence of two or more EWCs covering different international business divisions within a number of MNCs (Waddington and Kerckhofs 2003). This total represents not much more than a third of the 1,850 MNCs estimated to be covered by the Directive (prior to EU enlargement) (Kerckhofs 2002). Bearing out Ramsay's (1997) emphasis on the salience of contingent factors, variations in the diffusion of EWCs according to the country of origin of the MNCs covered, sector and type of company are evident. Differences are also apparent in the operational definition of 'Europe' among agreements.

EWCs are concentrated among MNCs headquartered in seven countries: companies based in France, Germany, the UK and the USA account for almost 60 per cent, with those based in the Netherlands, Sweden and Switzerland accounting for a further 20 per cent (calculated from Waddington and Kerckhofs 2003: 325–6). Differences in the 'strike rate' of agreements among MNCs according to their country of origin suggest some influence of national systems on the diffusion of EWCs. Among the large

European economies, for example, Germany has a relatively low strike rate at 25 per cent, whereas, at 40 per cent, the UK's is relatively high, with France (35 per cent) at around the overall average (34 per cent). Elsewhere, Spain is noticeable for a low (5 per cent) and Norway for a high (74 per cent) strike rate (Waddington and Kerckhofs 2003: 325).

The precedence the Directive accords to agreements negotiated between the parties leaves scope for EWCs that extend beyond the EEA in their geographical coverage. In a considerable number of cases, the outcome of negotiations goes beyond what minimal compliance with the Directive would require. In a sizeable minority, EWCs provide for representation from operations in European countries outside the EEA, and in a handful arrangements are worldwide. One in five agreements extend coverage to Switzerland and – some years prior to EU enlargement – a similar proportion to one or more of the countries of central Europe (Carley and Marginson 2000). Considerations of companies' production and management organisation within Europe, rather than the political boundaries of the EEA, seem to be driving the way in which 'Europe' is operationalised in EWC agreements.

As between sectors, manufacturing dominates the picture, accounting for almost 80 per cent of agreements; construction and the utilities account for 7–8 per cent; and services for just under 15 per cent. Here, there are considerable differences in the sectoral 'strike rate' of agreements concluded compared to the number of MNCs covered by the Directive. This is attributable to a range of factors, including the strength of trade union organisation within companies, the effectiveness of their European-level organisations, and employer strategy. Also important is the extent to which production is organised and integrated internationally. Overall, the 'strike rate' of agreements in the more internationalised manufacturing sectors is double that in the service sectors, where competition tends to be more nationally bounded (Carley and Marginson 2000). The same factor suggests why, within manufacturing, strike rates in the oil and chemicals sectors are markedly higher than those in paper and printing, and textiles, clothing and footwear; and why the strike rate in financial services is considerably higher than in any other service sector.

Differences in the penetration of EWCs according to type of company reflect the operation of three influences (Waddington and Kerckhofs 2003: 326) rising with company size (in employment terms); spread of the workforce across two or more countries (as compared with concentration in a single country); and the extent of internationalisation (the number of countries in which a given MNC operates).

Given that almost two-thirds of the MNCs covered have yet to establish an EWC, findings from research among Dutch-based companies concerned throw important light on the relevant influences. Blokland and Berentsen (2003) confirm the salience of company size, with smaller MNCs being markedly less likely to establish an EWC than larger ones. Frequently, this correlates with the concentration of the workforce in a single country: in the nine cases examined in depth, operations outside the Netherlands were small. The Dutch works council considered that existing national arrangements gave them sufficient information about, and influence over, group management decisions, while the employee representatives in overseas operations had not approached the Dutch works councils with a request to initiate the establishment of an EWC.

The Provisions of EWC Agreements

Four main influences on the content of the EWC agreements negotiated between central management and employee representatives are apparent (Gilman and Marginson 2002), further underscoring the perceptiveness of Ramsay's (1997) emphasis on the influence of contingent factors. First, there is a 'statutory model effect' – the influence of the terms of the EWC Directive itself, particularly the statutory fall-back model or 'subsidiary requirements', annexed to the Directive which are to be applied in the event that negotiations fail to result in agreement. For example, as compared with agreements concluded in the period before the implementation deadline of the Directive in September 1996, later agreements are more likely to contain provision for the employee side to have access to independent experts and to convene additional EWC meetings should extraordinary circumstances arise. Both these are matters covered directly in the Directive.

Second is a 'country effect' under which industrial relations arrangements in the European country in which an MNC is headquartered, and those for employee information and consultation in particular, influence the provision of EWC agreements. This is most apparent in the basic structure of EWCs (Carley and Marginson 2000). Following the French model of employee consultation, EWCs in French-based MNCs are almost all constituted as joint management–employee structures whereas, influenced by the German model, their counterparts in German-based EWCs are more likely to be employee-only structures, but not universally so (some two-thirds of relevant instances). Among UK-based MNCs, the great majority have opted for joint structures, arguably reflecting the existence of joint consultation arrangements in the UK. In the Nordic countries, as in Germany, a mixed approach is evident, with no single model predominating: two-thirds of the EWCs concerned are joint bodies, while the remaining third are employee-only. In part, this reflects variations in national practice between the four countries, but in Denmark and Sweden the constitution of a number of EWCs breaks with national traditions (Knudsen and Bruun 1998: 138–9). National systems, while being an important influence on this basic feature of EWCs, are not an overriding determinant. A further country influence stems from differences in corporate governance across countries and is evident in the incidence of confidentiality clauses in agreements. These are significantly more widespread among EWCs in UK-based MNCs than among their counterparts in French, German or Nordic based companies. More stringent confidentiality clauses, enabling management to withhold potentially detrimental information are also significantly more evident among agreements in UK-based MNCs.

Third is a 'sector effect', which cuts across countries. This arises from the similarities in production methods, employment practices and industrial relations traditions within sectors, but also from the influence of the European trade union industry federations that have played an important role in initiating and co-ordinating negotiations across MNCs within their respective sectors (Rivest 1996). Such an effect is evident, for example, in the basic structure of EWCs where, controlling for country, joint structures are significantly more evident in chemicals and food and drink compared with metalworking, arguably reflecting different industrial relations traditions in these sectors. Again controlling for country, sector differences are also evident in the incidence with which agreements provide explicitly for trade union officials to participate in the EWC, with such participation being more evident in EWCs in chemicals, food and drink, and textiles and clothing than metalworking, for example. Following Rivest (1996), this is attributable to the differing emphasis placed on such provision by the respective European industry federations.

Fourth, a 'learning effect' is evident, under which innovations in earlier agreements which come to be regarded by one or other (or both) of the parties as good practice become generalised in later agreements. Like the 'sector effect', the 'learning effect' cuts across countries and is evidenced by the growing incidence of clauses in agreements dealing with training for employee representatives and opportunity for employee representatives to convene their own meeting immediately following the EWC, both matters on which the Directive is silent.

Concerns about the limited nature of the consultation rights envisaged under the Directive would seem to be borne out by the provisions of agreements. As noted earlier, the overwhelming majority define consultation in terms of 'dialogue' or an 'exchange of views'; only one in ten agreements makes provision for more a more formal consultation process, including the right for the employee side to give considered comments or opinions or to make recommendations, and just 3 per cent of agreements anticipate a negotiating role for the EWC (Carley and Marginson 2000). There is also evidence suggesting that the provisions of some EWC agreements fall short of the requirements incorporated in the statutory fall-back model, notably on the questions of the rights of employee representatives to have an additional EWC meeting convened in the context of exceptional circumstances, particularly company restructuring, and to be assisted by experts of their own choosing (Marginson *et al.* 1998). Such shortcomings are mainly evident among the relatively large number of agreements signed in the two-year period between the Directive's adoption and its implementation deadline in September 1996. Subsequent agreements, negotiated under the Directive's 'special negotiating body' procedures, almost all conform to the minimum requirements on these and other matters laid down in the statutory fall-back model (Carley and Marginson 2000).

What in fact happens in terms of the practice of EWCs cannot simply be read off from the provisions of agreements. At best, these are likely to provide only an approximate guide to the actual practice evolved by the parties. Practice may differ from, or have moved beyond, the provisions laid down in agreements. None the less, the formal provisions of agreements are likely to facilitate or constrain the development of EWCs in particular directions. Accordingly, Marginson *et al.* (1998) draw a distinction between agreements whose provisions seem likely to constrain the EWC to a formal or 'symbolic' role, in which there is a ritual annual meeting but little or no contact between employee representatives in between, and none with management, and those whose provisions are likely to promote an EWC with an 'active' role, in which there is contact and networking among the employee representatives, and liaison with management, including the provision of information and dialogue, is ongoing.

The Practice of EWCs

Harvie Ramsay's third proposition emphasised that, only through empirical investigation of the ways EWCs operate in practice can a robust assessment of their significance be developed. There is a burgeoning literature on EWCs, reviewed extensively by Müller and Hoffmann (2001). This section highlights key strands of both survey- and case-study-based literature on the operation and impact of EWCs. Among other things, researchers have sought to assess management and employee-side views and expectations concerning the role of EWCs, and to analyse and explain the differing degrees of activism and influence exhibited by EWCs, focusing on issues such as the different types of EWC observable, developmental trajectories, and the key factors affecting their operation. Much of the literature confirms Ramsay's first and second propositions – that the practice of EWCs may bear only an indirect relationship to their formal remit and consultation rights, and will be shaped by a range of contingent factors.

A number of surveys of managerial opinion suggest that, in practice, EWCs have generally proved to be less of a 'threat' than many managers originally feared. Conversely, concerns have been voiced by trade union and employee EWC representatives about the 'ineffectiveness' of many EWCs, fuelling demands for the strengthening of the EWCs Directive's requirements on employers (Waddington 2003).

Wills (1999) survey of British managerial opinion of EWCs found that managers in companies that had established EWCs had a much more positive view about the role of EWCs than those in companies without them, but saw the benefits of EWCs primarily in terms of reinforcing corporate communications rather than their wider consultative or representative role. Respondents saw EWCs as playing a useful role in terms of two-way communication (88 per cent); getting management views over to employees (63 per cent); hearing the voice of employees (56 per cent); and involving employees in the business (50 per cent). But only a minority of respondents associated EWCs with the more concrete outcomes of 'aiding organisational change' (25 per cent) and 'enhancing productivity through employee involvement' (6 per cent). A UK Department of Trade and Industry survey (Weber *et al.* 2000), covering managers in ten companies with EWCs, six of them UK-based companies, produced similar results. Eight of the ten companies saw EWCs primarily as having 'symbolic value', and half the companies said that their EWCs had been beneficial in enabling them to exchange information with employee representatives and to involve employees more closely in the business. Again, few companies saw EWCs as 'aiding organisational change' or 'increasing productivity'. In terms of the major drawbacks of EWCs, other than the financial costs involved, the principal managerial concerns highlighted by both surveys included 'raised employee expectations' and 'increased bureaucracy'.

Such findings were echoed in a survey of managers in fourteen Japanese-based MNCs with EWCs (Nakano 1999), which found that a majority perceived them as providing a net benefit to the company through their role as a channel for information provision and/or fostering co-operation between management and employee representatives, and/or developing a wider corporate identity among employee representatives. In addition to the financial costs involved, respondents were again concerned that EWCs might raise employee expectations, and at the potential mismatch with decentralised management structures.

A more recent survey of twenty-four UK, US and Japanese multinationals by the American management consultants Organization Resources Counselors Inc. (ORC 2003) found that, in the majority of cases, management perceptions of EWCs were reported to be 'positive'. Three-quarters of the companies said that EWCs had 'added value'. However, while twenty companies said they had informed and consulted their EWC over instances of company restructuring, and most regarded this as beneficial, this was less for its impact on company decisions, which was 'low to non-existent' in the majority of cases, than for the positive influence it exerted in terms of enhanced management co-ordination. In 'only a few companies' had management accepted suggestions from the EWC and subsequently incorporated them into the company's final decisions, although two of the companies had negotiated framework agreements with their EWCs addressing specific aspects of restructuring.

A further survey by Vitols (2003) examined management attitudes towards EWCs in sixty-three European-based MNCs. While 30 per cent of respondents regarded their EWC as 'a necessary legal obligation', 19 per cent saw it as 'a responsible partner for co-managing the company', and 44 per cent chose 'other', with most responses indicating that the EWC was seen as 'an important or useful mechanism for information, exchange of viewpoints and dialogue within the company'. In terms of the 'effectiveness' of EWCs, respondents reported EWCs as having 'moderate positive effects' on the quality of communication with employees, the acceptance of management decisions by employees, the quality of management decision-making and, less than universally, the implementation of new business strategies, but also as having a negative impact on the speed of decision-making within the company.

Surveys of employee opinion of EWCs are rarer, but Waddington (2003) highlights widespread dissatisfaction among EWC representatives from six EU countries with the current practices of EWCs, particularly regarding the scope of the agenda and the quality of information and consultation. However, the extent of this dissatisfaction varies between EWC representatives from the UK and Ireland on the one hand, and those from continental Europe on the other, and between EWC representatives in 'Anglo-Saxon' companies and those in companies based in continental European countries. EWC representatives from the UK and Ireland, where there are only limited domestic information and consultation procedures, were more likely to report 'useful information and consultation' at EWC level than their continental counterparts, who have experience of more regulated national information and consultation regimes. The research also found that the agenda was reported to be narrower and the quality of information lower in EWCs in Anglo-Saxon companies than in those based in continental European countries, whereas Vitols (2003) found that the strength of 'partnership' traditions in the companies' home country had no significant influence on managers' assessment of EWCs' effectiveness.

This last question – the extent to which the operation of EWCs is influenced by the industrial relations traditions and practices in the company's home country – has been an area of considerable debate in the wider academic literature. A number of analysts have argued that employee representatives from the company's home-country workforce, by virtue of their established relations with group-level management and (usually) their numerical dominance, are likely to have a decisive influence on the internal dynamics and performance of EWCs. According to Streeck (1997: 331), rather than being an 'integrated European system of representation', EWCs are likely to be 'international extensions' of the national system of workplace representation in the company's country of origin. Lecher (1999) contends that 'home country' employee representatives are able to exert a decisive influence on the internal dynamics of EWCs and to drive or constrain the development of their role. However, such views derive largely from the experience of EWCs in companies based in continental European countries, especially Germany and France, where there are well-defined national works council institutions providing for information and consultation.

Hall *et al.* (2003) argue for a more differentiated approach to the influence of national industrial relations factors on EWCs to take into account the circumstances of companies headquartered in the countries, such as the UK, whose national industrial relations arrangements do not provide a strong institutional model for EWCs, and those headquartered outside Europe whose 'home' management and workforce are not involved in the EWC, as is the case with US-based companies. Case studies of EWCs in eight UK- and US-based companies carried out by Warwick University's Industrial Relations Research Unit found that headquarters management in the UK-based companies tended to maintain a minimalist or restrictive approach to the EWC – a reflection of Anglo-Saxon traditions in terms of industrial relations and corporate governance. In contrast, management policy towards the EWC tended to be more proactive in the US cases where the EWC was managed from a European-level management structure and the management EWC co-ordinators were European nationals with extensive experience of 'continental' works council systems. On the employee side, UK workforce representatives tended not to 'punch their weight' within EWCs. In six of the eight case study companies, the home or largest workforce, was the UK yet in four of these cases UK workers 'conceded' the employee-side leadership role to representatives from other countries. In each case, interviewees reported that the principal reason for this was British employee representatives' lack of familiarity with works-council-type structures and consultation with senior management about corporate strategy, and their limited infrastructural support at the workplace. This reinforces similar findings by Wills (2000), whose study of an EWC in a company formed by an a British-French-American merger shows that, while the UK and France had the same number of EWC members, the employee side tended to be 'dominated' by the French representatives because of their greater experience of consultation at national level in France.

The relative salience of national industrial relations factors is also central to the three 'lines of development' for EWCs identified by Lecher and Rüb (1999), based on research on the functioning of EWCs in multinationals based in four European countries. In the first category are EWCs in which employee representatives have an exclusively national frame of reference, regarding the EWC as an extension of national representation arrangements that provides an additional forum for pursuing domestic issues. A second category comprises those EWCs which have developed a supranational role, but whose agendas are driven primarily by representatives from the company's home country. Third, there are EWCs which are developing a 'collective European identity', less reliant on co-ordination by home-country representatives, and which are beginning to regulate some matters at European level. Lecher and Rüb (1999) found evidence of all three types of EWC, as did Stoop and Donders (1998) in a parallel study of ten EWCs. Crucially, even though many of the EWCs in question had only been in operation for two to three years, some were already evolving a transnational or 'European' mode of operation where the network of contacts and control of resources is not nationally centred.

The considerable variety of EWC practice is underlined in further work by Lecher and colleagues (Lecher *et al.* 2001). Their comparative, cross-national and cross-sectoral analysis of EWCs' role and functioning in twenty-three MNCs yields four empirically distinctive types of EWC, differentiated according to their 'capacity to act' (Lecher *et al.* 2001): 'symbolic EWCs' (as suggested by Marginson *et al.* 1998), involving a low level of information provision and no formal consultation, and little or no contact between employee representatives, or with management, between annual meetings; 'service EWCs' (in which EWC members exchange information but do not attempt to develop a common EWC policy); 'project-oriented EWCs' (in which the employee side focuses on the systematic development of its internal capacities and structures, independently of management); and 'participatory' EWCs (which engage in formalised consultative procedures and negotiations with management). In the three 'active' types, to differing degrees there is ongoing contact and activity between employee representatives, and regular liaison with management. Around half of the EWCs studied by Lecher *et al.* (2001) fell under the 'symbolic' heading, but in a minority of more advanced cases the EWC had developed a formalised consultative role going beyond the relatively limited rights envisaged by the Directive.

In terms of identifying the conditions that facilitate the emergence of an active rather than a symbolic EWC, Lecher *et al.* (1999, 2001, 2002) take an 'actor-centred' approach which emphasises such factors as the organising capacity of, and effective networking between, the employee representatives; strong links between the EWC representatives and those at national and local levels; close relations with trade unions providing resources and expert assistance; and co-operative, high-trust relations with central management. But the Warwick University research (Marginson *et al.* 2004) suggests that structural factors, particularly the degree of internationalisation of the business operations of the companies concerned, are also a crucial element in explaining variations in EWCs' 'capacity to act'.

In their study of EWCs in eight UK- and US-based companies, the Warwick-based team investigated the impact of EWCs on management decision-making. The research found that the capacity of EWCs to influence the outcome of transnational management decision-making is conditioned fundamentally by the nature of companies' business operations and the degree to which they are internationalised. The impact of the EWC on management decision-making was found to be greatest in single-business companies whose operations are spread across more than one country, and where production and other activities are integrated across European borders. No EWC impact on management decision-making was evident in multi-business companies whose operations tended to be concentrated in one country and/or where there was little or no cross-border integration of production.

EWC practice in the eight EWCs was additionally shaped by a range of further, structure and agency factors. Management structure and management policy are both important. How far EWCs are 'active' rather than 'symbolic' was facilitated or constrained by whether there was a European level management structure that in fact corresponded to the EWC. Where there was a close 'fit' between the management structure and the EWC, the latter was more likely to be active, and more likely to have an impact on management decisions, than where there was not. Moreover, EWCs were more likely to exercise influence where management's approach to the EWC was proactive, seeing it as a mechanism that could be utilised for management purposes – such as improving employee understanding of the rationale for business decisions and hence the legitimacy of management actions – than where management's approach was minimalist, concerned primarily with complying with its legal obligations but strictly circumscribing the role and remit of the EWC. The nature of pre-existing structures of employee representation are also important in facilitating the development of employee-side organisation and activity; in particular, the existence of representative structures at national group level in the main countries of operation and/or a pre-existing international network among employee representatives on which the EWC can build. In only one of the eight companies studied, a leading US-based automotive manufacturer, were all these factors present, and the EWC exercised the strongest influence of any of the eight we investigated, engaging both in formalised consultation and in the negotiation of European-level agreements with central management on the handling of restructuring.

These agreements are among the small number of joint texts negotiated via EWCs to date. Union hopes and employer fears that the EWCs Directive would provide a stepping stone towards European-level collective bargaining over substantive industrial relations matters have so far not materialised on any widespread basis. The most visible indication of bargaining activity involving EWCs is the number of written agreements or joint texts negotiated by, or within the context of, EWCs. Carley (2002) identifies just twenty-six such texts concluded by twelve EWCs (although a few additional cases have been reported more recently).

The subject matter of these joint texts and the nature of their provisions vary considerably. The most common themes addressed are the handling of company restructuring and social/trade-union rights. Other topics covered include health and safety, skills training and gender equality. Most establish general frameworks for company policy. In a number of cases the joint texts promote or require action on the issues concerned at lower levels within the organisation. Of these, agreements concluded over the 2000–3 period at three companies – Ford Europe, General Motors Europe and Danone – have established specific principles or procedures that are obligatory on the parties at lower levels, and come closest to 'traditional' collective agreements. The January 2000 agreement at Ford dealt with the consequences of the spin-off of Visteon for employees' status, representation rights, and terms and conditions of employment. Three framework agreements within GME have dealt with the handling of successive restructuring initiatives, and at Danone an October 2001 agreement dealt with the social standards applicable in the restructuring of its biscuits division within Europe. In Carley's view, the agreements in these companies 'may indeed be the first signs of genuine collective bargaining within EWCs'.

In very few of the companies where such texts have been negotiated do their EWC agreements envisage explicitly a negotiating role for the EWC (Air France, Danone and Sara Lee Personal Products are among the exceptions). Significantly, however, many of the companies that have concluded joint texts via EWCs are from sectors such as motor manufacturing and food, drink and tobacco, which are characterised by internationally integrated operations and well-organised trade unions and works councils within companies – structural features that tend to underpin the more advanced forms of EWC practice more generally.

Conclusion

Much of Harvie Ramsay's (1997) 'provisional and indicative' evaluation of the prospects of EWCs remains highly relevant today, in particular his conclusion that:

> In practice, [EWCs'] formal rights are at most a framework within which, just as in other levels of works council organisation, a wide variation of outcomes remains possible. At present the balance of possibilities suggests that management will be able to contain most EWCs and engage at least in successful damage limitation. Any exceptions may mark the longer-run potential of such bodies to challenge MNCs, however. (p. 320)

The research on EWCs to date certainly presents a mixed picture. It is clear that the practice of EWCs and the influence they wield varies considerably, ranging from 'symbolic' EWCs, more akin to 'paper tigers', whose role is largely confined to a ritual annual meeting, through more active bodies involving ongoing networking activity on the employee side and regular liaison with management, to those that exert a measure of influence over management decision-making and even engage in negotiation of joint texts or agreements with management. The most far-reaching of these agreements have established a binding framework for handling aspects of European-wide restructuring, with direct consequences for national and local negotiations, confirming their potential – if not their widespread actuality – as a 'Trojan horse' for European-level collective bargaining. This substantial variation in EWC practice and impact maps on to a diverse range of contingent influences, as suggested by Ramsay, including country-, sector- and company-specific factors, in which considerations of structure and agency interact.

Although only a small minority of EWCs would appear to have developed into effective means of employee interest representation at a transnational, European level, they remain relatively youthful structures that are taking both management and employee representatives into uncharted territory. 'Learning to walk before they can run' appears to be an appropriate metaphor, and one borne out by the trajectory of EWC practice in some (but by no means all) companies (Lecher and Rüb 1999; Hall *et al.* 2003). One crucial precondition shaping the evolution of EWCs into effective European-level means of employee interest representation – the international integration of companies' operations – is developing progressively across sectors, raising the prospect of more EWCs developing into active or influential bodies over time. The wider diffusion of a second such precondition – the capacity of trade unions and national works council structures to initiate and sustain effective cross-border forms of organisation within multinationals – is more hazardous to predict. Further legislative intervention does not seem likely to impinge greatly on current dynamics. Even though European trade unions are pressing for far-reaching amendments designed to generalise best EWC practice (Waddington 2003), a significant strengthening of the formal rights of EWCs as a result of the prospective revision of the Directive is doubtful.

References

Blokland, A. and Berentsen, B. (2003) 'Accounting for the "Missing" EWCs', *European Works Councils Bulletin*, 44, March/April, 17–20.

Carley, M. (2002) 'European-level Bargaining in Action? Joint Texts Negotiated by European Works Councils', *Transfer*, 8:4, 646–53.

Carley, M. and Hall, M. (2000) 'The Implementation of the European Works Councils Directive', *Industrial Law Journal*, 29:2, 103–24.

Carley, M. and Marginson, P. (2000) *Negotiating European Works Councils: A Comparative Study of Article 6 and Article 13 Agreements* (Luxembourg: Office for Official Publications of the European Communities/European Foundation for the Improvement of Living and Working Conditions).

EIRR (1993) 'The Hoover Affair and Social Dumping', *European Industrial Relations Review*, 275, December, 26–30.

Gilman, M. and Marginson, P. (2002) 'Negotiating European Works Councils: Contours of Constrained Choice', *Industrial Relations Journal*, 33:1, 36–51.

Hall, M. (1992) 'Behind the European Works Councils Directive: the European Commission's Legislative Strategy', *British Journal of Industrial Relations*, 30:4, 547–66.

Hall, M., Hoffmann, A., Marginson, P. and Müller, T. (2003) 'National Influences on European Works Councils in UK- and US-based Companies', *Human Resource Management Journal*, 13:4, 75–92.

Kerckhofs, P. (2002) *European Works Councils: Facts and Figures* (Brussels: European Trade Union Institute).

Knudsen, H. and Bruun, N. (1998) 'European Works Councils in the Nordic Countries', *European Journal of Industrial Relations*, 4:2, 131–55.

Lecher, W. (1999) 'Resources of the European Works Council – Empirical Knowledge and Prospects', *Transfer*, 5:3, 278–301.

Lecher, W. and Rüb, S. (1999) 'The Constitution of European Works Councils', *European Journal of Industrial Relations*, 5:1, 7–25.

Lecher, W., Nagel, B. and Platzer, H.-W. (1999) *The Establishment of European Works Councils: From Information Committee to Social Actor* (Aldershot: Ashgate).

Lecher, W., Platzer, H.-W., Rüb, S. and Weiner, K.-P. (2001) *European Works Councils: Developments, Types and Networking* (Aldershot: Gower).

Lecher, W., Platzer, H.-W., Rüb, S. and Weiner, K.-P. (2002) *European Works Councils: Negotiated Europeanisation* (Aldershot: Ashgate).

Marginson, P., Gilman, M., Jacobi, O. and Krieger, H. (1998) *Negotiating European Works Councils: An Analysis of Agreements Under Article 13* (Luxembourg: Office for Official Publications of the European Communities/European Foundation for the Improvement of Living and Working Conditions).

Marginson, P., Hall, M., Hoffmann, A. and Müller, T. (2004) 'The Impact of European Works Councils on Management Decision-making in UK- and US-based multinationals: A Case Study Comparison', *British Journal of Industrial Relations*.

ORC (Organization Resources Counselors, Inc.) (2003) *European Works Council survey*.

Müller, T. and Hoffmann, A. (2001) 'EWC Research: A Review of the Literature', *Warwick Papers in Industrial Relations*, 65. Accessed to http://users.wbs.warwick.ac.uk/irru/publications/papers.htm.

Müller, T. and Platzer, H.-W. (2003) 'European Works Councils', in B. Keller, and H.-W. Platzer (eds), *Industrial Relations and European Integration* (Aldershot: Ashgate), 53–84.

Nakano, S. (1999) 'Management views of European Works Councils', *European Journal of Industrial Relations*, 5:3, 307–26.

Ramsay, H. (1995) 'Le défi européen', in A. Amin and J. Tomaney (eds), *Behind the myth of the European Union* (London: Routledge), 174–97.

Ramsay, H. (1997) 'Fool's gold? European Works Councils and Workplace Democracy', *Industrial Relations Journal*, 28:4, 314–22.

Rivest, C. (1996) 'Voluntary European Works Councils', *European Journal of Industrial Relations*, 2:2, 235–53.

Stoop, S. and Donders, P. (1998) *EOR-en in functie*, English summary translated by P. Kerckhofs (Rotterdam: FNV).

Streeck, W. (1997) 'Neither European Nor Works Councils', *Economic and Industrial Democracy*, 18:2, 325–37.

Vitols, S. (2003) *Management Cultures in Europe: European Works Councils and Human Resource Management in Multinational Enterprises*, Forum Mitbestimmung und

Unternehmen Accessed at www.unternehmenskultur.org/mitbest/Vitols_
finalreport_komp.pdf.

Waddington, J. (2003) 'What Do Representatives Think of the Practices of European
Works Councils? Views from six countries', *European Journal of Industrial Relations*,
9:3, 303–25.

Waddington, J. and Kerckhofs, P. (2003) 'European Works Councils: What Is The
Current State of Play?', *Transfer* 9:2, 322–39.

Weber, T., Foster, P. and Levent Egriboz, K. (2000) *Costs and Benefits of the European
Works Councils Directive*, Department of Trade and Industry, Employment
Relations Research Series, 9.

Wills, J. (1999) 'European Works Councils in British Firms', *Human Resource
Management Journal*, 9:4, 19–38.

Wills, J. (2000) 'Great Expectations: Three Years in the Life of a European Works
Council', *European Journal of Industrial Relations*, 6:1, 85–107.

12
Theorising the State and Economic Democracy

Paul Boreham and Richard Hall

Introduction

The material standards and political rights of labour rise and fall with the viability of particular models of the relationship between capitalist economic organisation and the capitalist state. The choice of model is an intensely political one. The form it has assumed in different national settings has been contingent on a combination of institutional legacies, the balance of political forces, the policy autonomy of key political institutions, and changing international and economic conjunctures (see Jessop 2002: 259). It would be difficult to overstate the political importance for the labour movement of the outcomes of the debate about appropriate models for the organization of economic activity. In this context, some national labour movements expounded a highly policy-conscious 'strategic unionism' (see Korpi 1983). Explicit in this developing policy assertiveness were conceptions that labour movement participation in macroeconomic policy would be permanent and beneficial for economic outcomes such as full employment and social equality. The Keynesian prescription for democratic control over investment was a key element of this approach (see Meidner 1978). The democratisation of economic decision-making implicit in these labour movement strategies gives rise to a definition of the concept that provides a framework for the analysis that follows.

The concept of economic democracy can be traced back to Bernstein's theories of democratic socialism. More concrete manifestations of the practical import of economic democracy can be found, however, with the emergence of moves to introduce forms of economic democracy in western European, and in particular, in Swedish social democracy of the 1960s and 1970s. Pontusson and Kuruvilla (1992) argue that the broad parameters of such a project include the facilitation of a solidaristic wages policy that would limit wage inequality; a reduction in wealth inequality; the extension of industrial and economic democracy; the encouragement of 'societal influence over economic investment'; and the improved funding of pensions. Together, these motivations lead to a broader concept of economic democracy based on principles of decommodification – the distribution and access to socially and economically important goods, services and opportunities on the basis of universal rights rather than on market power. In societies where markets continue to be important, this also implies the absence of extreme inequalities in wealth and income.

This chapter assesses the institutional forms of economic democracy inherent in two contrasting types of capitalist economic organisation that have characterised the advanced capitalist states in the post-war era. Our additional aim is to comment on the ability of economic democracy to achieve positive social and economic outcomes for labour in these particular conjunctures of the state and capitalism. A central focus concerns the rise and *decline* of the nation state as the key agency of labour market, industrial relations and economic governance; a change that has been an important aspect of the wider shift in regimes of economic governance towards neo-liberalism. Leaving aside state led forms of capitalist organisation exemplified by Japan, the two models that have prevailed – neo-corporatism and neo-liberalism – have had very different outcomes for the labour movement and for notions of economic democracy.

Models of the State and the Capitalist Economy: Neo-corporatism

The political-economic model that prevailed during the post-war period in many, mainly European Christian democratic or social democratic, economies relied on the institutionalisation of permanent, negotiated approaches to the investment and production decisions and actions of economic agents. Based on a mutual, negotiated understanding of the linkages between their own economic interests and the importance of collective agreements to the stability of a socially embedded, socially regulated economy, the economic forces involved in these neo-corporatist arrangements sought to balance competition and co-operation (Jessop 2002: 261). This institutional framework entrenched a powerful market presence for organised labour and presented it with the ability to participate directly in economic decision-making. The resulting policy model was characterised by a focus on unemployment, labour rights and welfare provisions (Coates 2000: 10).

The development of institutions such as those outlined above proceeded unevenly and incrementally. Nevertheless, control of the economy that was formerly 'unregulated' (that is, regulated by markets) had become bargained or negotiated more explicitly. In particular, the kinds of institutions that were constitutive of changing modes of regulation represented an opening up to democratic processes of decisions previously made behind the anonymity and uncertainty of the marketplace. These institutional arrangements allowed the effective participation of labour organisations in the formulation and implementation of policy 'across those interdependent policy areas that are of central importance for the management of the economy' (Lehmbruch 1984: 66). The social democratic parties and labour movements promoting this view of corporatism were convinced that there were policy issues that were much more susceptible to public resolution when collective criteria were applied than when they were relegated to entrepreneurial or parliamentary processes. Hence there was an explicitly democratic rationale for the post-liberal arrangements advocated and formulated. In addition, as private investment decisions have public and long-lasting consequences, there was considered to be an economic as well as a normative rationale for subjecting them to democratic deliberation.

The view of economic democracy presented here rests on an understanding of the institutional relationship between the political system and the structures of extra-parliamentary political organisation. Important aspects of this institutional milieu include: the extent to which the political power balance between social democratic or labour parties and national labour movements is weighted toward the latter; the degree of concentration of labour movement confederations; the extent to which labour movements are representative of the workforce; and the degree to which trade union political action is focused on policy matters rather than industrial relations.

It was argued that trade unions had a direct interest in accepting a public role and participating in these institutions. In so doing they would not become merely instruments of an authoritarian state (Higgins 1985). The labour movement benefited organisationally by taking on legitimate public functions. But what were the material outcomes in terms of delivering better economic outcomes that conformed to labour interests? This question was to be addressed by empirical studies in comparative political economy undertaken in the 1980s and 1990s that focused on relationships between labour participation in economic decision-making and macroeconomic outcomes favourable to labour, notably employment and social welfare provision.

Economic Democracy and Unemployment

During the 1960s–1980s, policy development in many OECD countries involved major functional interest groups in key decision-making or policy formulation processes. The resulting institutional arrangements often provided for the formal participation of labour in the formulation and implementation of policy (see Keman 1984; Schmidt 1984; Schott 1984; Boreham *et al*. 1986, 1989; Tarantelli 1986; Hicks 1987, 1988; Calmfors and Driffill 1988; Paloheimo 1989). Such interventionist institutions ranged from centralised wage-fixing systems (Australia) to 'active' labour market boards

(Sweden), to broader economic planning institutions providing a formal role for labour in the formulation of national economic policy.

Research has documented the importance to institutions of economic policy making (and the strategic policy choices for which they were responsible) in producing macroeconomic outcomes that accorded broadly with labour movement objectives in various advanced industrial nations (see Cameron 1984; Keman 1984; Scharpf 1984a, 1984b; Clegg *et al.* 1986; Therborn 1986; Czada 1987; Keman and van Dijk 1987; Schmidt 1987). Different political/institutional factors were identified in various empirical analyses, including party government (Castles 1982; Schmidt 1982a; Boreham and Hall 1994; Alt 1985); unions (Griffin *et al.* 1989; Paloheimo 1990); and corporatism (Schott 1984; Therborn 1987; Hicks 1988). Studies focused on the articulation of political actors and political institutions in such domains as the efficacy of corporatist institutions in centralised and decentralised economies (Paloheimo 1990); the intersection of government partisanship and labour organisation (Alvarez *et al.* 1991); variations in the institutional rules and organizational structures of trade unions and their decision making processes (Golden 1993); trade unions' wage-bargaining strategies (Kenworthy 1990); wage-setting arrangements associated with wage flexibility (Calmfors and Driffill 1988; Rowthorn 1992); and conflicts centred on the nature and distribution of power resources between major collectivities (Schmidt 1988; Korpi 1991).

The key aspect of the forms of neo-corporatism suggested in these studies is that the class representation of labour in economic decision-making makes the shares accruing to profits and incomes overtly political. By placing corporate investment decisions in the public policy arena, political pressure on the part of labour to retain goals such as (low) unemployment as salient policy issues is likely to be associated with compatible interventions such as counter-cyclical demand policies in association with active labour market interventions, labour protection legislation, and an orientation towards employment issues in public infrastructural expenditure and in the regulation of private investment capital (Clegg *et al.* 1986: 340–55; Pampel and Williamson 1988; Griffin *et al.* 1989; Paloheimo 1990; Boreham and Compston 1992).

These comparative studies led to the conclusion that, where political actors representing labour had been accorded a formal role in the development and implementation of economic policy, there had been a major impact in reducing national levels of unemployment. In particular, the data presented by Boreham and Compston (1992) supported a number of quite specific conclusions about the relationship between the successful achievement of policies committed to low levels of unemployment and the institutional processes involved. This research showed that the critical pathway towards low unemployment was the formal participation of trade unions in the institutions of economic policy-making. Specifically, where trade unions had been able to assert their political power to achieve formal participation with governments in broader macroeconomic policy areas, quite dramatic achievements were evident in the data demonstrating a commitment to reducing unemployment.

Economic Democracy, the Welfare State and Decommodification

The essence of the welfare state takes the form of public intervention to preserve minimum standards of income, health, education and housing, with the former subsumed under programmes to secure against the risks to living standards associated with market dependence. The conceptual dimensions of this problem concern an understanding of the welfare state as being central to the articulation of the market's and society's roles in social provision. The redistributive role of the state described by Wilensky (1981) clearly involves an intervention in the cash nexus of individual provision of welfare through the purchase of welfare goods and services as market commodities. The extension of social citizenship rights in many capitalist economies has involved a relaxation of the pure commodity status of welfare, though the mere presence of welfare expenditure may not bring about significant decommodification unless it replaces market provision and market dependence – a concept referred to below as 'welfare effort'.

The organised labour movement has a structural interest in such policy outcomes. As Esping-Andersen (1990) contends, where workers are captive to labour market forces, they will be forced to seek income (social) security outside the market. It is therefore to be expected that wage earners' desire for emancipation from market dependency will constitute decommodification as a guiding principle of labour movement policy. This has provided the analytical focus of a number of studies that have sought to answer the question: can the extent of social as opposed to market development of welfare be attributed to labour movement mobilisation and its democratic participation in economic decision-making?

Comparative analysis of social policy outcomes has allowed both a detailed evaluation of variations in social welfare effort in the advanced industrial democracies as well as explaining the diversity of approaches within nations with similar political traditions and economic structure. The role of political institutions was only conceded within the comparative political economy literature since the 1980s, following the seminal works of Korpi (1980; 1983), Castles (1981; 1982), Wilensky (1981), Schmidt (1982b) and Esping-Andersen (1985). The body of work that emerged during the decade following these studies emphasised the role of political institutions in translating the power of key political actors into welfare effort.

The broad conclusion from the comparative analyses of the divergence that exists between different national social policy performances has been that particular institutional bases of decision-making have had a significant effect on final welfare outcomes (see also Swank and Hicks 1985; Esping-Andersen 1987; Griffin *et al.* 1989; Paloheimo 1990). However, quantitative analyses have differed in their explanation as to how democratic institutional roles matter for welfare spending. They have contrasted alternative explanations of welfare state development in terms of 'power resources' approaches (for example Korpi 1989); 'social democratic' and 'interest-group-politics' theories (for example, Pampel and Williamson 1988); or 'social democratic corporatist', 'political democratic' and 'statist' perspectives (for example, Hicks and Swank 1992; Boreham and Hall 1994).

Research findings have identified an association between higher levels of union strength and institutional power and significantly greater welfare effort in OECD countries (Esping-Andersen 1990; Pampel and Williamson 1990; Hicks and Swank 1992). More recently, Boreham *et al.* (1996) showed that increasing labour's participation in economic policy-making appears to lead to considerable increases in social security expenditure and welfare effort. As they concluded, 'elevating the participatory status of unions in the policy process from no participation to full participation could be expected to lead to a doubling of government consumption expenditure on social welfare from present levels' (1996: 221).

In general, the results of the comparative studies confirm that trade union strength, and to a greater degree the formal participation of labour in policy formation, have been crucial to welfare state effort and decommodification. The form of political and institutional structuring conducive to highly developed welfare decommodification is likely to be the combination of high rates of trade union density and extensive institutional participation by national labour movements. These analyses have illuminated some conduits through which economic democracy has reshaped economic and political relations. Clearly, both the existence and the nature of a democratic institutional milieu that has been forged through historical processes and contemporary strategic choices have been crucial in facilitating the achievement of labour movement objectives. The form of economic democracy facilitated by neo-corporatist institutions had created some significant tensions for national labour movements. However, the comparative data was unequivocal in demonstrating that economic democracy had achieved considerable gains in reducing unemployment and in developing decommodifying welfare state regimes.

The Fate of Neo-corporatism in the Contemporary Era

Business mobilisation against corporatism occurred in the advanced social democracies of northern Europe (see Gerlich 1992; Pontusson 1992; Kurzer

1993; Notermans 1993) and in Australia (Boreham *et al.* 1999). Business interests (whether formerly incorporated or not) have played a central role in the
decline of corporatist politics (Streeck 1984, Kurzer 1991, 1993; Streeck and
Schmitter 1991; Gobeyn 1993; Thelen 1994) as they no longer 'view corporatist arrangements as beneficial in an era of domestic structural economic
change and transformations in the global capitalist system' (Gobeyn 1993: 3).
These changes oversaw the structural weakening of labour, the growing
resistance of business to regulatory controls, and evidence that globally
mobile sectors of business have become less interested in the constraints and
restrictions imposed by 'national' structures of wage bargaining and labour
market regulation. By the 1990s, it was becoming clear that the benefits that
neo-corporatist forms of decision-making created for capital such as wage
demand moderation and the control of industrial militancy were now
perceived as being realisable through less restrictive, market-based, decentralised forms of labour-management relations.

New conditions of intensified global competition have placed levels of
labour remuneration and the erosion of labour rights at the centre of the
agenda for the achievement of international competitiveness. These strategies can take various forms. The policy vocabulary is one of flexibility for
management to redeploy labour outside the constraints of custom or legal
convention in order to reduce unit labour costs. Microeconomic reform also
concentrates on intervening in the social and historical structures that have
determined how work is done, and the social relations through which it is
collectively organised. Both developments are fostered by a deregulation of
employment and labour market conditions, and an accompanying shift from
more centralised regulatory structures for the control of wages and industrial relations to unregulated bargaining at the workplace level (see Boreham
2002).

These changes reflect both the pressures of economic adjustment and a
wider neo-liberal policy agenda. They have altered the landscape of labour
politics. Union attitudes and structures have been transformed, reflected in
a shift from labour's traditional distributional concerns towards employers'
firm-level interests in productivity, efficiency and flexibility. As Regini
(1992: 7) has argued: 'there has been a shift in the "centre of gravity" of
economic and industrial relations systems from the level of macroeconomic
management to the micro-level of the firm; and management, rather than the
state, has become the central actor in the process of economic adjustment'
(see also Thelen 1994: 108). These enterprise-level changes have an impact on
state capacity and the macro-political role of labour because, to the extent
that the role of the arbitration system is being downgraded, unions are
excluded from bargaining over societal level social and economic issues.
Micro-level outcomes can be expected to be less favourable to workers and,
while there is still uncertainty about the economic outcomes of enterprise
bargaining, there is no ambiguity about equity questions: workplace

bargaining favours the strong – those in a superior bargaining position (Peetz 1998: 343).

Models of the State and the Capitalist Economy: Neo-liberalism

Neo-liberal theory has as its core the view that economic development depends on competitiveness, which depends substantially on the control of labour costs. Inflexibilities created by successful labour movement organisation have focused legislative attention on cutting trade union powers and trade union participation in regulatory agencies. Neo-liberal approaches tend to have Anglo-American practices in which there is no significant role or voice for unions as their key referents. Contemporary economic policy debate is centred on a neoliberal orthodoxy that espouses the need to free market forces, resulting in differences in the quality and quantity of the factors of production, most notably labour. Regulation of the conditions of and returns to labour is regarded as the source of inflexibilities that need to be overcome to facilitate competitiveness. Orthodox neo-liberal economic theory is antithetical to labour (Coates 2000: 6) as it involves privatisation and the imposition of commercial criteria in the public sector, with deregulation and an imposed legal framework to expose decisions to market-based discipline in the private sector.

Economic Democracy in the New Century

In this section the effects of consolidation of the neo-liberal ascendency and decline of the power of organised labour are considered at the aggregate level. Recognition that the political-economic power of organised labour has declined is almost universal; the impact of this weakening of labour is, however, more debatable.

As noted above, orthodox neo-classical approaches tend to see marginalisation of organised labour as being consistent with the imperative of removing institutional and labour market rigidities in the interests of enhancing flexibility in the face of intensified global competition. These analyses are typically cloaked in a grim optimism – there is no realistic alternative to the pursuit of the 'Washington consensus' (Standing 2002: 26) for contemporary advanced economies, and while there is short-term pain for workers associated with the industrial restructuring, the resulting improvements in the efficiency of markets (including labour markets) and the performance of economies benefit all in the long run. Research utilising broader approaches than those inspired by neo-classical economics generally reaches a more pessimistic conclusion. This research and the empirical record of the performance of industrial states in the most recent period, particularly the 1990s, offers similarly gloomy conclusions. The neo-liberal ascendency has led to more than the restructuring of the institutional configuration of state institutions and the re-alignment of the power resources of key societal actors; it has had adverse consequences for workers and their families across a range of dimensions.

The delineation of the dimensions against which the outcomes of the neo-liberal ascendency can be evaluated is inspired here by the idea of economic democracy. Economic democracy in this sense implies that workers will have significant power in the sphere of production, exercising a strong voice, if not control over and ownership of, the means of production. For Swedish social democracy in the 1960s and 1970s this meant active participation of employees in enterprise ownership and the distribution of economic rewards. In discussing the motives behind the Swedish attempt to institute economic democracy, Pontusson and Kuruvilla (1992) hint to a broader definition of the concept of economic democracy, extending beyond capital and profit-sharing (Poole 1989), to one based on principles of decommodification. Drawing on these principles the following sections consider four general dimensions of economic and social performance.

Income and wealth inequality

Economic democracy in the context of market economies implies that levels of income and wealth inequality will be moderate rather than extreme. The greater the levels of inequality, the less likely it will be that poorer individuals and households will be able to purchase high-quality goods and services on private markets.

Social security and welfare

The welfare state has been one of the prime ways in which dependency on private incomes for the provision of socially important goods and services has been attenuated for the citizenries of advanced industrial states. Through direct provision of social services and goods, and through social security payments of various kinds, welfare state systems of different varieties have sought to provide for citizens unable to purchase sufficient socially important services and goods on private markets or cope with unemployment and other enforced absences from the labour market. Pensions, sickness benefits and unemployment benefits have been among the most prominent.

Employment, unemployment and the experience of work

In the advanced industrial economies, access to quality paid employment is a critical determinant of one's capacity to participate in the economy more generally. Beyond measures of employment, however, the quality and labour market status of employment are also critical and point to the importance of the dimensions of fragmentation and diversity in labour markets.

Training and skills development

Access to training and opportunities for the development of vocational skills are critical for both job-seekers and workers seeking advancement and access to higher paying and more rewarding jobs or careers. In addition to potentially improving incomes and life chances, access to quality training enhances the ability of workers to undertake work that is more intrinsically satisfying.

Income and Wealth Inequality – Deeper into the Mire

There is little doubt that levels of both wage and wealth inequality rose appreciably across most of the OECD from the mid-1980s to the mid- to late 1990s. Similarly, much research has found that, while moderating to some degree in the latter half of the 1990s, inequality has continued to increase since then. However, questions concerning the causes of increasing inequality and the ameliorating effect of what some have found to be lower levels of poverty in the advanced economies continue to be contested.

Since the 1980s, the share of national incomes going to capital has been increasing while the share going to labour has been declining (Standing 2002: 71). The rate of return to capital has increased with the boom in equity markets, while large groups of workers in many countries continue to complain that their incomes are inadequate. The trend has been compounded by changes to taxation regimes whereby taxation rates on capital and the highest earners have tended to decline while the social insurance burden on individual workers has mounted. This worldwide dynamic is reflected in the particular experiences of the populations of the OECD states.

Recent trends in income inequality for twenty-five countries are shown in Table 12.1. Incomes are defined here as all post-tax cash income including transfers. The decade from the mid-1980s witnessed more consistent increases in income inequality than had the previous decade. In the 1970s–1980s income inequality increased (strongly) in two economies (the USA and the UK), remained stable in eight, and actually fell in seven. In the later period (1980s–1990s), however, the picture is much more uniform: income inequality increased in twenty-four of the economies, and in fifteen of these the magnitude of the increase was over 7 per cent.

The rapid rises in income inequality seen in both the USA and the UK in the 1970s and 1980s continued into the early 1990s, although it is commonplace to observe that the rate of increase in inequality 'slowed markedly' in

Table 12.1   Overall trends in income distribution – summary results from national and cross-national studies

	Mid/early 1970s to mid/late 1980s	OECD Study 1980s	Mid/late 1980s to mid/late 1990s
Australia	0	+	+
Austria	0	0	+ +
Belgium	0	+	+
Canada	–	0	+
Czech Republic	na	na	+ + +
Denmark	na	na	–
Finland	–	0	+
France	–	0	+
Germany	–	+	+
Hungary	na	na	+ +
Ireland	–	0	+ +
Israel	0	0	+ +
Italy	– –	–	+ +
Japan	0	+	+ +
Mexico	na	na	+ +
Netherlands	0	+	+ +
New Zealand	0	+	+ + +
Norway	0	0	+ +
Poland	na	na	+ +
Russia	na	na	+ +
Sweden	–	+	+ +
Switzerland	na	na	+
Taiwan	0	0	+
United Kingdom	+ +	+ + +	+ +
USA	+ +	+ +	+ +

Notes:
+ + +   Significant rise in income inequality (more than 15% increase)
+ +   Rise in income inequality (7% to 15% increase).
+   Modest rise in income inequality (1% to 6% increase).
0   No change (–1% to +1%).
–   Modest decrease in income inequality (1% to 6% decrease).
– –   Decrease in income inequality (7% to 15% decrease).
– – –   Significant decrease in income inequality (more than 15% decrease).
na   No consistent estimate available.

Source: Smeeding (2002) table 3.

those two countries in the late 1990s (Smeeding 2002: 22). Nevertheless, the point remains that the levels of inequality in the two largest English-speaking countries continues to increase.

In the USA, the story of the late 1990s is an interesting one. Low levels of unemployment and a continuation of the 1990s boom saw wages at the low end of the distribution increase in real terms, thus reversing the historic stagnation of average wages. The median family income in the USA grew 2.2 per cent per year between 1995 and 2000, compared with just 0.4 per cent per year between 1973 and 1995. The ongoing rise in inequality in the USA as in a number of other economies, is largely a result of the dramatic increases at the top of the earnings distribution (Mishel *et al*. 2002: 3) rather than declines at the bottom. Some take heart from this – while the rich are certainly getting richer, the poor are not necessarily getting poorer.

Certainly, an examination of the more limited time-series data on poverty confirms that, generally, the proportion of the population in poverty has not been growing, and in at least some countries in recent times it has been declining. Tax transfer systems have clearly had some effect on poverty, although it is far from clear that the overall proportion of the population of advanced industrial economies in poverty has been declining. OECD analysis of poverty trends in five countries revealed that in four of these countries the level of poverty remained constant or had been reduced; the exception was the USA, where the proportion in poverty has continued to increase (Burniaux *et al*. 1998: 33). While conceding that the US economy has recently been making gains in reducing poverty levels, Mishel *et al*. (2002: 8–9) note that the share of the nation's poor is now about equal to the 1973 level – a modest achievement, given dramatic increases in productivity and real per capita incomes over the period.

Poverty levels in the USA have been slightly reduced recently, largely by encouraging more of the poor into the labour market through the strengthening of the Earned Income Tax Credit scheme and new 'welfare to work' legislation. The increased labour market participation among the poor has resulted in an estimated 3.3 per cent decline in the level of poverty in recent years. Offsetting the effects of this market-based response, however, has been the effect of sharp cuts to the cash assistance component, accounting for an estimated 1.6 per cent increase in the poverty rate (Mishel 2002: 10).

Not surprisingly, the pattern of rising levels of income inequality has been largely mirrored in the case of wealth inequality. In the USA in the period 1992–2000, for example, households in the top 20 per cent of income saw their share of aggregate net worth increase from 59.6 per cent to 62.9 per cent, while those in the bottom 40 per cent of the income distribution saw their share of wealth decline by 0.2 percentage points (Mishel *et al*. 2002: 280). Despite all the popular publicity surrounding the stock market boom of the 1990s, and the anecdotal stories of average people accessing on-line trading to cash-in, participation in direct share ownership remains largely the privilege of the wealthy. 'For most households rising debt, not a rising stock market, was the real story of the 1990s' (Mishel *et al*. 2002: 307).

Explanations for Increasing Income Inequality

The most popular explanation for the growing inequality in advanced economies in recent times has been that firms competing in increasingly globalised markets and utilising increasing levels of technology, particularly information technology (IT), has resulted in a shift in demand from unskilled to skilled labour. For example, the 'skill-biased technical change' argument asserts that the relative demand for highly skilled workers increased through the 1990s, and potentially increased at a faster rate than supply, pushing up wages for those workers as well as resulting in a compositional shift in favour of more high-skilled workers, and the thereby increasing earnings inequality. This argument can be coupled with the claim that, at the same time, the wage rates that can be demanded by lower skilled workers have been depressed by the emergence of competition from lower wage countries – the globalisation thesis. Both these arguments are problematic. The skill-biased technical change argument is weakened by the fact that there is little evidence that there has been any clear upskilling at the aggregate level (Morris and Western 1999: 634; Sheehan 2001: 52). Moreover, over the period when technology usage has allegedly driven a demand for more higher-skilled workers, productivity has been relatively stagnant (Morris and Western 1999: 635). The globalisation thesis, while superficially appealing, is also flawed. The moderating influence of foreign low-wage labour competition on domestic wage rates is plausible; however, only a relatively small proportion of the workforce is in fact employed in the traded goods sectors of contemporary economies (Sheehan 2001: 48).

In their review of the rise in income inequality in the USA, Morris and Western (1999) suggest that the arguments with the strongest evidentiary credentials are those relating to institutional factors, and in particular a relatively low minimum wage in the USA, which remained frozen throughout the 1990s, was seen to have a major effect on holding down low wages and contributing to increasing income inequality. Similarly, declining unionisation in the USA is correlated with increasing wage dispersion, accounting for around 20 per cent of the increase among males generally, and up to 50 per cent for male blue-collar workers (Morris and Western 1999: 645).

Social Security and Welfare – Rollback, Restructuring and the Workfare State

The restructuring and rollback of the welfare state is one of the distinguishing features of contemporary political economy. Quantitative studies of welfare-state expansion invariably focused on welfare state expenditure; however, there are well-documented problems with this approach (Esping-Andersen 1990), particularly in the context of understanding the dynamics and character of welfare state 'retrenchment' (Clayton and Pontusson 1998; Korpi and Palme 2001: 8). Across the OECD countries, expenditure on social security and welfare may have levelled off, or increased at a less rapid rate than in previous periods; however, this does little to suggest the magnitude of the changes and their impact on citizens.

Social protection systems across the affluent nations have been beset by a range of crises since the 1980s. The fiscal crisis of the welfare state – the perception that states could no longer afford the burden of a rigid and ultimately ineffective system of social protection – drove three trends: cutting benefits, either directly through lower payments or indirectly through a stagnation of the minimum wage system to which benefit levels might be tied; increasing targeting (particularly through more aggressive means testing in the Anglophone democracies) thereby disentitling many beneficiaries; and decentralising delivery by shifting the emphasis from direct state provision to the use of local authorities, community organisations and private-sector agencies. This last trend has also seen non-government organisations and private agencies being subjected to commercially oriented performance criteria and a generalised privatisation of social protection, particularly in the provision of healthcare, pensions and employment services (Standing 2002: 88–92).

Healthcare has seen dramatic privatisation, with benefits lagging behind inflation, and increased co-payments in the case of most OECD countries. The public share of expenditure began to decline in the 1980s; and further contraction was achieved in the 1990s with increases in waiting days for benefits, shortening periods for which benefits can be claimed, and decreasing the 'generosity' of benefits (Huber and Stephens 2000: 12).

In the case of pensions, there has been a degree of convergence across the OECD, with most countries moving to a multi-tiered system which increasingly differentiates benefit levels, tying them more directly to work incomes and stigmatising and lowering pension levels for the poor. While nine OECD economies (Australia, Canada, Denmark, Iceland, Ireland, New Zealand, Norway, Sweden and the UK) traditionally had tax-financed minimum pension schemes, by the mid-1990s, only three could still be classified as having those systems – the others had moved to multi-tiered compulsory contribution-based schemes (Standing 2002: 119). From a universalistic social protection perspective, these systems have multiple problems. The legitimacy of the minimum pension is threatened as the majority of wage-earners focus on the higher tiers. Second, the security and value of the pension entitlements for those dependent on the tiers is left to the investment wisdom of the pension funds and the vagaries of the equities markets.

Similarly, unemployment benefit systems have typically been restructured in a regressive fashion. Here the main trend across the OECD has been away from a heavy reliance on unemployment insurance schemes (where

contributions paid or credits provided give access to compensation) underpinned by a residual unemployment assistance scheme, to a heavier reliance
on an increasingly parsimonious unemployment assistance scheme
buttressed by extensive workfare requirements and conditions. Most states
have focused on developing increasingly stringent and complex tests for entitlement to unemployment benefits. As a result, the coverage rate for unemployment benefits (that is, the estimated proportion of unemployed people
receiving benefits) fell in most countries in the 1990s. In countries such as the
USA, the coverage rate has always been notoriously low – between 30 per
cent and 40 per cent in the 1980s and 1990s. Estimated coverage for a selection of European countries in 1994 and 1999 is shown in Table 12.2.

Table 12.2 also shows average net replacement rates (the value of average
benefits as a percentage of average earnings) for unemployment benefits for
several OECD countries as at 1995. Replacement rates vary significantly, but
are relatively modest in many cases and below 50 per cent in every
Anglophone country apart from the UK, where they were estimated to be 51
per cent.

**Table 12.2   Percentage of unemployed receiving benefits (coverage) 1994 and
1999 and unemployment benefit net replacement rates 1995**

	Coverage 1994	Coverage 1999	Replacement rate 1995
Australia	–	–	31
Austria	63.1[1]	74.2	–
Belgium	84.5	66.3	59
Canada	–	–	43
Denmark	64.2	62.6	81
Finland	67.6[1]	51.6	59
France	46.5	42.4	55
Germany	66.0	74.2	54
Ireland	–	–	37
Italy	7.0	5.1[2]	19
Japan	36.0	29.3	45
Netherlands	45.0	31.2	69
New Zealand	–	–	39
Norway	–	–	62
Portugal	25.3	28.4	–
Spain	28.1	16.6	49
Sweden	70.3[1]	55.4	67
Switzerland	–	–	62
United Kingdom	59.9	40.6	51
USA	–	–	16

Notes: [1] 1995; [2] 1998.

Source: Standing (2002), 149–50 from Eurostat data for coverage rates, and from OECD for
replacement rates.

Replacement rates have not just been falling in the case of unemployment benefits. Across eighteen OECD countries, replacement levels for various forms of social security peaked in the period 1975–85 (at approximately 65 per cent for unemployment benefits, 70 per cent for sickness benefits, and 85 per cent for accident insurance benefits) then declined by 10 percentage points for unemployment and around 5 percentage points for sickness and accident benefits (Korpi and Palme 2001: 11) by 1995. Korpi and Palme's contrasting analysis of the different fates of the Swedish and UK systems makes it clear that, while there has been a degree of convergence, politics still matters. The Swedish social insurance system had been significantly weakened by the mid-1990s however, with respect to unemployment, sickness and accident benefits at least, 'the British welfare state has ... been rolled back to a pre-Beveridge level, to the 1930s' (Korpi and Palme 2001: 12).

Much of the spirit and character of the restructuring of the social protection policies across the affluent capitalist democracies is captured by the shift from welfare to workfare. The principles have come to be applied in a range of social policy areas under the misnomer of 'mutual obligation', but have been most developed in the area of unemployment compensation and employment services. Workfare – the requirement that in order to access entitlements beneficiaries must undertake jobs or training – has had its most draconian expression in the USA. Federal legislation passed in 1996 capped welfare entitlements to a maximum of five years over a lifetime, and compelled recipients to accept a designated job after two years (as well as devolving welfare policy to the states, banning legal aid to immigrants and cutting food stamps). Workfare principles are now applied widely throughout Europe and in Australia. In the UK, Germany, Sweden, Denmark and Italy, various benefits are denied or cut if recipients fail to undertake training or job placement (Standing 2002: 177). In Australia, the 'work for the dole' scheme has been gradually extended. These systems invariably cut the costs of benefits and seriously curtail access: moreover, workfare is a long way from economic democracy – particularly when this implies universal access to adequate social protection as an entitlement of citizenship.

While the general trend across the OECD in the area of social protection policy and outcomes has been one of rollback, and restructuring limiting access and reducing the value of benefits, the degree of convergence should not be overstated. Varieties of capitalism persist (Hall and Soskice 2001) and welfare state regimes remain distinctive and are intimately linked to these varieties of capitalism (Hicks and Kenworthy 2003). While globalisation and ideology are possible explanations for the drift away from the classic welfare state model of social democracy (Bonoli *et al.* 1999), most recent studies serve to discredit these explanations in favour of those that highlight the role of politics and institutions (Huber and Stephens 2000). Recent studies question the extent to which the 'new politics' of welfare are in fact different from the 'old politics' (Korpi and Palme 2001; Allan and Scruggs 2002). There is little doubt that the perceived 'room to manoeuvre' for left-wing parties has been affected by 'contagion from the right'; however, the capacity for different states to defend, if not to extend, the social democratic character of social security policies is still likely to be related to the strength and mobilisation of labour movements (Hicks 1999).

Employment, Unemployment and the Experience of Work: Lower Unemployment, at a Price

At first glance, one of the few apparent gains for labour throughout the 1990s was lower unemployment. One of the most widely celebrated 'success stories' of the 1990s, the USA, saw unemployment fall from over 7.5 per cent in 1992 to just 4.0 per cent in 2000. This led to advocacy of the US neo-liberal model – low unemployment could be achieved and sustained with the right combination of weaker unions, low minimum wage rates, less generous social security benefits and lower taxes. However, closer inspection of the data suggests that lower unemployment has not been a unique achievement of the US neo-liberal model, and nor has lower unemployment been achieved (in the USA or in a number of other economies) without significant costs.

Between 1989 and 2001, unemployment fell in thirteen of the twenty OECD countries shown in Table 12.3. In comparative terms, the USA of the 1990s emerges as a low unemployment country, but a diverse range of other countries also showed unemployment rates of below 6 per cent by 2001 – Japan, the UK, Austria, Denmark, Ireland, the Netherlands, New Zealand, Norway, Portugal, Sweden and Switzerland. Since the low point of 4 per cent in the USA in 2000, unemployment has been rising (at the time of writing) with the latest recession, projected to be 6 per cent for 2003 (OECD 2003a: 23). This most recent rise in US unemployment has also been accompanied by slower growth in labour market participation, suggesting increasing numbers of 'hidden unemployed'.

Perhaps more importantly for labour, though, lower unemployment across the OECD generally appears to have come at a significant cost. A significant proportion of new jobs created throughout the 1990s in the OECD were part-time or temporary. Part-time jobs accounted for over half of all jobs created in the 1990s in half of all OECD countries. Temporary employment grew in two-thirds of OECD countries, and in five OECD countries more temporary jobs were created than permanent jobs (OECD 2003a: 20). While part-time and temporary jobs are not always inferior jobs, these data do suggest that many labour markets in the OECD are producing a significant proportion of jobs that offer less than full-time hours and limited job security.

Other data strongly suggest that job conditions worsened on a number of

Table 12.3   Standardised unemployment rates,
1989 and 2001

	1989	*2001*
Australia	6.2	6.7
Austria	–	3.6
Belgium	7.5	6.6
Canada	7.5	7.2
Denmark	7.4	4.3
Finland	3.3	9.1
France	9.3	8.6
Finland	3.3	9.1
Germany	5.6[1]	7.9
Ireland	14.7	3.8
Italy	10.0	9.5
Japan	2.3	5.0
Netherlands	6.9	2.4
New Zealand	7.1	5.3
Norway	5.0	3.6
Portugal	4.9	4.1
Spain	17.2	13.0
Sweden	1.6	5.1
Switzerland	–	2.5
United Kingdom	7.3	5.0
USA	5.3	4.8

Note: [1]West Germany.

Source: Mishel *et al.* (2002), 431.

measures. The European Survey of Working Conditions (ESWC), covering the fifteen European OECD countries in 1990, 1995 and 2000, indicates that while a declining proportion of workers see their jobs as posing a health or safety risk (as would be expected with blue-collar jobs constituting a declining share of employment), increasing numbers reported work-related health problems including fatigue and stress. Work intensification is also strongly suggested by increasing proportions of workers reporting that they are forced to work at 'very high speed' (up from 48 per cent in 1990 to 56 per cent in 2000) and to 'tight deadlines' (up from 50 per cent in 1990 to 60 per cent in 2000) (OECD 2003a: 46).

Finally, the suspicion that jobs are less secure is further supported by data on employee perceptions of job security. Comparable data on perceived job insecurity from the International Social Survey Programme is only available for two years (1989 and 1997) for seven countries. The proportion of workers who did not believe that their job was secure increased in all seven countries between those two years (OECD 2003a: 52).

Training and Skills

Comparative, time-series data on vocational education and training rates across the OECD are not readily available. In Anglophone democracies, however, there is evidence that the trend in vocational education and training, as well as in school and university education, has been towards heavier reliance on private markets rather than on public provision. Consequently, there has been some cost-shifting, away from the state and employers and on to individuals. It is also apparent that levels of employer-sponsored training provisions continue to be inadequate, and that more disadvantaged workers tend to receive less training.

Useful time-series data is available for expenditure on educational institutions across the OECD. These data tend to show that there has been no significant increase in expenditure on tertiary institutions (including universities, technical colleges and other vocational training institutions) in the second half of the 1990s. For twelve of the twenty-five OECD countries for which data is available, expenditure on tertiary institutions increased at a rate slower than GDP growth. Moreover, this net decline in tertiary expenditure relative to GDP was typical of many of the more mature advanced economies – the UK, Germany, France, Austria, Canada, Denmark, Finland, Norway, Australia and New Zealand (as well as the Czech Republic and Poland) (OECD 2002: 165). Disaggregation of tertiary education expenditure into public and private sources confirms the impression of privatisation (or 'marketisation'). In eleven of the eighteen OECD countries for which data is available, the share of expenditure on tertiary educational institutions shifted from public sources to private sources. In some cases the shift was quite dramatic – in Australia, for example, while 64.2 per cent of expenditure in 1995 came from public sources, by 1999 this had fallen to 52.4 per cent (OECD 2002: 190).

Comparative data on vocational education and training confirms that there continues to be significant inequality of access to vocational training opportunities. Immigrants and workers in smaller establishments receive less training, and the OECD estimates that demand for training outstrips the supply of employer-sponsored training for female workers, involuntary part-time workers, temporary workers and workers in lower-skilled occupations (OECD 2003b: 243, 251). Despite the rhetoric of the importance of skills in the new globalised world economy, training under-provision continues to be endemic to OECD economies (OECD 2003b: 248). In the latter half of the 1990s an estimated quarter of workers in the advanced economies wanted more training. Time and cost constraints were the main reasons given for not being able to access sufficient training – a consequence likely to be associated with low wages and long working hours. The impression given is that training under-provision is common, principally among workers most in need of training to improve their labour market prospects.

Conclusions

As the survey of economic outcomes across the OECD in the 1990s attests, the neo-liberal ascendency has, on balance, had disastrous consequences for workers. Standing has described the effects of the neo-liberal ascendency on work and workers as ushering in 'an era of intensified human insecurity' characterised by increasing insecurities in the labour market, employment, job, skill reproduction, work and representation (Standing 2002: 37–69). Others, however, have suggested that the record for labour has not been all bad. The trend of unemployment was lower throughout the 1990s, though at a considerable price in terms of the quality and security of work. Nevertheless, there is evidence that an increasing proportion of workers now report improved levels of autonomy and control over their work (Useem 1996: 164–7; OECD 2003a: 46), and it is claimed that many jobs have been enriched as a result of technological change, reorganisation and restructuring. In one sense, though, increased autonomy is a reflection of increasing responsibility and job enlargement – an explanation surely more consistent with widespread evidence of increasing work intensification.

While there is a range of potential explanations for the labour market, welfare state, training and work experience outcomes documented in this chapter, politics and political institutions continue to figure repeatedly in many studies as being among the most durable and consistent explanations. It is hard to avoid the conclusion that the decline of organised labour has been pivotal to the ability of capital to exploit the regulatory environment and the degradation of state institutions associated with the neo-liberal ascendency. With the decentralising and de-institutionalising of industrial relations in the 1990s, and the consequent reconfiguration of interest group representation and intermediation, unions faced the end of direct political engagement with the government over industrial relations, economic and labour market policy, and the advent of more direct bargaining on the terrain of the individual enterprise. However, while trends toward de-institutionalisation and deregulation of industrial relations have been replicated in many major industrial nations, there is no universal imperative towards the short-term profitability-oriented model of flexible production that these institutional changes oversee. Indeed, the complex social and economic outcomes of industrial relations are likely to require an institutional domain for the representation of large-scale interests, encompassing collective actors to achieve political ends such as anti-inflation targets, equity and low unemployment. Increasingly, in such instances, forms of representation and systems of collective negotiation which many observers identify as neo-corporatist (see Bordogna and Cella 1999; Grote and Schmitter 1999) have seen a selective resurgence, particularly in Europe, as states grapple with forms of intervention they have denied themselves in the contemporary neo-liberal environment.

Despite being weakened, organised labour and the political institutions that provide an opportunity for the expression and implementation of labour interests and claims continue to matter. The states with the strongest traditional social democratic credentials, have generally managed to weather the neo-liberal assault better than other states. It would not surprise us to see the resurgence of innovative forms of democratic social relations in capitalist societies. The promotion of neo-liberalism as a market-led transition to a new social and economic regime is unlikely to provide permanent solutions to the contradictions of capitalist market societies.

References

Allan, J. and Scruggs, L. (2002) *Politics as Usual? Political Parties and Welfare Regime Change in Advanced Industrial Societies*, Paper presented at 13th Annual Conference of Europeanists, Chicago, March 14–16.

Alt, J. E. (1985) 'Political Parties, World Demand and Unemployment: Domestic and International Sources of Economic Activity', *American Political Science Review*, 79, 1016–40.

Alvarez, R. M., Garrett, G. and Lange, P. (1991) 'Government Partisanship, Labor Organization, and Macroeconomic Performance', *American Political Science Review*, 85, 539–56.

Bonoli, G., George, V. and Taylor-Gooby, P. (1999) *European Welfare Futures: Towards a Theory of Retrenchment* (Cambridge: Polity Press).

Bordogna, L. and Cella, G. P. (1999) 'Admission, Exclusion, Correction: the Changing Role of the State in Industrial Relations', *Transfer: European Review of Labour and Research*, 5:1–2, 14–33.

Boreham, P. (2002) 'Governance of the Labour Market: The Declining Role of the State', in S. Bell (ed.), *Economic Governance and Institutional Dynamics* (Melbourne: Oxford University Press).

Boreham, P. and Compston, H. (1992) 'Labour Movement Organization and Political Intervention: The Politics of Unemployment in the OECD Countries 1974–1986', *European Journal of Political Research*, 22:2, 143–70.

Boreham, P. and Hall, R. (1994) 'Trade Union Strategy in Contemporary Capitalism: The Microeconomic and Macroeconomic Implications of Political Unionism', *Economic and Industrial Democracy*, 15:3, 313–53.

Boreham, P., Dow, G. and Leet, M. (1999) *Room to Manoeuvre: Political Aspects of Full Employment* (Melbourne: Melbourne University Press).

Boreham, P., Hall, R. and Leet, M. (1996) 'Labour and Citizenship: The Development of Welfare State Regimes', *Journal of Public Policy*, 16:2, 203–27.

Boreham, P. R., Clegg, S. and Dow, G. (1986) 'The Institutional Management of Class Politics: Beyond the Labour Process and Corporatist Debates', in D. Knights and H. Willmott (eds), *Managing the Labour Process* (London: Gower), 203–28.

Boreham, P. R., Clegg, S. and Dow, G. (1989) 'Political Organization and Economic Policy', in G. Duncan (ed.), *Democracy and the Capitalist State* (Cambridge University Press), 253–76.

Burniaux, J.-M., Dang, T.-T., Fore, D., Forster, M., d'Ercole, M. and Oxley, H. (1998) *Income Distribution and Poverty in Selected OECD Countries*, OECD Economics Department Working Paper No. 189 (Paris: OECD).

Calmfors, L. and Driffill, L. (1988) 'Bargaining Structure, Corporatism and Macroeconomic Performance', *Economic Policy: A European Forum*, 6, 13–61.

Cameron, D. R. (1984) 'Social Democracy, Corporatism, Labour Quiescence and the Representation of Economic Interest in Advanced Capitalist Society', in J. Goldthorpe (ed.), *Order and Conflict in Contemporary Capitalism* (Oxford: Clarendon Press) 143–78.

Castles, F. (1981) 'How Does Politics Matter? Structure or Agency in the Determination of Public Policy Outcomes', *European Journal of Political Research*, 9, 119–32.

Castles, F. (1982) *The Impact of Parties* (London: Sage).

Clayton, R. and Pontusson, J. (1998) 'Welfare State Retrenchment Revisited: Entitlement Cuts, Public Sector Restructuring and Inegalitarian Trends in Advanced Capitalist Societies', *World Politics*, 51, 67–98.

Clegg, S., Boreham, P. R. and Dow, G. (1986) *Class, Politics and the Economy* (London: Routledge & Kegan Paul).

Coates, D. (2000) *Models of Capitalism: Growth and Stagnation in the Modern Era* (Cambridge: Polity Press).

Czada, R. (1987) 'The Impact of Interest Politics on Flexible Adjustment Policies', in H. Keman, H. Paloheimo and P. F. Whiteley (eds), *Coping with the Economic Crisis: Alternative Responses to Economic Recession in Advanced Industrial Societies* (London: Sage), 20–53.

Esping-Andersen, G. (1985) 'Power and Distributional Regimes', *Politics and Society*, 14, 223–56.

Esping-Andersen, G. (1987) 'Citizenship and Socialism: De-commodification and Solidarity in the Welfare State', in M. Rein, G. Esping-Andersen and L. Rainwater (eds), *Stagnation and Renewal in Social Policy* (New York: M. E. Sharpe)

Esping-Andersen, G. (1990) *The Three Worlds of Welfare Capitalism* (Princeton, NJ: Princeton University Press).

Frank, T. (2002) *One Market Under God: Extreme Capitalism, Market Populism and the End of Economic Democracy* (London: Vintage).

Gerlich, P. (1992) 'A Farewell to Corporatism', *West European Politics*, 15, 132–46.

Gobeyn, M. J. (1993) 'Explaining the Decline of Macro-Corporatist Bargaining Structures in Advanced Capitalist Societies', *Governance*, 6, 3–22.

Golden, M. (1993) 'The Dynamics of Trade Unionism and National Economic Performance', *American Political Science Review*, 87, 439–54.

Griffin, L. J., O'Connell, P. J., and McCammon, H. J. (1989) 'National Variation in the Context of Struggle: Postwar Class Conflict and Market Distribution in the Capitalist Democracies', *Canadian Review of Sociology and Anthropology*, 26, 37–68.

Grote, J. R., and Schmitter, P. C. (1999) 'The Renaissance of National Corporatism: Unintended Side-Effect of European Economic and Monetary Union or Calculated Response to the Absence of European Social Policy', *Transfer: European Review of Labour and Research*, 5:1–2, 34–63.

Hall, P. and Soskice, D. (eds) (2001) *Varieties of Capitalism* (New York: Oxford University Press).

Hicks, A. (1987) 'Capitalism, Social Democratic Corporatism and Economic Growth', Unpublished MS.

Hicks, A. (1988) 'National Collective Action and Economic Performance: A Review Essay', *International Studies Quarterly*, 32, 131–52.

Hicks, A. (1999) *Social Democracy and Welfare Capitalism: A Century of Income Security Politics* (Ithaca, NY: Cornell University Press).

Hicks, A. and Kenworthy, L. (2003) 'Varieties of Welfare Capitalism', *Socio-Economic Review*, 1, 27–61.

Hicks, A. and Swank, D. (1985) 'Politics, Institutions and Welfare Spending in Industrialised Democracies, 1960–82', *American Political Science Review*, 86:3, 658–74.

Higgins, W. (1985) 'Political Unionism and the Corporatism Thesis', *Economic and Industrial Democracy*, 6, 349–81.

Huber, E. and Stephens, J. (2000) 'Welfare State and Production Regimes in the Era of Retrenchment' in P. Pierson (ed.), *The New Politics of the Welfare State* (New York: Oxford University Press).

Jessop, B. (2002) *The Future of the Capitalist State* (Cambridge: Polity Press).

Keman, H. (1984) 'Politics, Policies and Consequences: A Cross-national Analysis of Public Policy-formation in Advanced Capitalist Democracies (1967–1981)', *European Journal of Political Research*, 12, 147–70.

Keman, H. and van Dijk, T. (1987) 'Political Strategies to Overcome the Crisis: Policy Formation and Economic Performance in Seventeen Capitalist Democracies', in Keman, H., Paloheimo, H. and P. Whiteley (eds) *Coping with the Economic Crisis: Alternative Responses to Economic Recession in Advanced Industrial Societies* (London: Sage), 127–62.

Kenworthy, L. (1990) 'Labour Organization, Wage Restraint and Economic Performance', *Review of Radical Political Economics*, 22:4, 111–34.

Korpi, W. (1980) 'Social Policy and Distributional Conflict in the Capitalist Democracies', *West European Politics*, 3, 296–316.

Korpi, W. (1983) *The Democratic Class Struggle* (London: Routledge & Kegan Paul).

Korpi, W. (1989) 'Power, Politics and State Autonomy in the Development of Social Citizenship: Social Rights during Sickness in Eighteen OECD Countries since 1930', *American Sociological Review*, 54, 309–28.

Korpi, W. (1991) 'Political and Economic Explanations for Unemployment: A Cross-National and Long-Term Analysis', *British Journal of Political Science*, 21, 315–48.

Korpi, W. and Palme, J. (2001) 'The New and Old Politics of Welfare State Retrenchment: A Comparative Analysis of Cuts in Social Rights in 18 Countries 1975–1995', Paper presented to the ISA Research Committee on Social Stratification, Mannheim, 27–29 April.

Kurzer, P. (1991) 'The Internationalisation of Business and Domestic Class Compromises: A Four Country Study', *West European Politics*, 14, 1–24.

Kurzer, P. (1993) *Banking and Business: Political Change and Economic Integration in Western Europe* (Ithaca, NY: Cornell University Press).

Lehmbruch, G. (1984) 'Concertation and the Structure of Corporatist Networks', in J. Goldthorpe (ed.), *Order and Conflict in Contemporary Capitalism: Studies in the Political Economy of Western European Nations* (Oxford: Clarendon Press).

Meidner, R. (1978) *Employee Investment Funds: An Approach to Collective Capital Formation* (with Anna Hedborg) (London: George Allen & Unwin).

Mishel, L., Bernstein, J. and Boushey, H. (2002) *The State of Working America 2002–03* (Ithaca, NY: ILR Press).

Morris, M. and Western, B. (1999) 'Inequality in Earnings at the Close of the Twentieth Century', *Annual Review of Sociology*, 26, 623–57.

Notermans, T. (1993) 'The Abdication of National Policy Autonomy: Why the Macroeconomic Policy Regime Has Become So Unfavourable to Labour', *Politics and Society*, 21, 133–67.

OECD (2002) *Education at a Glance – Financial and Human Resources Invested in Education* (Paris: OECD).

OECD (2003a) 'More and Better Jobs? Aggregate Performance During the Past Decade', *OECD Employment Outlook* 2003 (Paris: OECD).

OECD (2003b) 'Upgrading Workers' Skills and Competencies', *OECD Employment Outlook* 2003 (Paris: OECD).

Paloheimo, H. (1989) 'Between Liberalism and Corporatism: The Effect of Trade Unions and Governments on Economic Performance in Eighteen OECD Countries', in R. Brunetta and C. Dell'Aringa (eds), *Labour Relations and Economic Performance*, Proceedings of a Conference held by the International Economic Association, Venice.

Paloheimo, H. (1990) 'Micro Foundations and Macro Practice of Centralised Industrial Relations', *European Journal of Political Research*, 18, 389–406.

Pampel, F. C. and Williamson, J. B. (1988) 'Welfare Spending in Advanced Industrial Democracies, 1950–1980', *American Journal of Sociology*, 50, 1424–56.

Pampel, F., Williamson, J. and Stryker, R. (1990) 'Class Context and Pension Response to Demographic Structure in Advanced Industrial Democracies', *Social Problems*, 37, 535–50.

Peetz, D. (1998) *Unions in a Contrary World: The Future of the Australian Trade Union Movement* (Melbourne: Cambridge University Press).

Poole, M. (1989) *The Origins of Economic Democracy, Profit Sharing and Employee Share-holding Schemes* (London: Routledge).

Pontusson, J. (1992) 'At the End of the Third Road: Social democracy in Crisis', *Politics and Society*, 20, 305–22.

Pontusson, J. and Kuruvilla, S. (1992) 'Swedish Wage-Earner Funds: An Experiment in Economic Democracy', *Industrial and Labor Relations Review*, 45:4, 779–91.

Regini, M. (1992) 'Introduction: The Past and Future of Social Studies of Labour Movements', in M. Regini (ed.), *The Future of Labour Movements* (London: Sage).

Rowthorn, B. (1992) 'Corporatism and Labour Market Performance', in J. Pekkarinen, M. Pohjola and B. Rowthorn (eds), *Social Corporatism: A Superior Economic System* (Oxford: Clarendon Press).

Scharpf, F. (1984a) 'Economic and Institutional Constraints of Full-Employment Strategies: Sweden, Austria and Western Germany 1973–1982', in J. Goldthorpe (ed.), *Order and Conflict in Contemporary Capitalism* (Oxford: Clarendon Press) 257–90.

Scharpf, F. (1984b) 'Strategy Choice, Economic Feasibility and Institutional Constraints as Determinants of Full Employment Policy During the Recession', in K. Gerlach, W. Peters and W. Sengenberger (eds), *Public Policies to Combat Unemployment in a Period of Economic Stagnation: An International Comparison* (Frankfurt: Campus Verlag).

Schmidt, M. (1982a) 'The Role of Parties in Shaping Macro-economic Policies' in F. Castles (ed.), *The Impact of Parties* (London: Sage).

Schmidt, M. (1982b) 'Does Corporatism Matter? Economic Crisis, Parties and Rates of Unemployment in Capitalist Democracies in the 1970s', in G. Lehmbruch and P. C. Schmitter (eds), *Patterns of Corporatist Policymaking* (London: Sage).

Schmidt, M. (1984) 'Labour Market Performance and the Inflation in OECD Nations: A Political-Institutionalist View' in K. Gerlach, W. Peters and W. Sengenberger (eds), *Public Policies to Combat Unemployment in a Period of Economic Stagnation. An International Comparison* (Frankfurt: Campus Verlag).

Schmidt, M. (1987) 'The Politics of Full Employment in Western Democracies', *Annals of the American Academy of Political and Social Science*, 492, 171–81.

Schmidt, M. (1988) 'The Politics of Labour Market Policy: Structural and Political Determinants of Unemployment in Industrial Nations', in F. G. Castles, F. Lehner and M. Schmidt (eds), *The Future of Party Government, Vol. 3, Managing Mixed Economies* (New York: de Gruyter).

Schott, K. (1984) *Policy, Power and Order: The Persistence of Economic Problems in Capitalist States* (New Haven, Conn.: Yale University Press).

Sheehan, P. (2001) 'The Causes of Increased Earnings Inequality: The International Literature', in J. Borland, B. Gregory and P. Sheehan (eds), *Work Rich, Work Poor: Inequality and Economic Change in Australia* (Melbourne: Centre for Strategic Economic Studies).

Smeeding, T. (2002) *Globalization, Inequality and the Rich Countries of the G-20: Evidence from the Luxembourg Income Study* (Luxembourg Income Study Working Paper No. 320).

Standing, G. (2002) *Beyond the New Paternalism: Basic Security as Equality* (London: Verso).

Streeck, W. (1984) 'Neocorporatist Industrial Relations and the Economic Crisis in West Germany', in J. Goldthorpe (ed.), *Order and Conflict in Contemporary Capitalism* (Oxford: Clarendon Press).

Streeck, W. and Schmitter, P. C. (1991) 'From National Corporatism to Transnational Pluralism: Organising Interests in a Single European Market', *Politics and Society*, 19, 133–63.

Swank, D. H. and Hicks, A. (1985) 'The Determinants and Redistributive Impacts of Welfare State Spending in the Advanced Capitalist Democracies 1960–1980', in N. J. Vig and S. E. Schier (eds), *Political Economy in Western Democracies* (New York: Holmes & Meier).

Tarantelli, E. (1986) 'The Regulation of Inflation and Unemployment', *Industrial Relations*, 25:1, 1–15.

Thelen, K. (1994) 'Toward a New Framework for the Study of Labor in Advanced Capitalism', *Comparative Politics*, 27, 107–24.

Therborn, G. (1986) *Why Some Peoples are More Unemployed Than Others: The Strange Paradox of Growth and Unemployment* (London: Verso) 14–36.

Therborn, G. (1987) 'Does Corporatism Really Matter? The Economic Crisis and Issues of Political Theory', *Journal of Public Policy*, 7:3, 259–84.

Useem, M. (1996) *Investor Capitalism: How Money Managers are Changing the Face of Corporate America* (New York: Basic Books).

Wilensky, H. (1981) 'Leftism, Catholicism and Democratic Corporatism', in P. Flora and A. Heidenheimer (eds), *The Development of Welfare States in Europe and America* (London: Transaction).

Name Index

Subject Index